Awaken 101

Praise for This Book

What Educators Are Saying

Awaken 101 offers readers a chance to explore what it means to pursue transformational education experiences. The authors' deep sense of commitment to student well-being and their quest for universities to be places that embrace an ethic of care are evident with every turn of the page.... A must-read for college students.—JACQUELINE EDMONDSON, CHANCELLOR, PENN STATE, ALLEGHENY

For members of the anxious generation who were born after 9/11, who grew up during the Great Recession, and who came of age in a time of climate emergency, here is a book unlike others. Not a study guide for the college entrance exams or a standard text for a major chosen with an eye on paying off educational debt, this book draws wisdom from a wide range of sources to invite young adults to awake, reflect, connect, and choose to live in more mindful, engaged, and satisfying ways. Themselves from different generations and genders, DiJulio and Uhl offer with clarity and concision a compelling call to *Awaken*.—JULIA S. KASDORF, PROFESSOR OF ENGLISH, PENN STATE UNIVERSITY, AND AUTHOR, *SHALE PLAY: POEMS AND PHOTOGRAPHS FROM THE FRACKING FIELDS*

"Who am I? Why am I here? How can I be of service to life? These are the kinds of big questions that readers are invited to explore in *Awaken 101*. As such, this book would be a great choice for college first-year seminar courses aimed at guiding emerging adults in the quest for self-discovery, as well as for teachers seeking ways to support young people in their development as engaged learners and citizens."—JEFF ADAMS, ASSOCIATE DEAN FOR UNDERGRADUATE EDUCATION, PENN STATE UNIVERSITY

What College Students Are Saying

This is one of the only books that I have had for a college class that I am truly enjoying. Each time I am assigned a chapter, I'm excited to discover what I will learn. It's a book that all college students should read.—LARYN JACKSON, SOPHOMORE, JOURNALISM, PENN STATE UNIVERSITY

This book has engaged my soul like never before.... Truly thought provoking... Truly life-changing.—MAGGIE WARD, SOPHOMORE, PUBLIC RELATIONS, PENN STATE

Each time I read from *Awaken 101*, I feel myself entering into a dialogue with myself about who I truly am and who I seek to become.—HANNAH SINGLETARY, JUNIOR, ENGLISH, PENN STATE

This book has allowed me to ask questions that have been pivotal for my development, while also gently challenging me to examine my beliefs and how they limit me.—NATALIE SCOHCH, SOPHOMORE, ENGLISH & COMMUNICATION ARTS AND SCIENCES, PENN STATE

Awaken 101 is inviting me into a deep relationship with myself. The blending of styles—narratives, inquiries, exercises and poems—is helping me to see things in exciting, often unconventional, ways.—EMMA ORLOSKI, SOPHOMORE, EDUCATION, PENN STATE

The teachings in this book have given me permission to experience what it means to be my authentic self. Not only have I begun to think in new ways, but I have also become more fearless and confident, a better listener and human being.—ASHLEY NOVOTNY, SENIOR, COMMUNITY, ENVIRONMENT AND DEVELOPMENT, PENN STATE

This book has offered me guidance in my most impressionable years, opening my eyes to not only my own truth and potential, but to my ability to bring out the best in the world around me. Inspired by *Awaken 101*, I now choose to perceive every fabric of my existence with new eyes, and I can only hope that it has the same incredible impact on other readers.—SAM SPIRGEL, SENIOR, COMMUNICATIONS, PENN STATE

This book makes me want to hug trees, run in fields, and howl at the moon. Life no longer seems abstract; instead it has become immeasurably special, messy and big.—MAGGIE WELCH, JUNIOR, ART AND ART HISTORY, PENN STATE

What Those Beyond College Are Saying

As a therapist working in the field of personal growth and development, I can attest that *Awaken 101* provides invaluable insight into the process of change, and how I can live a life full of truth, passion, and purpose. I feel enlivened by this book, and more supported in my pursuit of such change.—JAMIE QUAIL, REGISTERED PSYCHOTHERAPIST

When I first encountered Uhl's teachings a decade ago as a college student, my world cracked open. Focused on myself with a limited understanding of my place in the world, Uhl's provocations awakened my spirit. My transformation was uncomfortable and continues to be … and, yet, I now choose awakening as a way of life and consider myself lucky to have this book as a guide.—STEVEN J. GERVAIS, DIRECTOR OF FINANCE AND OPERATIONS, THE NATURE CONSERVANCY

A profound reminder to never settle for anything less than what makes us feel alive. *Awaken 101* helped me let go of the scripts I so rigidly clung to while living someone else's life. Because of this book, I now realize my authentic self has been there all along, waiting to be seen and loved.—ABIGAIL NELSON, INTERNATIONAL ADMISSIONS COUNSELOR, WESTERN CAROLINA UNIVERSITY

Awaken 101 is a captivating guide that challenges me to remain present and courageous as I reach goals in both personal and professional development. Each page offers opportunities to continue my inner work in applicable and intention-focused ways.—BEAONCA WARD, LIFE COACH

Being a year out of college and recently starting a small company has thrown me out of my element in the best of ways. *Awaken 101* has given me the confidence to harness this new beginning along with the peace of knowing that I always have the power to awaken.—ASHLEY JENKINS, SOCIAL MEDIA MANAGER, JENKINS SOCIALS

Taking in this book's teachings has encouraged me to place authenticity above fear, and to switch from pursuing law to enjoying an education degree and my role as an elementary school teacher. I am now able to work with and through my heart. I can guide, learn, laugh, listen, empathize… I can *feel*. I can play! I am stepping more fully into my role as a nurturer. I am living a life of fulfilling service. I am Awakening.—INDIGO MURRAY, M.S. ED., PUBLIC SCHOOL TEACHER, NYC

As far back as I can remember I searched for an answer to the question, "Who am I and what have I come here to do with my life?" As I sat in Chris's class in 2005, I realized that it wasn't answers I needed but questions. Chris's questions were an invitation to search inside, and with every question I answered a part of me awakened. Now expertly woven together in *Awaken 101* readers are guided to discover their own answers, and to give the greatest gift we have to give the world, being who you really are.—JODI LE MASURIER, COFOUNDER OF *BE MORE U* AND *THE PURPOSE PROJECT*

Awaken 101

Discovering Meaning and
Purpose in Uncertain Times

CHRISTOPHER UHL *and*
MELISSA DIJULIO

Foreword by Tressa J. Gibbard

Toplight

Jefferson, North Carolina

Library of Congress Cataloguing-in-Publication Data

Names: Uhl, Christopher, 1949– author. | DiJulio, Melissa, 1991– author.
Title: Awaken 101 : discovering meaning and purpose in uncertain times /
Christopher Uhl and Melissa DiJulio ; foreword by Tressa J. Gibbard.
Other titles: Awaken one hundred and one
Description: Jefferson : Toplight, 2020. |
Includes bibliographical references.
Identifiers: LCCN 2020035208 | ISBN 9781476682310 (paperback : acid free paper) ∞
ISBN 9781476640518 (ebook)
Subjects: LCSH: Self-actualization (Psychology) | Happiness. | Success.
Classification: LCC BF637.S4 U945 2020 | DDC 158—dc23
LC record available at https://lccn.loc.gov/2020035208

British Library cataloguing data are available

ISBN (print) 978-1-4766-8231-0
ISBN (ebook) 978-1-4766-4051-8

Cover art: "Tracks" (2002) by Jean Forsberg (jeanforsberg.ws)

Printed in the United States of America

Toplight is an imprint of McFarland & Company, Inc., Publishers

Box 611, Jefferson, North Carolina 28640
www.toplightbooks.com

Table of Contents

Part III: A Curriculum for Waking Up

Part IV: Awakening in Action

Part V: Personal and Cultural Transformation

We dedicate this book to the generative Earth that has birthed all of us into being and to today's young people who are inheriting a world plagued by climate chaos, violence, greed and injustice. May this book open them, and all readers, to the opportunities for transformation lying dormant within these uncertain times.

Foreword

by Tressa J. Gibbard

Dear Reader,

Do you know what you want to do with your one, unique and extraordinary human life?

Twenty years ago, as a student starting out at Penn State University, I certainly did not! Yet, the teachings in this book—*Awaken 101: Discovering Meaning and Purpose in Uncertain Times* by Chris Uhl and Melissa DiJulio—have everything to do with how I found my way.

As a sophomore in college, I took a groundbreaking course taught by Chris Uhl which fomented my own journey of awakening and dramatically changed my life by introducing me to the ideas, perspectives and insights that have now been brought together in this book. Chris became my mentor in college and a lifelong friend, so I was deeply honored when he asked me to read and critique the first draft of this book in 2016. I expected a stirring distillation of his class that had made such an impact on me, but I failed to connect with the original manuscript. I sent him my honest reactions, and he thanked me. Years passed with no further word, until, one day, completely unexpectedly, Chris sent me the final draft of *Awaken 101*.

The title immediately took my breath away as I registered, "Yes, of course: AWAKEN!" This term captured, perfectly, Chris' teachings and their influence on me. When I dug in, I discovered that Chris and Melissa had painstakingly re-worked and refined the whole book into a powerful masterpiece that positively made my heart sing. Drawing on the wisdom of prominent philosophers, educators and spiritual leaders, they had artfully blended personal stories and insights, together with thought-provoking exercises to create a compelling guidebook for becoming more fully and meaningfully alive.

While I was reading *Awaken 101*, I reflected on the person I had been when I was a student in Chris' class and how much I had changed because of it. At 19, I was a shy, sheltered suburban creature who got straight A's, did community service, played sports and tamely followed all of the rules of society. Beneath my model student façade, however, I struggled with low self-esteem and had no clue what I wanted to study. I also secretly yearned to travel the world and help the needy. Without knowing it at the time, I was unconsciously craving greater meaning and purpose in life.

Chris' course was a radical introduction to what it might mean to awaken to a more fulfilling existence. Just as this book does, he began by challenging me and my fellow students to question much that we had been taught to believe in: the necessity of a classroom-based education, a conventional career, and the accumulation of wealth as the means to success and happiness. This questioning was combined with many provocative invitations to experience our real relationship with the world as active participants in the biosphere.

In a particularly powerful example, Chris pointed out that our very breath connects us with all that exists. Incredulously, I realized that with every breath I took, I was exchanging matter—electrons, atoms and molecules—with everything around me all of the time. I realized that I was not separate from but an integral part of "the environment," and that "the environment" was much more than just rocks and dirt and plants and animals. I abruptly woke up to the simple, yet far-reaching, truth that "the environment" is, in fact, EVERYTHING! Thinking about the collective oneness and interdependency of all life thoroughly electrified me. My spine actually tingled with a deep body-based knowing that respecting and caring for "the environment" is truly a fundamental priority and responsibility that benefits *everything*.

It was encouraging, therefore, when Chris emphasized that, because we are all inextricably part of the biosphere, following our hearts to discover our unique talents and gifts will allow us to bring joy, peace and wholeness to the world and to ourselves. For me, these ideas, which are also central to *Awaken 101*, replaced my lack of direction with a passionate drive to seek out ways to leave a lasting, positive legacy, rather than following my culture's principles to seek out money, prestige and comfort.

The summer after taking Chris' class, I put my nascent awakening into action by undertaking a less conventional type of cross-country road trip: by bicycle! For the first time in my life, I unplugged from the mainstream. As I pedaled along—actively sensing and engaging with my surroundings—I felt like I was in communion with the land, with my companions and with my own wild spirit. Reading *Awaken 101* years later,

I realized that this was my first experience with how it feels to be "more fully human."

Awakening on that revelatory journey helped me to return to college with a new purpose: to use my education to pursue what mattered to me. I chose to create my own major to explore the interconnected pieces of our biosphere and ways to heal it. Moreover, I specifically sought out field-based courses to interact with and learn about the world directly. For example, I learned about natural history and animal behavior while trekking through national parks, sustainable agriculture by working on Penn State's experimental farm, and alternative building practices by designing and building with natural materials. These innovative classes sparked greater curiosity and connections through interesting discoveries, conversations and spontaneous adventures. As I embraced the world itself as an endlessly interesting and delightful classroom, I felt much more vibrantly and playfully alive—just as I had on my bicycle—and I knew that I was on the right track. I no longer had any interest in the rat-race I had been headed for!

Thanks to Chris' class, my awakening in college formed the foundation of a soul-satisfying way of life for me based on following my heart, learning by doing, trusting my intuition, taking risks, and opening myself to new perspectives. Today, I enjoy working in the realms of field biology, natural building, forest restoration and environmental education. I love learning about and stewarding our Earth's magnificently diverse natural and cultural landscapes through my work and human-powered adventures, and I am deeply grateful to have awakened to this as my life's work.

I know, of course, that we each awaken to our life's meaning and purpose in our own ways and at our own pace. I only hope that my story serves to illustrate how this book may be a catalyst for positive change in your own life, too. I sincerely believe that, if you let it, this book will lead you towards developing a more meaningful, creative, and connected existence. That is not to say that you will change overnight—but if you read this book with an open mind and let its insights and perspectives get under your skin, you may find, as I have, that you will be inspired to take your life in new and exciting directions. Are you ready to have the time of your life? I hope so! And I hope that you will cherish *Awaken 101* as your timeless guide, as I have.

Tressa J. Gibbard graduated from Penn State University in 2004. Since then, she has worked in field biology and conservation throughout the American West and on all seven continents. She now focuses on running a small nonprofit dedicated to forest stewardship, which allows a fun balance of work and play in the mountains and woods.

Prologue

All the time our warmth and brilliance are right here. This
is who we really are. We are one blink of an eye away from
being fully awake.

—Pema Chödrön[1]

This book is about awakening our minds and hearts so that we might
discover and experience what it means to be fully human. Indeed, waking
up is the biggest job, as well as the biggest opportunity, that we each face
as human beings.

Beginnings—Christopher: In my experience, AWAKENING becomes possible, as we summon the courage to ask uncomfortable
questions. For example, I can trace this book's origins to my teen years
when I began to wrestle with coming-of-age questions like: Who am I?
Why am I here? What's my purpose? My high school teachers tended
to frown on this sort of introspection, warning me that to be successful
in life I needed to be practical. This meant playing it safe by going to
college and picking a major that would guarantee me a well-paying job.
But the mandate to "be practical" seemed like a prescription for a life
centered on fear and conformity rather than one sparked by passion
and purpose.

This struggle to make sense of my life was compounded by the pol-
icies and priorities of my country. For example, in tenth grade, it seemed
crazy to me that the U.S. was spending tens of billions of dollars on a
race to the moon when that money could have been used to save the lives
of the millions of children, worldwide, who were dying of hunger and
malnutrition.

A few years later, the *craziness* was focused directly on me when I was told that I had to register for the draft. This meant that my government now had the authority to order me to go to Vietnam to murder teen-age boys who, simultaneously, were being ordered by their government to kill the likes of me.

This existential dilemma served as a wake-up call, prompting me to begin to assume authorship of my life by questioning my country's values. This meant summoning the courage to formulate counter-cultural questions like:

- Why does our government believe that amassing weapons and waging war is a viable path to fostering peace among nations?
- Why does our culture condition us to believe that spending our life energy working in the pursuit of more and more money will bring genuine meaning and purpose to our lives?
- How is that we have come to equate perpetual economic growth, with its associated unbridled consumerism and environmental havoc, with progress?

The more that I sat with these, and related, questions, the more I came to realize that the answers that my culture offered failed to align with the answers arising from within me.

Beginnings—Melissa: From before I was born, it was already an accepted fact by many in the scientific community that human beings were causing far-reaching and possibly irreparable damage to our planet Earth, as well as to each other. Growing up, the possibility of both human extinction and the total collapse of the biosphere was a palpable weight on me, especially as things continued to get worse instead of better.

Today, it seems that the responsibility to fix the mistakes of our predecessors falls to my generation, the Millennials, along with today's college students (Gen-Zers). But how are we to do this, especially when so many of us are already overwhelmed by fear and anxiety, as well as immobilized by numbness in the face of this seemingly impossible task? On top of these obstacles, we are subjected to ongoing societal pressure to conform to the expectations of our culture, even though doing so will only exacerbate the mess in which we find ourselves.

If it truly falls to the younger generations to address the crises now threatening our very survival as a species, then we will need to leave previously held mindsets and behaviors behind and pursue a new path, forged with new tools and requiring a new consciousness.

But stepping beyond the status quo will not be easy. I have certainly struggled in my own life to leave behind the safety of pragmatism and embrace the greater aliveness that comes with authenticity, especially when my interests tended toward the impractical, like becoming a writer or pursuing a master's degree in Transpersonal Ecopsychology. Still, to this day, I sometimes worry that my path is unrealistic and that I might even come to regret my choices. Yet, being practical often feels like forcing the square peg of me into the round hole of what my culture tells me I must do to become a "successful adult"; and this would require giving up essential parts of myself, which I refuse to do.

I know that I am not alone. There are others today, both young and old, who are also refusing to conform to a system that is, too often, bereft of meaning and purpose. Together, we are seeking a path of authenticity, trusting that somewhere, deep inside of all of us, there is a soulful part that calls us to awaken and discover our destiny and the gift, no matter how humble, that is ours to give to the world. To heed this call is to begin to live in a way that is wakeful and deeply interconnected with the rest of life. In so doing, we shake ourselves loose from the comfortable, but ultimately deadening, status quo, so that we might become fully alive and fully human. This is precisely what this book is about.

Stepping Stones Toward Awakening

In my (Christopher) role as a college professor for the past thirty years, I have been a daily witness to the anxiety, confusion, loneliness, and pain that young people experience, coming of age in these daunting times. Their emotional charge shows up in their eyes: sad eyes, frightened eyes, anxious eyes, expectant eyes, tired eyes. Eyes that plead: "Just tell me that I am OK, that I am enough. Tell me what I need to do, what I need to know, so I can find genuine fulfillment in life. Guide me toward what truly matters. Give me some stepping stones."

This book is an effort to offer such stepping stones. It challenges readers to experience their lives, not as spectators, but as reflective, courageous, and purposeful participants. Organized as a five-part journey, it explores, both cognitively and experientially, what it might mean to become fully alive and robustly human in these challenging times. Here is a quick preview:

Part I—Waking Up: Waking up is our main job, our shared calling in life. But how will we awaken if we don't know that we're asleep? And what would it even mean to wake up? The six stepping stones in Part I provide the groundwork for beginning to live these questions.

Part II—Breakdown—Stepping into the Unknown: When our lives are no longer working—perhaps because we're stuck in a life-sapping routine or confused about our life's purpose—we experience Breakdown. Insofar as Breakdown heralds a crisis of identity, it can be frightening. At the same time, it can set the stage for self-discovery. The six stepping stones in Part II—through stories, provocations, and case studies—will invite you to explore the catalytic role that Breakdown can play in personal awakening.

Part III—A Curriculum for Waking Up: In today's conventional school settings, the curriculum is mostly centered on providing the cognitive tools deemed necessary to meet the needs of our economy. Meanwhile, what often goes missing are the skills, attitudes, and dispositions that contribute to self-knowledge and human flourishing. The seven stepping stones in Part III address this void by offering perspectives and tools essential for becoming open-minded, imaginative, playful, introspective, and soulful human beings.

Part IV—Awakening in Action: It's one thing to read about and reflect on *awakening* (as we invite you to do in Parts I–III), but quite another to consider adopting lifestyle changes that have the potential to trigger awakening in your daily life. This is the challenge we offer through Part IV's six stepping stones.

Part V—Personal and Cultural Transformation: Whether we choose to be aware of it or not, we have all been born into a culturally mediated narrative that shapes our understanding of our life's meaning and purpose. Ideally, this story would call forth our best or highest selves; but today our dominant narrative often does just the opposite by engendering fear, greed, and alienation. This book's final stepping stones demonstrate how those choosing to awaken can act as pioneers in giving birth to a new cultural story—one that showcases what it means to be in open-hearted relationship with Self, Other, and World—i.e., what it means to be fully human.

As you read this book, we invite you to have a notebook or journal by your side so that you can record your insights and awakenings as you engage with the book's exercises, prompts, and provocations.

Now, if you are ready, please take three deep breaths: the first to notice and release any tension that you might be holding; the second to open your body and mind to what is to come; and the third to join this present moment.

PART I

Waking Up

Introduction

Waking up is our main job, our shared calling in life. But what would it even mean to wake up? The six stepping stones in Part I provide the groundwork for beginning to live this question.

A tentative knock reverberates through the quiet of my office.

"Come in," I call. (Unless otherwise indicated, "I" references throughout this book reflect Christopher's voice.)

The door opens and Emily, a student from my Freshman Seminar, asks if she might talk with me.

I nod and she begins: "It's nothing serious. It's just that I'm kind of lost when it comes to choosing a major. Sometimes I'm not even sure why I'm here."

I invite Emily to say more and she adds: "There's nothing that I'm super passionate about. All my life I've been pretty much told what to study and how to behave. It's like I've never stopped to figure out for myself what I want to do with my life. My parents tell me I'm smart and that I should major in Business or maybe Engineering, but those fields don't really interest me. For now, I'm just going to class, doing what I'm told, but it all seems like a waste."

Curious, I ask: "What would have to happen so that it didn't feel like a waste?"

After a long silence, Emily responds, "I really don't know.... I just want to feel excited, you know, passionate about what I'm doing here. It's not enough for me to just go to classes, do my assignments, and take tests. There's got to be more."

Emily's experience is similar to many young people today who have been told by their parents and teachers, and by their society, that college is what comes after high school and that it's where you go to become *marketable*. Although Emily appears to be stuck, her confusion could also be seen as an opportunity for awakening.

The six stepping stones in Part I serve as guideposts for Emily and the countless number of other people who are seeking to discover their life's meaning and purpose. Here's what's ahead:

1. Asleep or Awake? When it comes to discerning our life's meaning and purpose, many of us are lost and confused.

2. What We Believe We Become: The journey to authentic adulthood begins as we summon the courage to explore the origins of our beliefs and the ways that they often cripple our perceptions of ourselves and of the world.

3. Questions Rather Than Answers: It is the questions that arise from deep inside us that are the catalyst for our awakening. Rather than pushing life's big questions aside, we can choose to embrace them, to live them.

4. Education for What? Insofar as modern schools focus primarily on preparing young people for the workplace—emphasizing answers rather than questions—they fail to educate the whole person, ignoring key competencies relating to self-discovery, civic engagement, moral literacy, and emotional intelligence.

5. Truthspeaking as a Catalyst for Awakening: The more we summon the courage to stand up and speak our truth to each other and to ourselves, the more we awaken.

6. The Power of Story: We are stuck just now—both as individuals and as a society—because we are entrapped in a too-small story of what it means to be fully human, fully alive, fully ourselves.

Asleep or Awake?

We don't come into this world to sleep. We come to awaken
… and to grow and evolve.
—Stephen Gilligan and Robert Dilts[1]

We have all been born into this crazy, vibrating, stupendous, vexing, mysterious and unfathomable universe. Yet, who among us lives in a state of radical amazement? Who wakes up overjoyed at having been granted one more day on this magnificent planet? Who goes to bed brimming with gratitude for the breath of life that is so freely given to each of us?

What about you? Can you recall the last time you felt ecstatically alive, teeming with gratitude, breathless with wonder? Maybe you had walked down that same street in your neighborhood a thousand times, but on one particular morning there was something about the velvety softness of the air, the blending of light and shadow, the way that a particular willow leaf tumbled to the ground, that stopped you in your tracks.

Or suppose you are someone who is in the habit of scarfing down your food. You tell yourself that rushing through meals gives you added time for other, more important things in life. But then, one day, when entering the shower, you pause before a full-length mirror to behold yourself, naked, from head to toe. Rather than critiquing your body as you might be prone to do, you simply stand in awe of the mystery that is your body; and in that moment, you realize that your body is not an object—it's not a gas tank that you stuff fuel into each day. Instead, it's a miracle, a marvel, and, as such, it is worthy of your love and attention.

Connecting as a Catalyst for Awakening: I vividly recall a day a decade ago when I chose to hang out for a while in front of the Student Union Building on the Penn State campus. It was exam week, and as I watched students passing by, I became troubled by the stress that was etched on so many faces. In an effort to reach out to students, I wrote the question, "What are you going through?" on a piece of cardboard. Then, I settled in on a bench, holding the sign on my lap.

Some of the students passing by acknowledged my presence with nods and smiles; and a few even sat down to share some of what they were going through. In one sense, this was all rather ordinary: a college professor with a question and some young people responding; but, in another sense, it was unusual. After all, we were strangers, from different generations with different histories, and yet we were taking time to talk, to listen, and to connect with one another.

Walking back to my office an hour later, I felt energized, awakened. Making this simple gesture reminded me that opportunities for awakening are all around us, provided we are willing to let go of our patterned ways of being.

Awakening to Your Life: Human beings have an innate hunger for adventure and discovery, and I believe that it is this hunger that emboldens us to put aside our habitual ways of being from time to time. As we begin to let go of our patterns and routines, we step into the unknown, where new discoveries await and the possibility of awakening beckons. You can have an embodied taste of what I am getting at by pausing to consider the following three questions:

1. Why are you here? Really, why are you here? [I am here to...?]
2. When do you feel most alive? [I feel most alive when...?]
3. What is your greatest fear? [My greatest fear is...?]

Rather than rushing ahead, grab your journal and write down the one question, from among these three, that you are most curious about. For example, if you are most drawn to the second question, write down, "I feel most alive when...." Then, take a deep breath, releasing any tension that you might be holding, and begin writing, non-stop, for a couple of minutes. Don't filter, don't second-guess, don't judge, don't erase or even punctuate. Just keep your pen moving. And if it happens that you get stuck, just skip down a line, write the prompt again, and have another go at responding.

When you are done, shake out your hand and slowly take in the rawness of your words, beholding the truth that emerges when any one of us expresses ourselves freely, absent filters.[2]

Of course, it would be easy to skip this challenge, just as it is easy to enact our lives, stuck in our patterns; but, in my experience, nothing transformative happens unless and until we muster the courage to become intimate with ourselves. Indeed, this exercise is an invitation to open a channel to your own shy soul. Dancer and author Martha Graham expressed it this way:

> There is a vitality, a life force, a quickening that is translated through you into action, and because there is only one of you in all time, this expression is unique. If you block it, it will never exist through any other medium and be lost. The world will not have it. It is not yours to determine how good it is; nor how it compares with other expressions. It is your business to keep the channel open.[3]

The Wonder of Awakening—Melissa's Experience: When I was in college, I joined fifteen other students on a winter retreat in the mountains of Pennsylvania. On a cold, clear night, in the light of a crescent moon, we stood together on the edge of a vast marshland. The place felt ancient. And as we lingered in the ankle-deep January snow, our breath forming little clouds, one of us began to howl—a free, joyful, wild sound that pierced the stillness of that dark night. Like a wave rushing toward the shore, that sound surged up through me, filling me, spilling from my own lungs, as I joined the chorus. It lasted only a few moments, but it remained in the air, the echo of something both forbidden and right. We hummed with the energy of it. Spontaneously, we began to dance under that sliver of moon, and the feeling was like the howl—utterly liberated, untamed, and full of joy, connecting us to ourselves, each other, and Earth.

In that moment, I was fully awake to everything and everyone around me—my friends, the air, the night sky, the snow-covered Earth, and my own self. This deep, ancient call to awaken rises and flows through all of us, breaking down our notions of what is right, appropriate, and practical. We are thrown suddenly into the mysteries of the Unknown, offered the opportunity to be transformed into a dance of unadulterated joyfulness, a howling gift to ourselves and to those around us.

I wish I could tell you that walking the path to Awakening will be easy. I wish I could say, "You will love every second of it and have the time of your life." But if you're anything like me, you will not love every second of it. You *will*, however, have the time of your life, because you will be having *your* life, not somebody else's. I believe that is more than enough.

Wrap-Up

> Only that day dawns to which we are awake.
> —Henry David Thoreau[4]

We are each recipients of the gift of a human life. This gift comes with the challenge to wake up! Awakening starts as we begin to shake free of our preconceived notions about ourselves and about how things should be; it happens as we open ourselves to EVERYTHING—the beauty and the joy, as well as the pain and the heartbreak, that come with having a human life. This is the journey of a lifetime; and it's what this book is about.

What We Believe, We Become

Are you living or are you being lived?

We all came into this world without a map, rulebook, or game plan. But with time, we learned the ways of our people—e.g., learned to talk as they did, eat as they did, behave as they did, believe as they did. We also learned that if we deviated from our culture's norms—e.g., by choosing to sleep on the floor instead of in a bed or refusing to obey school rules—there could be consequences. For example, we might be chided by our family or labeled as a problem child by society. No wonder most of us go along with what our culture expects of us; it's easier and safer that way.

Yet, you probably don't regard yourself as someone who goes along with or conforms to your society's expectations. More likely, you pride yourself as someone who is free to make your own choices. But is this true? Certainly, we each have the freedom to choose between things like drinking a Coke or a Snapple, going to bed early or late, or texting versus video chatting with a friend. In each of these examples though, we are really just selecting from the very narrow band of choices deemed acceptable by our culture.

Meanwhile, there are lots of things we might never do for fear of being judged as weird. For example, suppose the next time you are in a supermarket, you are so happy that you feel moved to whistle and to skip up and down the aisles. Your culture has conditioned you to believe that doing this would create a scene and lead to embarrassment. But that's your culture. What about you? Could you unabashedly express joy by skipping and whistling among strangers in a public space?

Or say you are walking downtown with some friends. It's an unbearably hot summer day, and everyone is complaining. But then, you come upon a giant oak tree, offering cooling shade. Filled with gratitude, you have the impulse to embrace that oak and thank her for the shade that she is offering you. Could you act on this impulse, or would you rein yourself in for fear that your friends might make fun of you for being a tree-hugger?

To the extent that our behaviors are hemmed in by societal expectations and the judgments of others, we have to wonder: How free are we really?

It wasn't until I was in my late twenties that I got a glimmer of what I am attempting to express here. I was standing on a street corner on a brisk November afternoon when, out of nowhere, my mind was inhabited by the haunting question: "Is <u>THIS</u> it?" Embedded in my question was a wake-up call, issuing from my depths, that sounded something like:

> Chris, your whole life has become a pattern. All you are doing, year after year, is slogging along, enacting patterns—thought patterns, behavioral patterns, consumption patterns, and on and on. IS THIS IT? Will you continue to spend your life shackled in this way, or will you awaken?

Our Beliefs Shape Our Reality: In her book, *The Continuum Concept*, Jean Leidloff shares a personal story that illustrates how, without our conscious awareness, culturally seeded beliefs can control our behaviors. It occurred when Leidloff joined two Italian diamond hunters on an adventure in the jungles of South America. The three of them were traveling up the Carcupi River, with Tauripan Indians serving as their guides. Far into their journey, a massive waterfall blocked their progress, and to continue, they had to portage their cumbersome canoe over a tortuous trail strewn with boulders. In Leidloff's words, here is what happened:

> On the day we arrived at Arepuchi Falls we were primed to suffer and started off, grim-faced ... hating every moment [as we struggled to drag and push and pull our enormous wooden canoe over huge boulders[1]]. A quarter of the way across, all ankles were bleeding.
> Partly by way of begging off for a minute, I jumped up on a high rock to photograph the scene. From my vantage point, and momentary disinvolvement, I noticed a most interesting fact. Here before me were men engaged in a single task. Two, the Italians, were tense, frowning, losing their tempers at everything, and cursing nonstop in the distinctive manner of the Tuscan. The rest, Indians, were having a fine time. They were laughing at the unwieldiness of the canoe, making a game of the battle, relaxing between pushes, laughing at their own scrapes and especially amused when the canoe, as it wobbled forward, pinned one or the other of them underneath it. The fellow,

held bare-backed against the scorching granite, when he could breathe again, invariably laughed the loudest, enjoying his relief.

All were doing the same work; all were experiencing the strain and pain…. There was no difference in our situations except that we [foreigners] had been conditioned by our culture to believe that such a combination of circumstances constituted an unquestionable low on the scale of well-being, and we were unaware that we had any option in the matter. The brown-skinned Indians, on the other hand, equally unconscious of making a choice, were in a particularly merry state of mind, reveling in the camaraderie…. Each forward move was for them a little victory.

As I finished photographing and rejoined the team, I opted out of [my previous conditioning] and enjoyed, quite genuinely, the rest of the portage. Even the bruises I sustained were reduced, with remarkable ease, to nothing more significant than what they indeed were: small hurts which would soon heal and which required neither an unpleasant emotional reaction such as anger, self-pity, or resentment, nor anxiety at how many more there might be before the end of the haul. On the contrary, I found myself appreciative of my excellently designed body, which would patch itself up with no instructions or decisions from me.[2]

In Leidloff's story, the Italian men believed that the task of carrying an unwieldy wooden canoe over boulders would be terrible, and this belief shaped their reality. The Tauripans, by contrast, saw the task as a time for camaraderie, even fun, and this became their experience.

Upshot: The task was neither terrible nor fun. It simply was what it was. The differing experiences of the Italians and the Tauripans resulted from differences in their culturally scribed beliefs. And it's no different for you and me. Though our responses to life events may seem to arise from within us, they are mostly triggered by our conditioning. The good news is that, with awareness, we can each *choose*, as Leidloff did, to step beyond our conditioning.

A Thought Experiment: Imagine yourself snugly ensconced indoors watching television with friends on a frigid winter day. Noting that the outside temperature is a harsh five below zero, one of your feisty friends bets you twenty-five dollars that you couldn't last outside—barefoot and wearing just your underwear—for two minutes. You're a bit low on cash, so receiving twenty-five bucks for a mere two minutes of discomfort seems worth it; you decide to take the bet.

Picture yourself, now, all warm and toasty, as you prepare to step outside. Your past experience has conditioned you to brace yourself against the cold. So, the instant you step outside, your body goes rigid, your breath becomes shallow, your shoulders scrunch, your eyes narrow, and your jaw locks. But does it need to be this way? What if, before stepping into the cold, you chose to upend your conditioning by breathing deeply while voluntarily releasing any tension in your jaw, neck, shoulders, and chest. Then, open and relaxed, you chose to experience the freezing temperature, not as unbearably horrendous but as enlivening.

Though it may seem like a stretch, it is possible to undo one's conditioning. You could actually explore this the next time you are in the shower by turning the water from hot to warm to chilly to cold in four stages, at 60-second intervals. Do all this while maintaining your focus on your breath, taking long, slow inhalations and with each exhalation, releasing the tension in your body. With a bit of practice, chances are good that you will discover that you don't need to be a pawn to your conditioning. You have a choice. We all do!

The Belief Effect: Once there was a man who was terribly sick with severe abdominal pains and a rash covering his belly and back. Unable to withstand the pain any longer, he was rushed to the Emergency Room where a doctor examined him. After a few moments, the doctor confidently announced that the man was suffering from an ailment that could be easily cured. She then gave him a small bottle of red pills and assured him that if he took three pills a day, he would be back to normal within a week. The man took the medicine as prescribed, and, lo and behold, a week later he was completely cured. Here's the catch: The pills didn't cure the man; they were made of sugar. The man was healed because he believed in the power of the pills. Indeed, medical research reveals that, not infrequently, cures that appeared to result from medical interventions were actually the result of the placebo effect—i.e., the belief effect.

Remarkably, the placebo effect even extends to surgery. For example, Dr. Bruce Moseley of the Baylor School of Medicine performed an experiment in which he compared the results of three alternative treatments for patients suffering from debilitating knee pain. In all three treatments, a local anesthetic was applied to numb the knee region, and then incisions were made to provide entry to the knee joint. In Treatment 1, Moseley flushed out the knee joint, removing any material that might have been causing inflammation. In Treatment 2, he went a step further by snipping away any damaged cartilage after the flushing process. In the final treatment, Moseley simply pretended that he was performing the full surgery—e.g., by simulating the sounds of the washing and clipping procedures.[3] As might be expected, the patients in Treatments 1 and 2, who received real surgical interventions, improved, but remarkably, those who received the fake or placebo treatment improved every bit as much as those in the first two groups. Moseley concluded: "My skill as a surgeon had no benefit on these patients. The entire benefit of surgery for osteoarthritis of the knee was the placebo effect."[4]

The placebo effect is often seen in negative terms, but rather than being embarrassed that a sugar pill or a fake surgery can sometimes cure what ails us, what if we were to see this as a testament to the power of our beliefs to affect both our minds and our bodies?

Depersonalizing Your Beliefs: Insofar as our beliefs influence how we experience ourselves, they impact our self-understanding. Yet, we often have little awareness of how all this works because we overlook the fact that our beliefs aren't so much "ours" as they are cultural hand-me-downs.

If it is self-discovery and awakening that you are seeking, it can be liberating to depersonalize your beliefs, treating them as assumptions or interpretations, rather than as capital "T" Truths. You can experience this liberation right now by writing down in your journal the first thing(s) that come to mind in response to the following ten open sentences.

1. My culture has taught me to believe that failure is _____

    _____.

2. My culture has taught me to believe that to be happy I should

    _____.

3. My culture has taught me to believe that the purpose of my education is _____.

4. My culture has taught me to believe that to be successful I should

    _____.

5. My culture has taught me to believe that my body is _____

    _____.

6. My culture has taught me to believe that the reason I am alive is to _____.

7. My culture has taught me to believe that my feelings are _____

    _____.

8. My culture has taught me that it is my responsibility to _____

  _____.

9. My culture has taught me to believe that other people are _____

  _____.

10. My culture has taught me to believe that planet Earth is _____

  _____[5].

When you are finished, look over your belief statements and pick one that feels especially true. Then, write down that statement along with its opposite:

Your Original True Statement: _____

_____.

The Opposite of your True Statement: _____

_____.

For illustrative purposes, suppose you completed the first prompt with: "My culture has taught me to believe that failure <u>should</u> <u>be</u> <u>avoided</u> at <u>all</u> <u>costs</u>." Though you may agree with the sentiment in this response, take a moment to explore what it would be like to believe the opposite—i.e., that failure *should be welcomed with open arms*. Granted, this tends to go against what our culture teaches us, but maybe our culture has it wrong? What if failure is important, necessary even? For example, rather than shunning failure, inventors welcome it, firm in the knowledge that the process of trial and error often leads to new discoveries.

Dear Reader, at this juncture, you might be inclined to move forward, reading more words, more paragraphs, more pages. After all, our culture teaches us to believe that we make *progress* by moving forward, always forward. But what if, instead of continuing to read, you were to stop, right now, with the intention of deepening your quest for awakening. How? By picking up your journal again and turning your responses to each of your belief statements (above) inside out, trusting that a willingness to playfully explore your beliefs will, in some measure, bring you greater freedom.

Clutching onto our beliefs and associated opinions can be exhausting, insofar as it leads to rigidity and self-righteousness. So if it's freedom of thought that you seek, it might be enough to simply exercise curiosity, openness, and humility in the face of all that arises. This way, when someone voices a belief that you disagree with, you can choose to simply take a long deep in-breath and, on the out-breath, in a gesture of humility, to respond with, "Could be."

Wrap-Up

> Man's last freedom is his freedom to choose how he will react
> in any given situation.
> —Viktor Frankl[6]

The fact that our beliefs are usually not so much our own as they are artifacts of our social conditioning is not a new idea. During childhood and adolescence, these cultural hand-me-downs help to ensure that we fit into society. But how is it for you today? Is being secure and comfortable what you most aspire to in life? Will conforming to the status quo uncork your energy and passion? Will it invite forth your full humanity?

Questions Rather Than Answers

The unexamined life is not worth living.
—Socrates[1]

When I ask the students in my Freshmen Seminar, "What comes to mind when you hear the word 'question?'" they frequently respond with words like "answer," "test," "interrogation," and "stress." Sadly, the word "question" is seldom associated with words like "open," "curious," "discovery," or "delight."

Our attitudes toward questions, whether positive, negative, or neutral, are rooted, in part, in our childhood experiences. For example, if, as a child, your questions were often ignored, or worse, ridiculed—or if your parents reprimanded you for asking too many questions—today you may tend to shy away from questions. But consider this: The more reluctant we are to embrace and delight in questions of all sorts, the more we mute our lives, forfeiting opportunities for awakening.

University professor Tobin Hart illustrates this point in a story about a bright, albeit unmotivated, high school kid named Gunner, growing up in New Jersey in the 1950s. In an effort to stimulate Gunner and other disaffected kids at his school, they were sometimes taken by bus to Princeton University to attend presentations by distinguished physicists of the day, including Albert Einstein. Amid a particularly confusing lecture, one of Gunner's classmates asked the assembled scientists if they thought ghosts were real. Two of the physicists quickly dismissed the possibility on the grounds that there was no hard evidence for the existence of ghosts. That might have been the end of it, but J. Robert Oppenheimer, famous for his role in developing the atomic bomb, responded, "That's a fascinating question. I accept the possibility of all things." He went on to say that "it is necessary to find one's own required evidence" before accepting or rejecting any possibility.

"For Gunner [who later became a college professor] this was a revelation. Instead of closing down and accepting the world as fixed, Oppenheimer's perspective opened it back up to mystery, to the possibility of all things...."[2] Indeed, when we mindlessly grasp onto pre-packaged answers to life's questions, we flatten the world, stunting our curiosity while forfeiting opportunities for discovery.

Might Answers Be Overrated? In the role of students, we learned to demonstrate our knowledge by providing correct answers to our teacher's questions, but consider that this practice of always focusing on the "correct answer" can get in the way of our learning. Think of it this way: Imagine that I have just handed you a bottle of water and asked you to tell me what's in the bottle. You unscrew the top, smell the contents, take a sip, and declare that the liquid is "water."

But I frown and respond: "Water may be the correct label for the liquid, but this doesn't really answer my question. So, what's this stuff that you are calling water?"

You reply, "Okay, it's an atom of oxygen combined with two atoms of hydrogen."

But I shake my head, saying: "All you have given me are more words, more concepts, more labels. Look deeper."

Your face clouds with perplexity as you try to figure out what I want to hear. Noting your mounting frustration, I ask you to consider that you will not know what water really is until you admit that all of your standard—i.e., conditioned—responses to my question separate you from the possibility of discovering, for yourself, what's in the glass.

Indeed, if any of us wishes to discover the deeper, fuller truth of things, we first must be willing to admit to ignorance. Of course, our culture teaches us that "admitting to ignorance" is tantamount to revealing weakness. And admitting weakness is something which we must never do! But could it be that all of those stock answers that we learned in school, deplete, in some measure, the world of its mystery; and could it be that by admitting ignorance, we might actually achieve a deeper and more profound understanding of the world?

Find out for yourself! Pour yourself a glass of water right now and devote ten minutes to exploring what's really in that glass. Investigate with the innocence of a child, using all of your senses, clear in the understanding that we can't truly awaken to the world if we think we know everything already.

Safe Versus Unsafe Questions: In the spirit of self-discovery, I find it useful to make a distinction between unsafe questions—i.e., those that shake us up by inviting us into unfamiliar states of mind—and safe questions—i.e., those with ready-made, prescribed answers. If it helps, think of safe questions as those fill-in-the-blank, multiple-choice, or true-false questions that frequently show up on school exams. They don't call for much active thinking; either we have memorized the "correct" answer, or we haven't. Unsafe questions, by contrast, don't have ready answers. You could ponder one all night long and still not find a satisfying response, though you'd be better off for having tried. Here are some examples:

- What secrets do you keep from yourself?
- What longings are at the core of your life right now?
- What door in your life are you afraid to open?
- What would it mean for you to be fully and unapologetically yourself?
- What breaks your heart about being alive in these times?
- Who are you when nobody is looking?

Notice that these questions cannot be answered with a quick trip to Google or a neatly pre-packaged response. They are more like fine wine to be deliberately sipped and enjoyed, turned over on the tongue, slowly revealing new and surprising perspectives in little glimpses, during quiet moments of contemplation.

Sadly, during all my years of compulsory schooling, I don't recall ever being challenged by a teacher to consider that the best questions—i.e., the ones with the power to trigger awakenings—don't have ready answers. Rainer Maria Rilke framed it this way:

> I want to beg you, as much as I can … try to love the questions themselves like locked rooms and like books that are written in a very foreign tongue. Do not now seek the answers, which cannot be given you because you would not be able to live them. And the point is to live everything. Live the questions now. Perhaps you will then, gradually, without noticing it, live along some distant day into the answer.[3]

Rilke knew that to actually live a question we must submit to the discomfort of not knowing. This submission takes courage, especially insofar as we have been conditioned to seek comfort in knowing—i.e., comfort in the Known. But if we accept culturally mediated answers to life's big questions, we will never set our own course. By contrast, as we muster the resolve to embrace our life as a journey toward awakening, we may discover that it is the questions that arise from the core of our being that point us toward our destiny.

Permission to Ask Yourself Questions: Geniuses, from Plato and Socrates to Leonardo da Vinci and Einstein, have known that cultivating a questioning mind leads to self-knowledge and wisdom. I invite you to experience this insight by making a list of questions directed toward yourself. How many questions? If I suggested ten, your questions would probably be the familiar ones that you have been asking yourself for years. So, to make this exercise worthwhile, I challenge you to come up with one hundred questions!

In the spirit of "free writing," note down any kind of question, from "What's that spot on my toe?" or "How can I have more fun?" to "Who am I becoming?" Anything goes so long as your questions are directed toward yourself and bubble up spontaneously from within you. Give yourself a half hour to create your entire list; write quickly, without filtering or judging.[4]

When you are done, reflect on your list by considering: (1) the patterns or unifying themes among your questions, (2) the things your questions reveal about you, (3) the questions that are most unexpected, and (4) the steps you might take to "live" those questions that hold the most energy for you.[5]

Awakening Your Curiosity: Recent research reveals that people who are curious tend to orient their lives toward growth and are predisposed to engage in novel activities.[6] Furthermore, "they don't shy away from tough questions…. Instead of sleepwalking through life or doing what's expected, they are wondering how to get the most out of their days and the most of themselves."[7]

How might exercising your innate curiosity help you to ensure that you get the most out of your days? Find out by using your journal to note down five things that you are deeply curious about.

I am deeply curious about _____

_____.

I am deeply curious about _____

_____.

I am deeply curious about _____

_____.

I am deeply curious about _____

_____.

I am deeply curious about _____

_____.

If you can't think of five things right away, be patient, lightly holding this question for a day or two. Answers will come. Once you have your five items, consider how, collectively, they could be beacons pointing you toward self-discovery. For example, perhaps, ever since elementary school, for one reason or another, you have been deeply curious about: (1) corn, (2) drums, (3) eggs, (4) magnets, and (5) clouds. Instead of dismissing these five items as random categories, what if you were to playfully consider that each one is a metaphor, providing you with hints about your life's meaning and purpose. For example, you might associate "corn" with food, "drums" with rhythm, "eggs" with fertility, "magnets" with bonding, and "clouds" with transformation, suggesting that your destiny—your calling in life—might, somehow, involve a conjoining of food, rhythm, fertility, bonding, and transformation. How? Who knows? It's enough for now, just to be curious, open, and playful!

The Power of Why: When I encounter a young person who doubts that curiosity-driven questions can lead to self-discovery, I introduce them to a practice from author Derrick Jensen.[8] It's easy to do—you just have to persist in asking "Why?" over and over again. For example, suppose a friend expresses a belief that you find perplexing. Normally, to maintain harmony, you might just let it pass. But, this time, because you truly want to understand your friend, you inquire: "I'm really curious to know <u>why</u> you believe that?" There is no judgment hidden in your question. Instead, you simply want to know how your friend has come to believe as she does. When she finishes explaining her rationale, rather than jumping in with your own thoughts, you continue to ask *why*, inviting your friend to explore the events and factors that have shaped her belief. In effect, you are offering your friend a gift, helping her along the path of self-discovery.

To better appreciate how the power of why can foment self-discovery, consider this hypothetical exchange between a college advisor and her student:

ADVISOR: "How's it going?"

STUDENT: "Okay."

ADVISOR: "Can you say more?"

STUDENT (looking down): "Well, actually, things aren't going so great. My grades have taken a dive, and I'm bored with my classes. The only thing I'm enjoying is my social life."

ADVISOR: "So, the only good thing about college right now is your social life?"

STUDENT (uncomfortable at hearing his own words reflected back): "No, there's more to it than that."

ADVISOR: "Okay. So, tell me, I'm curious: Why do you wish to remain in college?"

STUDENT (looking down again): "I guess because this is where I'm supposed to be?"

ADVISOR (still wanting to understand): "Why do you believe that you're supposed to be in college?"

STUDENT: "Because my parents expect me to be here."

ADVISOR: "I get that. But why do you believe that you have to do what your parents expect you to do?"

STUDENT (a bit shocked by the question): "Because they are my parents! Because they would be upset if I dropped out."

ADVISOR (from a place of genuine interest): "Help me to understand: Why would your parents be upset?"

STUDENT: "Because they want me to be successful."

ADVISOR: "OK, I get that. But can you explain to me why you think going to college will make you successful, especially given that you are not having a successful time while you are here?"

STUDENT (a bit defensive): "Because getting a college degree will help guarantee that I make a lot of money."

ADVISOR: "Thanks, that's helpful, and it leads me to want to know why you believe that making a lot of money is necessary in order to have a fulfilling and successful life?"

STUDENT (exasperated): "You're driving me crazy with all of your WHY questions."

ADVISOR: "Sorry, I am just curious about what you're going through. These questions are about you—your life! Why do you suppose they are upsetting to you?"

STUDENT: "Because … because … I don't like thinking about all this. Please stop."

With each successive *why* question, the advisor was inviting her student to discover the assumptions that shaped his thinking regarding: (i) the meaning and purpose of his life, (ii) what it means to be successful, (iii) the legitimacy of his parent's authority in directing his life, and (iv) whether college was the right choice for him at this time.

I grant you that this sort of inquiry can be unsettling, and may cause the one being questioned to bristle. But bold, direct questions, even those that can't be satisfactorily answered in the moment, sometimes take root in the mind and heart and, with time, yield insights that blossom into fruitful action.

Wrap-Up

> Once you have learned how to ask questions—relevant and appropriate and substantial questions—you have learned how to learn and no one can keep you from learning whatever you want or need to know.
> —Neil Postman and Charles Weingartner[9]

School culture often transmits the messages that a student's job is to learn the answers to the teacher's questions and that it's not OK for students to be asking questions all the time—i.e., it is not OK for them to exercise their innate curiosity. *Dumbed down* in this way, it's no wonder that so many of us believe that we have to rely on others to tell us who we are and why we are here. But consider this: If the person you have been schooled to be is not the person you have been born to be, then to become that person, you must be willing to question everything.

Education for What?

The previous stepping stone on "Questions" ended with the statement: "If the person that you have each been *schooled* to be is not the person you have been born to be, then to become that person, you must be willing to question everything." So, now, in the spirit of self-discovery and awakening, we invite you to reflect on and question your own schooling.

Begin by noting that by the time you completed your K–12 schooling, you had spent roughly 14,000 hours in classrooms. Do the math: 180 school days/year × 6 hours/day × 13 years = 14,040 hours. By any measure, that is a significant chunk of your life.

So, what do you have to show for it? Certainly, the experiences, relationships, and knowledge you acquired have contributed to the person you are today, but how, exactly? What did you learn? Was your time well spent? How might you assess this?

These questions may seem odd insofar as we are seldom encouraged to examine the merits and shortcomings of the practices that comprise(d) our schooling. As a result, we simply assume, without question, that school attendance is vital to our success in life. Similarly, we assume that we need outside authorities (professional educators) to tell us what we need to learn and how to learn it. But is all of this really true?

Take a moment, now, to recall your high school experiences. You are the authority when it comes to evaluating the educational merits of those years; you were there the whole time. You could do a quick assessment now by using your journal to record your responses to the following open sentences.

1. What I mostly learned in high school was _____

   _____.

2. If I allowed myself to speak my full truth about my time in high school, I would say _____

   _____.

3. The times that I felt most alive during my high school years were when _____

   _____.

4. By the time I finished high school, I was _____

   _____.

5. If I'd never gone to high school, today I would be _____

   _____.

When I invite students at Penn State into this inquiry, many, though certainly not all, complain that the classroom portion of high school was often a waste of their time. When pressed, they opine that something essential was missing. In many cases, it seems that the "missing piece" may have been the students, themselves, insofar as their life force, their questions, their passions, their curiosity, and their creativity, and their enlivened spirits were too often exiled from the classroom.

The Shadow Side of Schooling: Ideally, we hope that what we learn in school will deepen us, making us better informed, more aware, more competent, more thoughtful, more whole. But school, for all its good intentions, can actually condition—i.e., teach—us to be less inquisitive, less confident, less willing to be open and vulnerable, less spontaneous, and less whole. To the extent that this might occur, it is mostly linked to the structure of modern schooling, with its set curriculum, specified learning objectives, rigid schedules, standardized evaluation procedures, and so on.

Though K-12 learning experiences vary widely, there is one thing that almost all of us learn, without realizing it. That "one thing" is *conformity.* Yes, during those 14,000 classroom hours we were all socialized, to varying degrees, to be obedient, to follow the rules, to color inside the lines.... In this light, it may be that the most significant thing that school teaches us is to surrender to outside authorities, and in so doing to separate, in some measure, from ourselves—i.e., from our own inner authority.

Award-winning high school teacher David McCullough shares a story that illustrates what I am getting at here. On the first day of class each year, McCullough invites his students to write a short essay in response to three questions: (1) Are you a hammer or a nail? (2) Are you a pitcher or a catcher? (3) Are you a rake or a leaf?

How would you answer these questions? If you are at all like McCullough's students, you would probably choose hammer rather than nail, pitcher rather than catcher, and rake rather than leaf. After all, responding with hammer and pitcher and rake allows us to see ourselves as active agents out in the world, making things happen and directing our own learning.

But McCullough sees it differently. So it is that after everyone hands in their papers, he ceremoniously drops them into a trash bin, declaring that his students are not hammers but nails; not pitchers but catchers; not rakes but leaves. When they ask why he has trashed their work, McCullough replies, "Because against your preference, you bowed to my authority and scribbled out your essay … and you have been doing the same throughout your entire schooling."[1]

Through this demonstration, McCullough is, in effect, inviting his students to consider that conformity is at the center of schooling's hidden curriculum.

Erica Goldson—valedictorian at Coxsackie-Athens High School in New York—gave voice to the domesticating impacts of schooling when she said in her valedictorian address:

> In retrospect, I cannot say that I am any more intelligent than my peers. I can [only] attest that I am the best at doing what I am told…. I have no clue about what I want to do with my life. I have no interests because I saw every subject of study as "work," and I excelled at every subject just for the purpose of excelling and not learning. And quite frankly, I'm very scared.[2]

Goldson won the game of school; she became the valedictorian, and she did this by bending to the expectations of the system. And, yet, to her credit, on graduation day, she realized that what she had mostly learned in school was obedience and conformity. By virtue of this awakening, Goldson took a brave step toward self-authorship.

Upshot: It is undeniable that most of us have gained valuable knowledge in school settings in the cognitive realms of reading, writing, math, history, science, and so forth. However, what modern schooling often neglects is the education of the whole person, which entails cultivating student capacities for mindfulness, empathic listening, metacognition, moral discernment, civic engagement, and creative expression, among other things. Lamentably, these arenas of self-knowledge and actualization are largely missing from today's schools. For example, there are few, if any, high school or college courses bearing titles like: The Practice of Mindfulness, The Art of Peacemaking, The Power of Truthspeaking, The Development of Ecological Consciousness, The Cultivation of Emotional Intelligence, or The Call to Political Activism.

Significant Learning Moments: It is a common assumption in the U.S. that without schools we'd all be doomed! But is this true? You could explore this assumption right now by creating a chart in your journal (see mockup below) where you list: (i) the *three most significant things* that you've learned in your life, (ii) *where* each of these significant learning experiences took place, and (iii) *who and/or what* facilitated each learning experience. Fill in the chart below as you arrive at your answers.

The Three Most Significant Things I Have Learned?	*Where Each Learning Took Place?*	*Who/What Facilitated Each Learning?*
1.		
2.		
3.		

When you are done, look over what you have written with an eye to detecting patterns. Then, consider these words from Donald Finkel (author of *Teaching with Your Mouth Shut*): "Most people's significant learning—the learning that has really mattered ... did not take place as a result of intentional teaching ... more than likely, no teacher [or classroom] was even present."[3]

Finkel's thesis—i.e., that a lot of significant learning occurs outside of school settings—challenges the naïve assumption that learning has to occur in specific places (schools) under specified conditions and within set structures. Instead, as educator Matt Hern suggests, "Learning is something that happens all the time, whether we intend it or not. Learning is what people do. We learn, take in new information, gain new knowledge, pick up new skills and insights constantly."[4] In short, learning and living are inseparable.

Freedom to Learn on Our Own Terms: What if, growing up, rather than being subjected to compulsory schooling, you had been given the freedom to decide what you wanted to learn and when and how you would learn it? In other words, what if you didn't have to conform to a system of education, but you could instead have that system conform to you?

Believe it or not, this is the philosophy at Sudbury Valley School in Framingham, Massachusetts. Sudbury Valley is essentially an "unschool"— i.e., it is everything that a conventional school is not.[5]

For example, the students at Sudbury have full autonomy to decide what they want to learn and when they want to learn it. If they wish to hang out all day with their friends or binge on video games, they are totally free to do that. Even if they choose to do this for days or weeks or months on end, it's not a problem. This is because the staff members at Sudbury know that as humans, we are all innately drawn to learning. It is what we do; it's how we survive and thrive.

Secure in this wisdom, the job of the "teacher" at Sudbury is to simply wait until a student becomes interested in learning something and then to facilitate their learning. By way of example, Sudbury teacher Daniel Greenberg tells the story of how a bunch of kids, between the ages of nine and twelve, came to him one morning asking to learn arithmetic. They'd been attending Sudbury for several years, but until then, they had had very little need for arithmetic and therefore little desire to learn it. Of course, in a conventional U.S. school, having fourth, fifth, and sixth graders who had not learned basic arithmetic would be seen as scandalous. Talk about children left behind! But Sudbury doesn't classify children as "behind" or "ahead." Decades of experience has taught Sudbury teachers that genuine learning only occurs when a student feels a strong desire to master a new skill or body of knowledge.

Those 9–12 year olds were seeking out Greenberg because they truly wanted to master arithmetic. When they first asked, Greenberg actually tried to dissuade them, saying, "You really don't want to learn this. Your neighborhood friends, your parents, your relatives probably want you to, but you, yourselves, would much rather be playing or doing something else."[6] But those kids were not to be deterred. They pressed the issue, promising that they would work hard and never miss a homework assignment. Eventually, they convinced Greenberg, and he told them that he would meet with them every Tuesday and Thursday for a half hour, during which time he would instruct them. If they were even five minutes late, he warned, the class would be canceled. If they missed two classes, the whole deal was off. The students agreed to these terms.

When it came to picking a text, Greenberg selected a book written in 1898 because it was filled with practice exercises that would help the kids master basic math skills. After only two classes, those kids exhibited proficiency in the whole gamut of basic addition including what Greenberg calls "long thin columns, short fat columns, (and) long fat columns." Two classes later, they had a handle on subtraction. Next, they learned multiplication tables, which every student was required to memorize and was tested on over and over during class meetings. Greenberg reports:

> They were high, all of them. They could feel the material entering their bones. Then division. Fractions. Decimals. Percentages. Square roots. They came at 11:00 sharp, stayed half an hour, and left with homework. They came back the next time with all their homework done. After twenty contact hours, they had covered it all. Every one of them knew the material cold.[7]

In twenty weeks, they mastered what traditionally takes six years for public school students. And these students weren't geniuses; they were just regular kids.

It's important to register that Greenberg's students weren't cajoled, forced, or bribed, much less shamed, into learning arithmetic. They sought it out. They learned arithmetic because they wanted to. This is true for all of us: When we are allowed to follow our innate curiosity in its own organic timing, we learn effortlessly and find the process deeply fulfilling. It is our internal motivation that propels us to succeed in ways that conventional, top-down models of education often preclude.

Recall that the point of this Sudbury School example is to examine the beliefs and expectations that we tend to take for granted around schooling. This doesn't mean that these beliefs are wrong! After all, it sometimes seems like kids need lots of structure in order to learn. But what if what kids need most—far more than arbitrary rules and demands—is to be seen, appreciated, trusted, and respected? What if there is a seed of greatness within each child and the job of the teacher, as is the case at Sudbury School, is to nurture that seed with patience, trust, and love?[8]

Wrap-Up

> Whatever an education is, it should make you a unique individual, not a conformist; it should furnish you with an original spirit with which to tackle the big challenges; it should allow you to find values which will be your roadmap through life; it should make you spiritually rich, a person who loves whatever you are doing, wherever you are, whomever you are with; it should teach you what is important, how to live and how to die.
>
> —John Taylor Gatto[9]

It can be discomforting to look critically at our individual schooling histories and, in so doing, perhaps, to experience feelings of dissonance, confusion, or even anger. But remember: It is through fearlessly questioning EVERYTHING that we awaken; and, really, could there be any more noble goal for education than this?

Truthspeaking as a
Catalyst for Awakening

> Honesty is more than not lying. It is truth telling, truth speaking, truth living, and truth loving.
> —James E. Faust[1]

These days it often seems as if speaking the truth is not really the purpose of communication. For example: We are inundated by "news" stories and social media posts that often conflate and distort the truth; we are badgered by advertisements designed to manipulate our thoughts and feelings; and we are governed by leaders who often seem to regard lying as a legitimate political practice. No surprise, then, that by the time we reach adulthood, many of us have become experts at finessing, skirting, and compromising the truth. We may even lie to our very selves, without knowing it.

You could begin to explore how this pertains to you by recalling a time when you began a sentence with the words, "To be brutally honest…." For example, maybe in an attempt to be candid with a friend, you said: "To be brutally honest, that outfit doesn't look good on you," or "To be brutally honest, you don't really know what you are talking about." Perhaps you weren't saying these things to be cruel; you were simply being truthful. But were you?

Awakening to What's True: You are sitting with a friend at a restaurant, catching up and enjoying each other's company. But, after a while, you begin to feel irritated because you think that your friend is talking too much. So, you summon your courage and say: "Sorry, but I really need to speak my truth here and tell you that you are dominating our conversation by talking too much." It might even feel cathartic to speak out like this. After all, you're telling it like it is, standing up for yourself, speaking your truth. But, again, are you?

Imagine, instead, that you were able to have the presence of mind to realize that your thought—i.e., my friend is talking too much—is just a passing reaction to the frustration that *you* are feeling and that to discover *your* real truth, you will need to awaken to the root of your upset.

Genuine Truthspeaking, in the words of teacher/writer Tamarack Song, requires stating "clearly and simply what one thinks and feels." He continues on to explain, "[t]here is no judgment or expectation, no disguise of humor or force of anger. The manner of speech is sacred, because it wells up from the soul of our being rather than from our self-absorbed ego."[2]

Holding Song's definition for Truthspeaking in mind, return to that restaurant scene, where you were sitting with your friend who is "talking too much." This time, rather than voicing your frustration, you take a deep breath and then go inside and ask yourself: "What does my judgment that my friend is talking too much reveal about what I am feeling and needing in this moment?" By reflecting in this way, you might discover that you are frustrated because you are needing the very same thing that is causing your friend to "talk too much"—i.e., you are needing to be heard, appreciated, and seen by your friend.

Saying to your friend "you talk too much" is not your real truth; it is simply a judgment born of your frustration. To express your full truth you would need to speak in the first person, perhaps saying something like: "Hey, I <u>notice</u> I'm <u>feeling</u> frustrated because I have a <u>need</u> to be included in our conversation. Might you bring me in by asking me a question?" In this scenario, you would be making yourself transparent by expressing your *feelings* (frustration) and your *need* (to be brought into the conversation), together with *a clear request* (ask me a question).[3]

If Truthspeaking, as it's being presented here, strikes you as strange and/or awkward, that's understandable. Indeed, this kind of communicating is as unfamiliar in our culture as breathing underwater or sleeping upside down. As a result, most of us employ a variety of strategies to avoid making ourselves vulnerable in this way. For example, we might use humor to sidestep a touchy topic or harsh language to disguise our own truth—e.g., lashing out with "Go to hell" instead of truthfully saying, "I strongly disagree with you." But consider: As we each develop the capacity to be radically honest with ourselves, we gain the ability to be honest with each other.

Diving Deeper—James' Story: James was a Penn State student who had an assignment to speak nothing but the truth for 48 hours. When I talked with him on the afternoon of his first day, James was buzzed as he told me: "For the first time in my life I am only speaking what is true." Curious, I asked him if he could give me an example.

"Sure," he said. "Just an hour ago I ran into my roommate, and he looked really bad. So, I told him the truth. I said, 'Dude, you look really bad.'"

Hearing this, I asked James, "What was beneath your statement to your roommate that he looked really bad?" James looked perplexed, so I tried again: "When you told your roommate he looked 'really bad,' what is it that you, yourself, were needing?"

James replied, "I guess I was needing him to not look bad?"

"Yes, and why were you needing your roommate to not look bad?"

James thought for another long moment, and then, his face transforming as if something finally clicked, he exclaimed: "I've got it! I was feeling good earlier today, but when I ran into my roommate and saw how stressed and tired he looked, I started feeling stressed and tired, myself. So, I guess I just wanted to get away from feeling that way."

I reflected his words back, saying: "So, your real truth wasn't that your roommate looked bad; it was that you began to feel bad in his presence and wanted to escape."

James nodded in affirmation.

These two examples illustrate that Truthspeaking is not about saying the first thing that pops into our heads. It is not a knee-jerk reaction or a snap judgment. When we Truthspeak, it has almost nothing to do with the other person. Instead, real truth comes when we are aware and awake enough to tune into the truth lying within ourselves.

Authentic Conversation: There are few things more joyful and transformative than authentic conversation! Yet, it seems that this joy often goes unrealized today. In this regard, Joseph Campbell wrote, "The cave you fear to enter holds the treasure you seek." I see Campbell's words as an invitation to think of each and every conversation as an unexplored cave. We can remain at the entrance of the cave, stuck in our habitual, comfort-seeking conversational roles and behaviors. The alternative is to fearlessly step into the cave, leaving all artifice at the door. This means setting aside all forms of pretending, deflecting, judging and blaming.

But what does authentic conversation actually look like? Consider this scenario: You are sitting with a friend over lunch. Normally, the two of you would engage in chit-chat for a half hour as you eat, but today something different is about to happen. On this occasion your friend wants depth rather than surface-level chitchat. So, he looks you in the eye and asks: "What is true for you right now?"

At first, you are taken aback and consider making a joke to change the subject. But your friend presses you a bit, adding: "Come on, every day—in every moment—we each have something that is true for us. What's true for you right now?"

You hesitate, feeling uncomfortable and at a loss for words. You look down at the floor; then up at the ceiling. You begin to perspire. In the midst of your anxiety, you look at your friend and are surprised by the openness and kindness so apparent in his eyes. Even though you have not yet spoken, you sense that he is already listening to you, holding space for you.

Then, instinctively, you put your hand on your belly and the tension begins to ease. After several minutes of stillness, you begin to speak, your words arising from a place deep inside: "What's true for me is that I am unhappy, and I have been hiding my unhappiness from myself. I am bored with my job and my life is crap."

There you are, sharing things that you haven't even fully acknowledged to yourself and your friend is right there, listening, his presence open and reassuring.

Fortunately, he knows better than to think that he can fix your situation. What he can do, though, is to ask you open-ended, honest questions. I am *not* referring to those well-meaning questions that we sometimes pose to a troubled friend. You know, the kind that sound like: "Have you considered such and such?" Such questions are really just ways of telling the other person what we think they should consider. By contrast, with open-ended questions, we have no idea how the other person will respond—i.e., no hidden agenda.

For example, imagine your friend asking you questions like: (i) What does it feel like to acknowledge, out loud, that you are unhappy and bored and that your life is crap? or (ii) What possibilities or changes might be possible now that you have admitted all this to yourself?

Like a stone cast into a pond, these questions create ripples both outward and downward. As such, they are gifts. This is true for all open-ended questions when they are triggered by genuine curiosity and a willingness to listen. It is both powerful open-ended questions and the bravery to be real and vulnerable that create the possibility of authentic conversations.

Wrap-Up

> There is a price to pay for telling the truth. There is a bigger price for living a lie.
>
> —Cornel West[4]

Genuine Truthspeaking is hugely challenging, which is why it seems to be something of a rarity in our culture. Sadly, the more we remain separate from our truth, the more we remain estranged from ourselves. So, pause now to ask yourself: What's really true for you, right now? Turn your gaze inward to create space for your truth to arise. Be patient, knowing that by asking this question, you are developing the habits of heart and mind essential for awakening.

The Story That Lives Us[1]

Those who do not have power over the story that dominates their lives, the power to retell it, rethink it, deconstruct it, joke about it, and change it as times change, truly are powerless....
—Salman Rushdie[2]

Stories are central to human existence because it is through stories that we endeavor to bring meaning to our lives. For example, the ancient Greeks created an extensive set of stories, involving a wide cast of characters: the lightning bolt–wielding Zeus, the armor-clad Athena, not to mention cyclopes, centaurs, dragons, and sea monsters. Today we might regard these ancient stories as mere entertainments, failing to recognize that their primary intent was to provide the people of that time with ideological frameworks for grappling with life's challenges.

The role of stories in shaping culture is also apparent in the Middle Ages. This was a time when Christians lived by the narrative that God had placed the Earth—and therefore humans—at the center of the Universe. But history reveals, over and over, that culturally crafted stories eventually lose their power as new discoveries and perspectives emerge. This is what happened in the 1400s and 1500s when astronomers and mathematicians (e.g., Copernicus, Kepler, Galileo) discovered that, in reality, neither humans nor Earth were at the center of the Universe. Just imagine, now, how profoundly destabilizing it would have been for those living at that time to have had their reassuring story of an Earth-centered/human-centric universe suddenly pulled out from under them!

Or consider the period from 1500 to 1700 when Europeans were beginning to colonize the New World. The colonists came bearing the story of Manifest Destiny, rooted in the Genesis story from the Christian Bible that instructed believers to: "Be fruitful and multiply and fill the earth and subdue it, and have dominion over the fish of the sea and over the birds of the heavens and over every living thing that moves on the earth" (Genesis 1:28 [ESV]).

Emboldened by this story, the white settlers saw the New World as unclaimed property—i.e., as a commodity to be demarcated, owned, exploited, bought, and sold. However, American Indians—i.e., the "First Peoples"—had a very different story. For them, the Land was the cornerstone of their identity: the source of all that sustained them, the home of all their non-human kinfolk, and an umbilical cord connecting them to their ancestors.[3] Indeed, from the Native American perspective, claiming to own parcels of land was ludicrous because their story told them that it was Land—Earth—that contained, supported, and possessed humans, not the other way around.

The clash of cultural stories often results in conflict and suffering. For a more recent example, take Germany in the 1930s, when Adolf Hitler was in ascendancy. History reveals that Hitler's charismatic power was rooted in the story he told the German people about how the White (Aryan) race had been spat upon and oppressed by lesser mongrel races over the course of history. This story captured the attention of impoverished Germans who were looking for scapegoats for their defeat in World War I. Indeed, without Hitler's story, the vile acts of the Holocaust would not have been possible. This is what makes cultural stories so powerful, as well as frightening: They make it possible for humans to justify almost anything—even committing mass atrocities.

What's Our Story Today? Perhaps you're thinking, "Today we're beyond all this. We're modern, discerning, rational. We are no longer entrapped in stories." But consider these words from Daniel Quinn:

> Like the people of Nazi Germany, [we, too] are the captives of a story. Of course, we don't even think that there is a story for us. This is because our story is so ingrained that we have ceased to recognize it as a story. Everyone knows [this story] by heart by the time they are six or seven. Black and white, male and female, rich and poor, Christian and Jew, American and Russian … we all hear it … incessantly because every medium of propaganda, every medium of education pours it out incessantly…. It is always there humming away in the background like a distant motor that never stops.[4]

So, I ask you: What story could possibly be "humming away in the background" for those of us alive in the U.S. today? Here is a thought experiment that might help you answer this question. Begin by imagining yourself as a member of a team of extraterrestrials cruising through deep space in search of sentient life. Several months into your journey, your team comes upon a planet ablaze with artificial light. Given your civilization's technological and biological sophistication, you are able to descend to the United States (the most lit up region of the planet) undetected and blend in seamlessly.[5]

Your first task is to simply observe the Americans as they go about their lives in every imaginable setting—schools, neighborhoods, supermarkets, office buildings, farms, sporting events, hospitals, prisons, churches, factories—noting the amount of time they devote to their various daily pursuits.

As your team compiles its results, you are struck by the centrality of *work* in American culture. For adults, the daily routine usually consists of eight hours of work, followed by eight hours of recovery, and then eight hours of sleep. In exchange for their work, the Americans receive something called "money" that they use to acquire all manner of things: cars, clothes, food, gadgets, furnishings, and much more.

By eavesdropping on tens of thousands of conversations, you conclude that these people believe that it is access to material goods (to *stuff*) that ensures their well-being. This leads your team to summarize the story of American culture with the formula: Work → Money → Stuff → Success.

You name their story "Economism," because everything in their culture appears to be focused on economic activity—i.e., on working, consuming, investing, inventing, manufacturing, marketing, etc.—all with the intent of promoting GROWTH.[6] Even the underlying purpose of schools is to teach children the skills they will need as adults to help ensure that American businesses are competitive in the global economy.

Eventually, your team goes on to visit other countries and confirms that Economism is a global phenomenon. And it is at this point Mission Control directs you to determine how well the story of Economism is working. Are people truly happy? Do their lives have meaning and purpose? Do they extend care and generosity toward one another? Is their home, planet Earth, becoming ever-more healthy, vibrant, and beautiful?

Your team addresses these questions by surveying all available research outlets and media archives. Though this is a monumental task, it soon becomes evident that planet Earth is in trouble: Climate chaos, sharp rises in species extinctions, ocean acidification, sea level rise, freshwater contamination, massive deforestation, catastrophic soil loss, and the pro-liferation of toxins in all of Earth's biomes—provide unequivocal evidence for Earth's sickening.

As for Earth's human inhabitants, your team notes gross inequalities in wealth, with the richest 1 percent possessing more wealth than the rest of humankind combined.[7] Meanwhile, armed conflict divides nations, and strife and violence plague both households and communities.

The conclusion is inescapable: The story of Economism embraced by Earth's people tends to create separation rather than connection, suf-fering rather than healing, stress rather than happiness. In light of all of this, your team concludes its report with these words: "Humans are un-wittingly engaged in ecocide on a massive scale. Unless they wake up, it is inevitable that they will destroy Earth and themselves."

You and Economism? Might you be a devotee of Economism? If you're not sure, here is a way to find out. Start by removing a dollar bill from your wallet. As you hold that dollar in your hand, notice the thoughts and feelings that arise. Then, when you are ready, strike a match and light your dollar on fire, tracking your thoughts and feelings as the dollar dis-integrates to ash.

Recently, I did exactly this, and in front of my students no less! Many were shocked. Some pointed out that I could have given my dollar to char-ity instead of burning it—and that was certainly true. But I chose, as a kind of investment in awakening, to burn that piece of paper. I suspected that this counter-cultural act would be upsetting, but I hoped that the dis-comfort might prompt some in the room to question if their attachment to, and, perhaps even holy regard for, money might be misplaced, insofar as it seems to be sidetracking many of us from awakening to the true meaning and purpose of our lives.

After class, several people pointed out, quite correctly, that what I had done was illegal. This led me to wonder why it's against the law in America to burn one's own money. After all, a dollar bill is just a piece of paper. The American flag is just a piece of cloth, and it's not against the law to burn it. But burn a dollar that you earned, and you will be committing a criminal act.[8] This prohibition highlights, like nothing else, the sacred role that money plays in the story that lives us—the story of Economism.

Upshot: The ideology of Economism has become so deeply stitched into the American psyche that most people experience it simply as reality—i.e., as the way life is and must be! For example, if you happen to be a college student, ask yourself: Why am I in college? If your answer centers on the acquisition of money and financial security, you are an adherent of Economism. Why? Because like other followers, you ascribe to the belief that your success and happiness in life will be determined, primarily, by having ready access to money and all that money buys. And, yet, this view was not generally held by earlier generations of college students. For example, in the 1960s, fully 86 percent of college freshmen registered that their primary concern in college was "developing a meaningful philosophy of life," whereas today fewer than 50 percent of college students share this motivation.[9]

It would be easy to interpret this last statistic as evidence that today's college students tend to be shallow and crass, but from where I sit, this would be a mistake. For example, when I ask students to share what they most value in life, many speak of family, friendship, spirituality, education, service, and freedom. By contrast, when they characterize the values of contemporary American culture, they often use words like *competition, status, wealth, power, greed,* and *control,* underscoring the dissonance between their professed personal values and their perceptions of their culture's values. And, yet, in the conduct of their daily lives, many young people appear to be too harried, too busy, and too self-absorbed to act for the common good. Translation: Like most of the rest of us, it appears that they are mostly conforming to the status quo.

What Now? The story of Economism tells us that if we hope to flourish, as individuals and as a society, we must keep growing … and growing … and growing. More often than not, this translates to working more and more, exploiting more and more, rushing more and more, all so that we can consume more and more! But does this really make sense? Is it wise?

For example, what if, instead of continuing to grow in economic terms, we are now being called to grow in terms of kindness, humility, compassion, creativity, generosity, interdependence, social justice, wisdom, and restraint? Similarly, what if we are being called to turn toward one another, as brothers and sisters, and in so doing, to create a steady-state economy—one designed to meet everyone's fundamental needs without compromising Earth's ecosystems?[10] Such an economy would bring us genuine wholeness and well-being—e.g., whole bodies, healthy minds, heartfelt relationships, deep connections.

Though we have been conditioned to reject such propositions as impractical, consider that what's really impractical is continuing to give our life energy to stories, like Economism, that wreak havoc on ourselves, each other, and Earth.

Wrap-Up

> It's all a question of story. We are in trouble just now because we do not have a good story. We are in between stories. The old story … is no longer effective. Yet we have not learned the new story…. We need a story that will educate us, a story that will heal, guide, and discipline us.
> —Thomas Berry[11]

There is no denying that our present story of Economism has generated material benefits. However, today, the colossal environmental impacts of this story on planet Earth and its wrenching psychic costs on our minds and hearts is far exceeding this story's benefits.

The time has come to imagine a new story—one grounded in humility rather than entitlement, peace rather than domination, openheartedness rather than greed, honesty rather than deceit, and interdependence rather than separation—i.e., a story that invites us to dwell ever-more deeply and respectfully in the world we now have, rather than recklessly transforming our larger body, Mother Earth, into a wasteland.

Coda

Waking Up

No one can build you the bridge on which you, and only you, must cross the river of life.

—Nietzsche[1]

Shortly after graduating from college, I (Melissa) volunteered to serve as a guide at a youth camp on Assateague Island off the Virginia coast. My first day on the job, I remember sitting in the craft tent weaving a rainbow bracelet when sixteen-year-old Meghan came in and sat beside me. I helped her start her own bracelet, and while we worked, I asked about her plans for the future and whether or not she would go to college.

She shrugged, "I'll probably just go to Penn State because my parents work there, and we get a big discount. I don't really know what I want to study, so I won't choose a major right away. Hopefully I'll just figure things out."

Sensing her uncertainty, I asked Meghan if she had considered waiting for a couple of years before going on to college. She immediately dismissed the idea, saying that her parents wouldn't allow it. While she spoke, there was a perceptible weight on her; her whole being seemed uninspired, closed, defeated. Slumping further, she told me that she hated school, but her parents insisted that she go to college anyway.

I felt a rising agitation, and unable to contain myself, I said: "Meghan! I went to Penn State. And yeah, you could go and take some different classes, and maybe if you're lucky, one of them will touch something in you. But more likely, you'll resent going to classes you don't enjoy, and you'll feel most connected and alive when you're out socializing with friends, not jumping through hoops for your teachers. I don't think college is the place to find yourself if you 'hate school.'"

50

A "yeah" might have accompanied Meghan's shrug. But underneath, she didn't believe her parents would settle for anything less than seeing her enrolled in college following high school.

Seeing Meghan's despair broke something inside me. I had seen so many in her situation while I was in college, people who really didn't want to be there. Not knowing what they wanted, they had let their parents decide for them. Meanwhile, their parents, wanting a secure future for them, had said, in effect: "Get a degree that will land you a good job. You have to be realistic and support yourself, otherwise you'll end up living on the street!"

I don't mean to say anything against parents or guardians. I understand that their job is to look after their children and keep them safe. They think, "This worked for me; it will work for you."

Many of us grew up being told that we can be whatever we want, that we have endless potential. But how many of us learned how to forge our own path? Certainly, some of us have always known what we were truly called to do, but that's not the norm. I worry that our modern schooling, centered on passing tests, has programmed us to earn a high GPA, but not to know who or what we are.

So, what's the solution? I don't know. But, a year later, I was back on Assateague with that same youth group, and once again Meghan found me in the craft tent. As we sat weaving together, she reminded me of our conversation the previous year and told me how deeply it had affected her. Until then, no one had challenged her assumption that she must go to college immediately after high school or given her permission to imagine something different. Inspired by our earlier conversation, she had sought out alternatives to college and found a program that would allow her to live in South America, where she would learn Spanish and assist marine biologists in conservation work.

As Meghan shared this news, her whole being was alight with energy. Through the strength of her own spirit, the slumped, defeated individual that I had sat with a year earlier was now transformed into an alive, excited young woman. She was the one who had let our conversation mean something. She had found an alternative path, convinced her parents that it was right for her, and mustered the courage to go through with it.

Notice, now, how Meghan's story, from resignation to awakening, recapitulates the six stepping-stones of Part I:

- Stepping stone 1—Living Asleep: Meghan was lost, confused, and asleep.
- Stepping stone 2—What We Believe, We Become: She was stuck in the life-sapping belief that she *must* go to college immediately after high school.
- Stepping stone 3—Questions Rather Than Answers: Triggered by Melissa's prompts, Meghan began to ask herself questions about what she—not her parents—wanted for her life.
- Stepping stone 4—Education for What: In so doing, Meghan acknowledged that she was mostly bored by classroom learning.
- Stepping stone 5—Truthspeaking as a Catalyst for Awakening: With this clarity, Meghan moved toward self-authorship by Truthspeaking with her parents.
- Stepping stone 6—The Story That Lives Us: Letting go of her old story of helplessness, Meghan was now able to begin to create new possibilities for herself.

Personal Applications: In closing, Dear Reader, we leave you with six questions. May you receive each one as a potential stepping-stone to self-discovery.

- Stepping stone 1—Asleep or Awake? Where might you be asleep—i.e., stuck—in your life right now?
- Stepping stone 2—What We Believe, We Become: What limiting belief(s) might be contributing to your stuckness?
- Stepping stone 3—Questions Rather Than Answers: What questions have you been avoiding asking yourself? Why?
- Stepping stone 4—Education for What? What would happen if you were to put yourself in charge of *your* education?
- Stepping stone 5—Truthspeaking as a Catalyst for Awakening: How might you be lying to yourself, silencing yourself, holding yourself back? Why?
- Stepping stone 6—The Story That Lives Us: What's a new story for your life, a new way of seeing yourself, a new way of being yourself?

Gentle reminder: There are no free passes for those committed to awakening. We've all got to do the work. So, go on! Jump in and get started! And when you're ready, take the leap into Part II.

Breakdown: Stepping into the Unknown

Introduction

When our lives are no longer working—perhaps because we're stuck in a life-sapping routine or we're confused about our life's meaning and purpose—we are in Breakdown. This can be frightening insofar as it heralds a crisis of identity. At the same time, Breakdown can set the stage for self-discovery. The six stepping stones in Part II—through exercises, provocations, and case studies—are an invitation to explore the catalytic role that Breakdown can play in personal awakening.

In the spring of my 17th year I (Christopher) had a small awakening. It happened when my dad invited me to join him on a short road trip to the Blue Ridge Mountains, close to our home in Charlottesville, Virginia. I agreed and early the next morning we headed out.

I still recall the moment we arrived and stepped out into the cool mountain air, how good that felt. Then, without saying a word, my dad located a faint trail and walked into the woods. I followed.

He seemed to be on a mission. Neither of us spoke. Eventually, we came to a well-worn cross trail. It was there that my dad stopped and faced me. There was a glint in his eye. This was not like him. I wondered what was going on.

Still holding his silence, he positioned himself behind me on that cross trail and with his hands firmly planted on my shoulders said: "Go South on this trail, Son, and in a thousand miles you will reach Springer Mountain in Georgia. No roads, no cars, just your own two feet and this trail will take you there."

Will take you there…. What was my dad saying? Will take me where? In silence, I looked as far as I could down that rocky trail, struggling to imagine where it could take me. What was out there? What might I discover? Was it safe? Was I being told to leave home?

After what seemed like a very long time, my dad rotated me 180 degrees so that I was now facing North and, leaning in close, said: "Walk North, Son, and in a thousand miles you will reach Mt. Katahdin in Maine. No roads, no cars, just your own two feet and this trail will take you there."

That was all he said. And though I wasn't sure how to respond, I do know that on the drive home I was suffused with a bone-deep excitation.

Only now, many years later, am I able to see that on that spring morning my dad was opening a door, giving me permission to turn toward wild nature for adventure and freedom and self-discovery. In the months and years following that mountain moment, my hunger for authenticity and self-discovery grew as I was increasingly drawn to wild places: clambering up mountains, canoeing down boulder-strewn rivers, sleeping under the stars, taking shelter in caves. And with this, my crimped understanding of what it meant to have a human life expanded. It was a start.

Breakdown as a Catalyst for Self-Discovery

Sometimes it takes an overwhelming breakdown to have an undeniable breakthrough.

—Unknown[1]

I remember, as a young child, hearing my parents talk in hushed tones about a man in our neighborhood who had suffered a "nervous breakdown." I didn't know what that was, but I sensed that the man's situation was shameful and needed to be hidden. A taboo around breakdowns is still prevalent today. This is why, when it feels like everything in your life is falling apart, you might be told to keep it together and put on a brave face. But what if the symptoms of Breakdown were understood as calls to awaken?

It's possible to experience a Breakdown at almost any age. Perhaps you are nineteen and in college. You've decided on a particular major because you were told that it would guarantee you a secure future. You go to your classes and study hard, but the material really isn't very interesting to you. You keep telling yourself that if you just persevere for two more years, you'll have your diploma; but eventually the effort to align with a major that simply is not right for you becomes too much. Your life feels empty, small, and meaningless. You are in Breakdown!

Or maybe you're forty, and you've been in a lifeless marriage for ten years. You mostly blame yourself for your marital woes, yet you lack the motivation to make changes. You used to be only an occasional drinker, but now you're at the bottle daily. Breakdown!

Or perhaps you're sixty. You've had a successful life by societal standards: good salary, nice house, and two grown kids; but your life feels more empty than full. There is an ache inside; you feel more lost than at any other time in your life. Breakdown!

So, what's been your experience with Breakdown? While you may never have named it as such, consider that you are in the territory of Breakdown any time you experience your life as arid, dull, heavy, and soulless.

It could be that you are living in the land of Breakdown right now. The six questions below could provide a quick diagnostic:

- Do you usually wake up with enthusiasm for what your day will bring?
- Are you regularly filled with curiosity and wonder?
- Do you enjoy being alone—i.e., do you appreciate your own company?
- Do you frequently play and laugh and experience joy in the community of others?
- Do you make time to speak about matters of the heart with close friends?
- Do you regularly feel gratitude for the gift that is your life?

If you are unable to respond with a full-throated "Yes" to most of these questions, you may be floundering in the territory of Breakdown.[2]

Breakdown as a Catalyst for Awakening: In his book, *Soulcraft*, Bill Plotkin tells the story of Tom, a college student who was caught in the web of Breakdown. As his interest in school waned, Tom could barely get himself up in the morning. He recalls, "I really did not care if I lived or died. As far as I could tell, it was simply the momentum and inertia of my family's expectations that had brought me this far. Being a student was not my life. It was a wish or demand that others had for me. I felt trapped."[3]

One summer day, in the midst of his anguish, Tom overdosed on drugs and alcohol. He teetered on the edge of death, knowing with perfect clarity that he could simply let go and die. But Tom chose to live. "What astonished me," he later recalled, "was that there was something to actually hold on to, a something that was almost tangible. I realized in that moment that there was an essence of me beyond the compilation of my nerves and tissues. There was a me I could hold on to. I could feel my will, myself, my soul. It was as if I was experiencing the essential force at the center of life itself. I knew holding on would be tough—I had taken a lot of drugs and could feel how badly I had abused my body. But I knew I had to hold on."[4]

After Tom fully regained consciousness he received a phone call informing him that a close childhood friend had been killed in a terrible accident. Tom was devastated by his friend's death and equally appalled, knowing that, just hours before, he had almost ended his own life.

When classes began a few weeks later Tom returned to school. But one morning, as he left his apartment to go to class, he turned away from campus and made his way to a nearby lake. Gazing out over the water toward the mountains in the west, Tom recalls: "I fell into a trance. I became keenly aware of the beauty—the reflection of the mountains in the calm, glassy water; the birds circling and calling; the dramatic gray clouds. I noticed that in one spot the sun was shining through a blue hole. Rays of splintered sunlight struck the high peaks across the lake…. I knew without a doubt I was being called to go through that hole and over the mountains."[5]

A few days later Tom left school and wandered westward. In a sense, he was on a life and death journey. We all are! If we fail to make our journey, we may die to ourselves—i.e., to the essential force at the center of our lives. But even when we choose to take the journey, there is also a death to be faced—e.g., dying to old ways of being, to old social roles, to old habits of relating to ourselves and others.

Callings[6]

Do you hear yourself being called to places that are far away, beckoned by landscapes
Intimately unknown and unimaginable?

Does it feel as if only strangers can speak your name?
You must leave home.

You must leave HOME!

Escape the walls of your upbringing any way you can.

Caterpillars do it.

Travel far and wide, get lost, be robbed, over and over again, realize that the world is big,
you are small.

Forget who you believed yourself to be, who you thought others thought you were.

Become someone who can't answer simple questions like, "What do you do?"

Fail.

Totally and completely fail to reach your intended destination, though carrying
a map and
compass.

You are where you need to be the moment after you give up on all the land-
marks.

Sit down and cry out all of your laments.

Cry out the laments all your ancestors feared to cry.

You are indeed walking in circles, downward, inward, along a path marked
"Grief and
Despair" that leads directly to Soul.

You have arrived.

Arrived at the place you began, that it killed you to leave.

There is no entrance, nor exit. Never was.

When people ask you to tell the story of your travels, your journey, of the road
you have taken,
do so by living your Life,

Ecstatically.

Now you are human.
—by Jamie Reaser

Fear and the Unlived Life: It is fear that most often keeps us from turning our Breakdowns into Breakthroughs. Sociologist and author Martha Beck clarified the role that fear plays in influencing our decisions by distinguishing between what she calls the "social self" and the "essential self."[7] Your social self is concerned with conforming to societal norms and expectations, whereas your essential self, akin to the soul, is that sense of is-ness that resides at the core of your being. Beck posits that these two selves are often in opposition to one another, because our social self seeks to keep us safe, while our essential self calls us to awaken and transform, which is inherently unsafe. So it is that when a desire for bold action arises from our essential self, our social self often squelches it out of fear.

For example, your essential self might stir you to quit an unsatisfying job in order to do work that you are truly passionate about; or it could prod you to leave your church in search of a different form of spiritual nourishment; or it might call you to take a strong stand on a controversial issue. But if you begin to move in these "unsafe" directions, your social self will flood your mind with fear, warning that if you do these things, everybody will disapprove of you. Your "everybody" though, as Beck points out, is invariably composed of only a handful of people. This means that if you summon the courage to significantly change your life, there will be some who will applaud you, loads of others who will take no notice, and a few who will be upset. As for those few, they'll get over it!

Breakdown and the Essential Self: Some years back, Jean, a Penn State student, took my Field Ecology course. At the time, Jean was a biology major in the second semester of her senior year. As the semester progressed, she expressed her growing disenchantment with Biology; but, in spite of her misgivings, she was still applying to biology graduate programs, reasoning that it was the practical thing to do because she had already committed so much time to biology.

Although her grades were solid, Jean was rejected by all seven of the graduate programs to which she applied. When she called to tell me this, I suggested that she see her setback as an opportunity to pursue something that would truly make her heart sing. In effect, I was encouraging her to ignore the fear-generating murmurings of her "social self" and, instead, to tune into her "essential self."

A month later Jean sent me an email saying, "I'm being forced to re-think, well, everything! I won't lie though. It is probably for the better, seeing as how my interests have been evolving. But I'm pretty overwhelmed about what to do in the immediate future and don't even know where to start. I'm just treading water until I find some clarity."

A year passed before I heard from Jean again in the form of a hand-written letter with a Maine postmark. She wrote, "I have fallen in love with this state." Of her job at Maine's Ferry Beach Ecology School, she wrote, "The workdays are 14 hours long, and I make little money. But I have a room overlooking the ocean, and when the waves crash my bed shakes. I am meeting amazing people who work for the love of it and spend all their time in the present moment, with little concern for long-term plans. And it freaks me out! But slowly all the pressure I was putting on myself to figure out my future is melting away, and for once, I am totally happy." She concluded, "What happens after this is uncertain, but the current moment is a wonderful gift."

Like Jean, when we are in Breakdown, our essential self calls us to awaken. In this sense, Breakdown is akin to a self-imposed rite of passage, guiding us toward our life's deeper meaning and purpose.

Wrap-Up

> Life arranges things so that all of us, young or old, eventually arrive at a point in time where the map we have been given does not match the territory we find ourselves in … we must lose any fixed notions about ourselves and about the true nature of this world. The reason for undertaking the soul's adventure is to become completely other than who we have been so far.
>
> —Michael Meade[8]

As a child, I was conditioned to see Breakdowns as shameful. Now I know that when we find ourselves sleepwalking through our days, numb to life, it is Breakdown that has the power to awaken us. The hymn, "Amazing Grace," says we must be lost before we can be found. In choosing to embrace our lostness—i.e., our Breakdowns—we create opportunities for self-discovery. It is always a choice.

Rites of Passage as Gateways for Awakening

> Every positive change—every jump to a higher level of
> energy and awareness—involves a rite of passage. Each
> time, to ascend to a higher rung on the ladder of personal
> evolution, we must go through a period of discomfort, of
> initiation. I have never found an exception.
>
> —Dan Millman[1]

Rites of passage mark transitions from one stage of human development to another. It was your birth that constituted your first rite of passage. Can you imagine (or perhaps even recall) the very day when—like someone caught in a storm at sea—you were pushed from your mother's womb, out onto dry land?

That was an awakening day like no other! And every day, month, and year since then has been presenting you with more opportunities to expand and awaken.

Your awakening intensified as you began to crawl and then walk away from the security of your caregiver's arms. Much like the mythic hero of old who set off from home to face unknown obstacles and challenges, you, too, were stepping into the unknown. Your daily explorations, discoveries, risks, conquests, and failures were akin to mini ordeals, introducing you to the rigors, wonders, and mysteries of life.

This process continued into your puberty. In an ideal world, this would have been the time when elders in your community would have begun to initiate you into adulthood, helping you to fathom your life's meaning and purpose. But today there are few elders with the know-how and wisdom to serve the young in this way.

In the absence of meaningful rites of passage, adulthood, today, is often framed in legalistic terms—e.g., permission to drive at 16, permission to vote at 18, permission to drink at 21. Meanwhile, the young, in their search for something more embodied and visceral, seek out powerful music, extreme sports, a wide pallet of drugs, adventurous sex, tattoos, and more. And, yes, they sometimes get into trouble—at least that's what the authorities call it. But this trouble is really an artifact of their struggle to bring about their own transformation. As Michael Meade explains, "The inevitable troubles of youth are a kind of second labor of life intended to birth a revelation of the inner nature or innate gifts of the soul."[2]

A Modern-Day Rite of Passage: Fortunately, there are still small pockets of culture in the U.S. where meaningful rites of passage exist for young people. For example, not long ago, I joined with several elders in my community to offer a rite of passage ordeal for fifteen high school males. To get a taste of what happened, put yourself in the place of one of those young men.[3]

It's an evening in late spring, just after sunset. An elder from your community knocks on the door of your home. He greets your parents and then blindfolds you and guides you into a van. You sense that there are others already in the van, but no one speaks. After a long drive, the vehicle stops, and your blindfold is removed. Emerging from the van, you are buffeted on all sides by the sounds of crickets and chorusing frogs.

You are given a sealed envelope and told to walk forward in silence until you see a fire. You obey. Already, you can hear the faint sound of drums, and soon you see flickering flames through the trees.

When you and your peers reach the fire, the drums stop, and each of you is greeted by an elder and told to open the sealed envelope that you have been carrying. It contains a letter from your mother. She writes that her job is done and that it is now time for you to forge your own way in the world. She gives you her blessing and sets you free. But are you ready to let go of your Mother? A lump forms in your throat as you grasp, as never before, that your very life has come to you through her.

The drums begin again, slow and soft, then building, pounding. Determined to take responsibility for your life, you symbolically sever your dependency on your mother by releasing her letter into the fire.

It is then that the elder who will be your guide for the next 24 hours presents you with a drum, and though you have never drummed, your hands begin to pound, instinctively knowing what to do. You feel more alive than perhaps you have ever felt. Then, with a pop and a resounding slam-slap, the drumming stops. You finish in that same instant and wonder how you knew to stop.

Now, the crackling fire is the only sound breaking the silence. The head elder stands and, holding a tree branch high in the air, declares: "Death is already here; it is a foregone conclusion."

A deep silence descends; there are no more calling crickets, no more peeping frogs. You mull over the elder's words, wondering what it would mean for you to fully accept your death as a foregone conclusion. In so doing, it occurs to you that you could choose to take on death as a teacher.

The sound of a solitary drum lifts you from your reverie. An elder stands before you. He looks straight into your eyes. You look away, but he lifts your chin and meets your eyes with his own. Then, he speaks your name and says with serene clarity, "You are dust, and to dust you shall return. Tonight, you shall die." After a long pause, he smears your forehead and chest with ashes and signals for you to follow him. You stumble along behind him through the forest. Eventually, he stops, thrusts a shovel into your hands, and instructs you to find a spot—a sacred space—and to dig your grave.

After he departs you wander in the darkness until you find a flat area by a small tree. You begin to dig. It is not easy. After an hour of scrapping and digging you have managed to make a shallow depression in the ground. The darkness deepens.

Eventually the elder returns, inspects your grave, and declares, "It is good enough." Next, he hands you a box of warm ashes (gathered from the fire that burned earlier), declaring: "These are the ashes of both life and death. The time has now come for you to die." He instructs you to lie down in your grave with the ashes and to harbor in your heart—through the remaining night—the question: What is it time for you to die to?

Can you imagine this: the stillness, the darkness, the chill at 2:00 a.m., and the festering question, "What is it time for me to die to?"

You curl up on the cold ground and drift into intermittent slumber; your dreams are disorienting, and at times you experience a kind of mild delirium.

At first light, you hear drums—the tempo, a funeral dirge. The elder comes and gives you a black t-shirt. You put it on, and he motions for you to follow him. Ahead, you see a fire that, at first, you mistake for the rising sun. The other young men, somber and bedraggled, are also arriving. You notice the presence of a large wooden casket by the fire, with a human silhouette etched on top.

With the sun just beginning to appear above the horizon, an elder stands and speaks: "Today is a day of grief. The child has died."

In the light of this new day, death has become more real to you. Through your ordeal, you have come to realize that there are things to which *you* must die—things that you must let go of—if you are to grow up. You etch these things on a piece of paper. Then, along with others, you place your paper into the open casket, declaring, aloud, what you are now ready to let go of.

The drumming begins again as the elders carry the casket to the fire. You act as witness, feeling both macabre fascination and soulful mourning as flames slowly consume the pine casket. At length, you drop to the ground: empty, depleted, broken; your previous life, in some measure, rendered into ash.

Later, you are instructed to return to your grave and to shovel the soil back into the depression, mixing in some of the ashes from the fire. As you shovel and mix, you sense a shift deep inside. There are no words for this.

I witnessed fifteen young men open themselves to this ordeal. For that dark night and early morning, they were dwelling in liminal space—a realm where time was suspended and where significant awakening became possible.

A Personal Letting Go Ritual[4]: Even if you don't have the option of joining others in a rite of passage like the one just described, it is possible to fashion such ceremonies on your own. One way to start is to ask yourself: What are some things in my life that are sapping my energy? What might it be time for me to let go of? For example, perhaps it's a belief about yourself that you continue to hold even though this belief makes you feel small, weak, and ashamed. Or maybe it's a habitual way of acting that leaves you feeling more like a performer than an authentic person. Pause now to give this some serious thought by completing the following open sentence, three times, in your journal:

I am finally ready to let go of: _____.

I am finally ready to let go of: _____.

I am finally ready to let go of: _____.

Now, imagine the freedom you might experience if you were to muster the resolve to actually let go, once and for all, of one of these self-sabotaging aspects of yourself!

Then, go a step further and summon the courage to walk into a forest, in the dead of night, carrying a satchel containing a symbol representing that one habit or way of being that you are determined to let go of. Maybe it's a pack of cigarettes (reminding you of your addiction to tobacco) or a tattered marriage certificate (symbolizing your readiness to end an abusive relationship) or a hundred-dollar bill (representing your addiction to shopping). Whatever it is, you know that the time has finally come to free yourself from its life-crushing effects.

Once you have journeyed deep into the forest, stop and build a fire. Then, sitting by that fire, rock back and forth as you cradle the object that represents the life-sapping habit that you are now prepared to let go of. Then, as your resolve crescendos, release the object to the fire, emitting a full-throated primal scream as the flames devour it.

As the fire burns down, you acknowledge that you will need great strength if you are to truly free and heal yourself. With this awareness, you remove a second object from your satchel—a small, smooth stone. For you, this stone symbolizes the strength and determination that you will need if you are to remain firm in your resolve to let go, once and for all, of what has been robbing you of your life force.

Touching the stone to your forehead, you intone, "May the power of my mind free me from this life-crushing habit." Then, after a long silence, you press the stone to your heart and whisper to yourself, "May the tenderness of my heart free me of what no longer serves my life." Finally, pressing the stone between your feet, you intone, "May the wisdom of my feet lead me, today and always, toward what is healing and life-sustaining."

The ceremony complete, you tuck the stone into your pocket, with the knowledge that it will be there, always, as a touchstone, guiding you and steadying your resolve.

Wrap-Up

> Let things go. Release them. Detach yourself from them....
> Not because of pride, incapacity or arrogance, but simply
> because [they] no longer fit your life. Shut the door, change
> the record, clean the house, shake-off the dust. Stop being
> who you were and change into who you are.
>
> —Paulo Coelho[5]

We awaken as we let go of ideas, habits, beliefs, behaviors, and stories that no longer nurture, challenge, and enliven us. Each letting go marks a kind of dying that, understandably, brings anxiety, fear and loneliness. But with time, we come to realize that there is a "yes" as well as a "no" encoded in each act of letting go. The "no" is to an old way of being that is life-denying, and the "yes" is to a newfound path leading to authenticity and wholeness.

Success from the Inside Out

Don't ask what the world needs. Ask what makes you come alive and go do it. Because what the world needs is people who have come alive.

—Robert Thurman[1]

Physician and author Rachel Naomi Remen tells a story about a special dinner she attended when she was a medical student. It was a black-tie affair to honor a Nobel Laureate on the medical faculty who, at age 80, was approaching the end of his life. Following the dinner, this man gave a speech describing all the astounding medical advances that had occurred during his lifetime. When he finished, he was greeted with a standing ovation.

After everyone sat down, the laureate remained at the podium for a long time. Then, he addressed Remen and the other young doctors-to-be, saying: "I have been a physician for 50 years, and I don't know anything more about life now than I did at the beginning. I am no wiser. It slipped through my fingers...."[2]

Though there is great pathos in this man's statement, it is a powerful reminder that genuine success is not measured by accolades or by other people's praise or by material wealth. Instead, genuine success is something that is experienced from within, as we summon the courage to full-heartedly pursue our life's deep meaning and purpose.

In this sense, that Nobel Laureate was warning, not just those medical students, but all of us, to be wary of the constricted ways in which our culture teaches us to understand and pursue success. Absent this guidance, we might risk spending our days ladder-climbing, only to realize, after it is too late, that our "success ladder" was leaning against the wrong wall.

Society's Success Ladder: By the time you graduated from high school, you had already received your culture's prescription for success. It's been humming in the background your entire life, showing up in movies, television shows, books, advertisements, tweets, and more. Pull it into the foreground, now, by taking a moment to complete the following open sentence, five times, in your journal:

1. In our society, successful people are _____
_____.

2. In our society, successful people are _____
_____.

3. In our society, successful people are _____
_____.

4. In our society, successful people are _____
_____.

5. In our society, successful people are _____
_____.

When I invite my students at Penn State to do this, they often come up with words like *important, effective, powerful, popular, rich,* and *respected.* Yes, it seems that most of us have been conditioned to believe that success in life is largely the result of how others judge us—specifically, how they view us in terms of our ability to amass influence, wealth, power, and prestige. But what if these socially mediated metrics have little to do with genuine success?

The Cost of Conformity: The recently deceased Buddhist teacher/ writer Ram Dass used the parable of *Zumbach the Tailor* to illustrate how our culture can mislead us to mistake conformity for success.[3] The story begins with a humble farmer coming to Zumbach's shop to buy his first suit ever. This was a really big deal because Zumbach was recognized for his extraordinary craftsmanship.

Feeling nervous and out of place, the farmer entered Zumbach's shop. After choosing a fabric and being measured, Zumbach sent him away and told him to come back in a week.

As instructed, the farmer returned to pick up his suit the next week, but when he tried it on, he noticed that the right sleeve was two inches longer than the left sleeve. When the lowly farmer pointed this out to Zumbach, the famous tailor proclaimed that the problem was not with the suit, but with how the man was standing. He then proceeded to push down on the farmer's left shoulder until both sleeves were of equal length. But when the farmer examined himself again in the mirror, he pointed out that the suit was bunched up in the back, near his neck. Irritated by this second complaint, Zumbach shoved the man's head forward until the fabric bulge in the back was rendered smooth, and, again, pronounced the fit "perfect."

The farmer, in a state of bewilderment, paid for the suit and left the shop. Walking down the street, with lopsided shoulders and his head straining forward, the man encountered a stranger who complimented him on his "gorgeous suit," surmising, aloud, that, "It must be the work of Zumbach."

"Why, yes, how did you know?" responded the farmer.

"Because only a tailor as skillful as Zumbach could make a suit that would fit a body as contorted as yours," came the response.[4]

The "lopsided man" in this story serves as a metaphor for what can happen to each of us when we allow our culture—symbolized by Zumbach the Tailor—to jam us into a "one-size-fits-all" mold!

This seems to be occurring, to varying degrees, for all of us. Just look around! Look into the eyes of those you pass each day. Look into your own eyes. Are the people around you brimming with aliveness, living their lives free of shackles? Are you? Is your light burning brightly? Or are you, like too many of us today, unwittingly allowing yourself to be stitched up and separated from your life by our culture's narrow depiction of success?

A Different Notion of Success: In the realm of sports, I was taught that there are successful teams—those that win—and unsuccessful teams—those that lose. But one day I was challenged to see it differently. It occurred on a Saturday afternoon at the final game of my ten-year-old daughter's basketball season. When the game ended in a tie, the referee announced that the team that scored the first basket in overtime would be the winner.

My daughter Katie's team had been winless the entire season. Now, they finally had a chance for a victory—for success! I assumed that Katie's coach would put his five best players on the court, but, for this coach, it was more important to give each of his players equal playing time—i.e., for him success had more to do with team spirit and fairness than winning. So, when play resumed, he substituted in two girls who had been sitting out during the first half. One of the two, Jenny, was the least skilled player on the team. And it was Jenny who, to my surprise, took the initiative to bring the ball up court. Katie's coach could have signaled for a more adept dribbler to take over but he chose to remain silent.

The instant Jenny dribbled over the mid-court line, the other team's coach yelled to his players, "GET 'ER!" and immediately three defenders descended on Jenny, easily knocking the ball away and converting their steal into a basket. Game over!

After the game, I watched and listened as Katie's coach gathered his team together, taking time to carefully call attention to specific examples of good play demonstrated by each of the girls. Clearly for this man, success wasn't about winning at all costs; instead it was about learning the game, improving, and supporting one another.

As I left the gym, I mused that many of those watching the game that day probably regarded this coach's behavior as foolish insofar as he was enacting a "success" story—one based on fairness and inclusivity—that is at odds with our dominant culture.

Failure as a Catalyst for Success: It was 1982 when I accepted a faculty position in the biology department at Penn State University. Arriving on campus, my department head informed me that I would be teaching a general education course called "Man and the Environment" with an enrollment of 600 students. Being new to teaching, I assumed that to be successful I would need to adopt the same teaching approaches that I had experienced as a college student. This meant lecturing to my students and then giving them tests to assess their level of mastery.

I selected a thick environmental science textbook and got to work preparing my lectures. During each class, I focused on a different environmental problem—e.g., tropical deforestation, burgeoning population growth, soil erosion, chemical pollution, ozone thinning, climate change, etc.—always with the intention of alerting my students to the deteriorating health of Earth. In my mind, I was becoming a serious professional—hardworking, demanding, and always well-prepared.

But all of this began to change on the final day of class in my seventh year of teaching. From my perspective, it had been my most successful semester to date. I had incorporated new material into the course and was becoming a more skillful lecturer. So, there I stood in a self-congratulatory stance, while my students sat laboring over their final exam. As the hour wound down, they came up, one by one, to hand me their test sheets. I was excited to wish them well and to thank them for taking my course, but most of my students barely acknowledged my presence, with only a handful making eye contact. Something was terribly wrong.

A few days later, still feeling unsettled, I strapped on my backpack and headed to the mountains for a weeklong walkabout. Having that time to ramble in the woods reminded me of the wonder, kinship, and full-bodied delight I had experienced in my youth on outdoor sojourns. It also led to the realization that I had been asking my students to care about something—NATURE!—with which many had little direct contact. How ridiculous of me to expect them to care about something that was more abstract than visceral! And how foolish to imagine that I was a successful teacher, when all I was doing was conforming to my culture's crimped prescription for proper teaching!

This awakening triggered a new question—namely: What would happen if, instead of limiting my teaching to facts and figures, I was to anchor it in curiosity, compassion, vulnerability, connection, spontaneity, and wonder? What if my intention was to help students fall in love with Earth—i.e., to open their senses to the wild and wonderful planet that has birthed all of us into being; and, in so doing, to experience themselves, not as apart from Earth, but as a part of Earth? And what if instead of expecting them to provide me with the correct answers to my test questions, I was to mentor them to seek answers to their own questions?

Since that walkabout, twenty years ago, I have mostly let go of my culture's story for correct teaching and, in so doing, come to discover, as well as to experience, what successful teaching looks and feels like.[5]

Success on Our Own Terms: Success is personal. We each have to define it on our own terms. You could begin to do this, right now, by responding, five times, in your journal, to the following open sentence:

1. For me to be successful in my life means _____

   _____

   _____.

2. For me to be successful in my life means _____

   _____

   _____.

3. For me to be successful in my life means _____

   _____

   _____.

4. For me to be successful in my life means _____

   _____

   _____.

5. For me to be successful in my life means _____

   _____

   _____.

Be forewarned that in creating your five statements, you may discover—as I did when I began to define successful teaching for myself—that your inner criteria for success may differ from those proclaimed by your culture. Bringing awareness to the contradictions between your culture's story of success and your own understanding of success could spur you to assume the rightful authorship of your life. And what might that look like? A great example came to me a while back in this excerpt from a letter from a past student, Annamarie DiRaddo:

> I've recently made a whole lot of shifts in my life. I left a fabulously paying office job to go back to teaching preschool. I LOVE teaching children. I know this job will make me happy, and I am passionate about it. I just can't settle for working in a cubicle, no matter how good the pay.... Unfortunately, my family views me as a failure. To them I am not adjusting to the "real world." And maybe I'm not, but I feel so certain that the things that I'm supposed to be doing are just not for me. I don't want—much less need—a big house. I want to be doing something that matters to the world.... I only have this life.

Reading Annamarie's letter, it was clear that she was turning down the cultural static and tuning into her own heart. Yes, we may regret that those around us (be they family members or friends) disapprove of our path, but there comes a time when we must set aside the opinions of others and appreciate that it is only by following our heart's deep yearnings that we will discover our true meaning and purpose.

Wrap-Up

> The plain fact is that the planet does not need more "successful" people, but it does desperately need more peacemakers, healers, restorers, storytellers, and lovers of every kind. It needs people who live well in their places. It needs people of moral courage willing to join the fight to make the world habitable and humane. And these qualities have little to do with "success" as our culture has defined it.
> —David Orr[6]

Our success won't be measured by the wealth, power, and status that we amass but by how we choose to live, day by day. If we fail to engender wholeheartedness, kindness, love, and gratitude in our daily life, then, at life's end, our lament—like that of the Nobel Laureate quoted at the beginning of this chapter—might also be: "I don't know anything more about life now than I did at the beginning. I am no wiser. It slipped through my fingers."

The Seed in Each of Us

We are human by lot and divine by origin ... each person a
living puzzle as well as a divine experiment.
—Michael Meade[1]

In the above quote, mythologist and storyteller Michael Meade suggests a new story for what it might mean to have a human life. But is his idea—that we are each a divine experiment true? In the spirit of playful inquiry, consider how you might experience your life differently if you held the mindset that you were a "living puzzle," born with a unique purpose and destiny.

Many past cultures, and some still today, hold that each human comes into the world with a pre-ordained mission. For example, Sobonfu Some, a member of the Dagara tribal people of West Africa, relates that when a woman in her culture is pregnant, a "hearing" ritual is performed. In this ceremony, elders gather around the pregnant mother and ask the unborn child questions like: Who are you? Why are you coming into this world? How might we prepare for your arrival? The child responds to these questions by taking over her mother's voice, perhaps announcing her purpose this way: "The ancestors are sending me to you to serve as a healer," or "I come bearing messages from the winged ones," or "I am coming to bring stillness and wisdom." After the child is born, and as she matures, the same elders who attended her birth are present to nurture and guide her so that she might realize her destiny.[2]

It doesn't really matter if it's literally true that the unborn Dagara child can announce her calling through words spoken by her mother. What matters is the effect that believing and living within this story has on the lives of the Dagara people. The result of such a belief is that everyone in the Dagara community knows their reason for coming into the world;

they know that they belong and that they are needed. Now, consider that for you, too, there might also be a story about why you are here and what is yours to bring to the world. Though this story may not be apparent to you, what if it's there, nonetheless, exercising a subtle influence on the trajectory of your life?

The Blank Slate Theory: Early schooling plays a significant role in sculpting who we become as adults.[3] In many school settings, students are regarded as "empty buckets" that need to be filled with information in accordance with the dictates of a prescribed curriculum. This "empty bucket" metaphor echoes the so-called "Blank Slate Theory," which holds that we each come into the world needing to be etched with the knowledge and behavioral rules that our society deems necessary for our success.[4] All of this harkens back to Economism, the cultural narrative introduced in Part I, that defines success in terms of work, money, and stuff— i.e., Work →Money →Stuff →Success.

But Economism can be a hard sell, especially for a young person who is discerning enough to see that most adults in our culture are often more harried and agenda-driven than relaxed, joyful, and fulfilled. High school teacher and author David McCullough captures the situation this way: "Even those [adults] with the luxury of options, [often] have … little passion for, or gut-level belief in, what they do for a living…. Years of toil have yielded little beyond what the bank statement attests…."[5]

McCullough goes on to lament that by the time today's students reach high school, they have already been conditioned to follow Economism's script: "…the lesson they learn is do what you do for the material reward. Do this to get that. Hold your nose, grit your teeth, bleed if you have to, leave happiness on the sidewalk if you must, even peace of mind, but earn, baby, earn. Get yours."[6]

The problem with following Economism's nose to the grindstone script is that it creates confusion when it comes to discerning the deeper meaning and purpose of one's life. Author Bo Lozoff offers a story that provides insight into this conundrum. It begins when a rabbi asks a man, who regularly attends his synagogue, when he might have the time to devote himself to the study of the Torah. The man, who is engaged full-time in his business pursuits, responds that he really wants to give time to the Torah but can't afford to because he has to work to save money for his son's future.

Years go by, and when that father's son becomes a grown man, he, too, becomes fully engrossed in his work. Finally, one day when the rabbi is approaching old age, he asks the son when he might have time to study the Torah. But, like his father before him, the son responds that he must work long hours to provide for his own son's future. In time, that son's son grows up, and the story is the same. So it goes generation after generation … each father giving the same excuse, unwilling to devote time to explore the deeper meaning and purpose of his life because he is worried about the future welfare of his child.

"Somewhere then," the old rabbi laments, "perhaps at the end of time, we will find that ultimate child for whose welfare countless generations have so toiled…. Where [oh] where is that ultimate child? Is he not but a fiction? A non-existent endpoint? An illusion that has driven the entire world into an insane striving toward futility?"[7]

The message in this story, as I hear it, is that we are each seeded with a gift to give the world. However, to discover our gift requires that we step beyond the soul-numbing story of Economism that socializes us to believe that "fitting in" and striving for security are what most matter in life. It is in this context that the rabbi's request to the father to devote time each week to the study of the Torah can be seen as an invitation to awaken to the bigger story of what it means to have a human life. In accordance with this bigger story, the most important thing that a father (or a mother) can do to guide their child toward a full, joyful, and meaningful life is to be living such a life themselves, day by day.[8]

Upshot: No matter what we do for a living, what most matters is the energy, presence, and awareness that we bring to our doing. So, for example, if it is your calling in life to farm the land or to bake bread or to repair furniture or to care for refugees, and you actively engage with your work with skillfulness, good cheer, humility, and kindness, this will be enough.

I observed this firsthand through my acquaintanceship with a mail clerk named Mike. For many years Mike worked at the Penn State Post Office. His job was straightforward. He listened to what his customers wanted, and then he provided it. But what was remarkable was HOW he performed his job. You see, Mike had an uncanny ability to "see" his customers, and he used this gift—his acute sensitivity—to uplift virtually everyone who stepped up to his counter. For example, he extended gentle humor to the young man with the dour expression, compassion to the student with tear-streaked cheeks, and patience and warmth to the elderly man with crippling arthritis. Though we were all at a major university with four-thousand-plus teachers, Mike the Mailman modeled the most fundamental teaching of all—the art and practice of being awake, curious, compassionate, and fully present. Thank you, Mike!

Nurturing the Seed Within: Thirty-odd years ago when my son, Jake, was three, I remember watching him at a distance, as he played with a dump truck in our backyard sandbox. With excruciating slowness, he pushed his truck up a sand mound, his head bent low, just inches from the truck's rolling wheels. Then he, painstakingly, guided the truck backwards, down to the bottom of the mound. He repeated this up and down action, dozens of times, very slow, very focused.

Though Jake was barely out of diapers at the time, I sensed that something significant was happening; but I didn't know how to interpret it until I encountered these words from author and poet David Whyte: "Each of us, somewhere in the biography of our childhood, remembers a moment where we felt a portion of the world calling and beckoning to us…. Somewhere inside us, that child is still running enthusiastically toward a horizon it once glimpsed. Our future life depends on finding this original directional movement in our lives…."[9]

So, what has become of Jake? Well, his early fascination in the sandbox with how things are put together and how they work showed up in middle school when he spent months on end designing cityscapes with the video game "Sim-City." It surfaced again in high school, where Jake's big passion was designing and making furniture in shop class. And it blossomed further, after high school, when he spent a year constructing low-income housing with Habitat for Humanity in Miami. Now, approaching forty, Jake manifests the "original directional movement" of his life in Denver, where he remodels interior spaces and designs and builds furniture.[10] In one sense, you could say that Jake's life calling was seeded in the sandbox.

And you? What are some of your early childhood memories, and how might these memories point, however obliquely, to your life calling? If you struggle to recall such significant moments, it doesn't mean that they didn't occur for you. Perhaps they have simply been suppressed. For example, imagine that you are six years old and your no-nonsense second-grade teacher asks you: "What do you want to be when you grow up?" After a long pause you respond, dreamily, "I want to live in the sea and swim with the whales." Hearing this, your teacher responds: "That's nice, but it's not a real job. You need to be practical." Taken aback and not quite sure what "practical" means, you try again, saying, "I want to build houses high up in giant trees, like in *Swiss Family Robinson*." But to this, your teacher shakes his head and says: "That's sweet, but people don't really live in trees. When you get big, you will have to get a real job that pays good money so you can take care of your family."

By the time we reached middle school, chances are that most of us had already received numerous admonitions like this, coaxing us to be practical, taming our imaginations, cutting us off from the deeper stirrings of our souls. But it doesn't need to be this way. For example, Hawaiian poet and community organizer Puanani Burgess tells of a time when she asked a group of high school students to tell each other three stories—first, the story of their name; second, the story of their community; and third, the story of their gift. It was going well until Burgess came to a certain young man who did fine with the story of his name and the story of his community, but when it came to the story of his gift, he bristled: "What, Miss? What kind gift you think I get, eh? I stay in this Special-Ed class, and I get a hard time read and cannot do that math. And why you make me shame for, ask me that kind question, 'What kind gift I have?' If I had gift, you think I be here?" In that moment Burgess felt awful for having shamed the young man.

A short time later, she saw him at the local grocery store, and still feeling deep regret, she tried to flee; but he caught up with her and said, "You know, I've been thinking, thinking, thinking. I cannot do that math stuff or read so good, but Aunty, when I stay in the ocean, I can call the fish. The fish he come, every time. Every time I can put food on my family table. Every time. And sometimes when I stay in the ocean, and the Shark he come, he look at me. I look at him, and I tell him, 'Uncle, I not going take plenty fish. I just going to take one, two fish, just for my family. All the rest I leave for you.' And so the Shark he say, 'Oh, you cool, brother.' And I tell the Shark, 'Uncle, you cool.' And the Shark, he go his way, and I go my way."

This is a story of a young man with a special gift that might have gone unrecognized were it not for Burgess seeding the idea that each of us is born with unique sensitivities—special talents—giving us the potential to be successful in our own unique ways.[11]

> This might be a good place to pause and reflect, in your journal, on how all of this relates to your own calling in life…

The Acorn Theory: This notion that each of us is born with a unique gift to offer the world is sometimes referred to as "The Acorn Theory." Eminent psychologist James Hillman articulated this idea, in its modern form, when he posited that each human being comes into the world uniquely *seeded.* In other words, just as an acorn has within itself the potential to become a one-of-a-kind oak tree, so it is that each person has within them the capacity to become an unrepeatable expression of humanity.[12]

The forester doesn't put the oak into the acorn; it is already there. The forester's job is to nurture the acorn and, in so doing, to ensure that a unique oak tree emerges from each acorn. It is the same with humans. The parent or teacher or elder doesn't need to "put" anything into the young person. Instead their job is to gently draw forth and affirm the uniqueness that is already there.[13]

In this context, consider that just as we each have a thumbprint, with its unique pattern of swirls and curves, we also have a unique soul print, acting as an identification marker of the deepest kind.[14] From a biological perspective, this makes sense, insofar as we each came into this world with a one-of-a-kind nervous system, unique in the density and distribution of nerve endings in our eyes, ears, nose, mouth, skin, and everywhere else throughout our bodies. This means that we each take in and experience the world in ways that are uniquely our own, implying that we each possess sensitivities and sensibilities that have never existed before within any other human being.

This is a lot to take in. Indeed, as Michael Meade points out, "the hardest thing in life may be to learn to truly trust that there is something noble and generative in ourselves…. To truly believe in oneself [in this way] is to uncover the inner core of imagination and authenticity that can also be called the genius within us."[15]

Wrap-Up

Discovering your unique gift to bring to your community is your greatest opportunity and challenge. The offering of

that gift—your true self—is the most you can do to love and
serve the world. And it is all the world needs.
—Bill Plotkin[16]

We live in a culture that often conditions us to see ourselves as *blank
slates*—i.e., as cogs within a larger economically driven system; but we are
actually more akin to one-of-a-kind acorns—each with a unique destiny,
no matter how humble. This shift in self-understanding is a prerequisite
for our awakening.

Hearing the Call

The privilege of a lifetime is being who you are.
—Joseph Campbell[1]

It is hard beyond measure to pursue an authentic, awakened life insofar as we live in a culture that seduces us toward security, comfort, and conformity. Author Ron Jones highlights our challenge in the following story about his father, who worked for 35 years selling televisions, refrigerators, and glassware in a San Francisco department store:

> One day my father was told that the store was closing. In those days there were no golden parachutes or retirement benefits, and when they asked if there was anything they could do for him, my Dad's only request was to have the chair he'd been sitting in all those years. They sold it to him.
>
> He brought that chair to my house on his back one day and placed it in my living room and told me about all the years he had sat in it, and then he made me promise that I would never sit down in that chair, ever. It's in my living room to this day, and I never sit in it. I just tell the story, and the lesson my father passed on to me through it: Don't sit down in life. All through your life you're going to be asked to sit down, to conform, comply, and compromise, and it can be very deadly if you get in the habit of doing that. Be leery of the price of conformity, my father told me. Stand up, create things, do things.[2]

We all experience, in subtle and not so subtle ways, this pressure to conform. If you aren't sure about this, consider what happens for you when you feel called to take an action that puts you at odds with a societal norm. For example, suppose you are contemplating changing your diet by going vegan or taking a year off from school to hike the Appalachian Trail. These possibilities excite you, but when you share your plans with others, they warn you of possible dangers to your health or physical well-being, while stressing the importance of avoiding unnecessary risks. They may believe that the things they say are for your benefit. However, when you take this kind of advice—for all its good intentions—you run the even greater risk that comes with playing it safe—namely, the risk of being blocked from wholehearted engagement with your own life.

Discerning the Call: If you hope to discover your life's true meaning and purpose, you must be willing to summon the courage to tune into the murmurings of your shy soul. Here are five practices that can help you along your way:

(i) Hushing: Most of us are so busy rushing about that we are reluctant to take time to be present with our own sweet selves. In fact, when challenged to slow down, many of us balk because keeping busy is what our culture expects of us.

But the way to connect with ourselves—with our life's meaning and purpose—is not through speed but through slowness, presence and awareness. You can get a taste, right now, of what I am suggesting by putting this book down and sitting still for several minutes with no agenda. The challenge is to do nothing so that you might experience what it's like to just be.

Author Gregg Levoy calls this "hushing," because it resembles what happens when we leave a busy street and enter into the quiet of a cathedral or another spiritual domain. There we experience a different realm of time. All need to rush or hurry falls away, replaced by stillness, allowing space for deeper, more soulful feelings, intuitions, and leadings to arise.[3]

Through the simple act of "hushing," we create the conditions wherein we might hear and actually feel what it is that is tugging at our heartstrings—e.g., what we are being called to say, do, and be. This "tug" can be just as palpable as what you may have felt as a child when flying a kite. Go back to that time, now:

> It is a beautiful windy day, and in your exuberance, you are letting out more and more string. Then a moment comes when you look up, and you can no longer see your kite. At this point a man comes along and, seeing you running happily with a string in your hand, asks, "What are you doing?" You explain that you are flying a kite. But the man says, "I don't see a kite. How do you know there is a kite?" You stop and look up at him and gravely explain, "I know there is kite on the end of my string because I can feel the tug."

As author Marc Gafni explains:

> When we were kids it was relatively easy to feel the tug, that precious pull of our youthful souls toward meaning. Our world was small, the rules fairly clear and the joys of childhood abundant. What happens when we grow up? How often do we lose the magic of the tug—the tug that tells us that life is exciting and worth living even if we can't always see the flying kite…? When you are truly connected with the nature of your soul … when you know how you can leave its inscription on the world, then you feel the tug.[4]

Granted, this suggestion to simply take time to hush might seem scary because, in so doing, we may run the risk of discovering a hollowness or loneliness at our core. But perhaps this is why it is so important that we explore "hushing." For if we avoid creating openings for intimacy with our innermost self, we may never discover who we truly are.[5]

(ii) Where Deep Gladness and Deep Hunger Meet: Theologian Frederick Buechner described one's calling in life as that place "where our deep gladness and the world's deep hunger meet."[6] If you're curious, you can begin to locate that "place" right now for yourself by making three columns on a blank sheet of paper. Then, close your eyes and move your awareness from your head down to your body core. Staying grounded at your center—in your pelvic bowl—open your eyes and begin to consider the things in your life that bring you deep gladness. You will know these things by the feelings of well-being, peace, and expansiveness that arise within you. Write down whatever comes to mind in the first column on your paper. Take your time.

When you are ready to proceed, move your awareness back down to your core and reflect on "the world's deep hunger." If you're having trouble, call to mind things that, upon hearing or witnessing, create a sudden constriction in your throat or cause you to tear up or make you want to look away. Record these heartaches in the right-hand column of your paper. Again, take your time.

Now, as you consider your two lists, ask yourself: "Where are the places that my deep gladness (left column) and my heartbreak for the world (right column) meet?" Stay grounded in your body and be gentle with yourself, as this will require patience, stillness, and an open heart. As responses arise, jot them down in the middle column, all the while holding in mind Buechner's counsel that our life's purpose is to be found in those places where "our deep gladness and the world's deep hunger meet."

See your jottings in the middle column as whispers emanating from your soul, calling you to live wholeheartedly with full authenticity.

(iii) Using Art as a Catalyst for Coming Home to Yourself: When it comes to attuning to the whispers of one's soul, art can be among our best allies. As Bharati Mukherjee reminds us: "All artistic practices are satellite dishes for hearing the signals the soul sends out."[7] Sadly, many of us have forgotten that to be a human is to be an artist. Our ancestors knew this. Many nature-based cultures have no word for art, because expressing ourselves through art is simply part and parcel of what it means to be human. Today, art continues to offer us the possibility of moving beyond everyday left-brained (analytical) approaches to life's challenges, toward more right-brained (fluid, intuitive) responses.

So, simply gather some art supplies—whatever you happen to have on hand—crayons, paints, pastels, colored pencils, mud, etc., as anything will do. Then, settle into a relaxed state. This might entail sipping a cup of tea while listening to some soothing music or sitting outside by a favorite tree. Once you are open and relaxed, consider the following questions, one at a time:

- Where are you now in your life?
- Where are you going—i.e., What might be a next step toward your awakening?
- What obstacles stand in your way?
- What resources, lying within and around you, will allow you to take your next step?[8]

Sit with each question, creating space for responses to arise; but this time, instead of writing out responses in your journal, consider using art supplies to depict images or symbols or energetic impulses that arise in response to these questions. Be open. You are fishing the waters of your soul. You may get some nibbles—perhaps even some tugs!

(iv) Creating a Personal Mission Statement: At a time of confusion in my life, I spent a day at a workshop led by my friend David Tait. The aim was for participants to create a mission statement for their lives. My first attempt at articulating my life mission was four pages long, filled with hopes and platitudes. David listened patiently as I read each page and, then, without comment, told me to pare it down to a mere half page. I dutifully cut out all the fluff and returned triumphant. Again, David listened as I read and then told me to whittle it all down to a quarter page. I complied.

As the day unfolded David continued to push, requesting fifty words, then twenty-five, and, finally, just three words. David instructed me to write my three words on a small card and to keep this card in my wallet. "That way," he said, "any time you are presented with a decision in life, you can use your three words to ensure that your choice is in alignment with the essence of who you are coming to understand yourself to be."

Right now, Dear Reader, you too can benefit from David's teaching. Begin by settling into a comfortable chair with your journal. Then write "My Mission Statement" at the top of the page and proceed to write down whatever comes to mind, scribbling away for fifteen minutes without pausing. Then read aloud to yourself what you have written, circling words that hold special power for you. You are looking for words that touch you to your core; words that land in your body with a click or a boom; words that perhaps give you goose bumps, provoke tears, or cause a chill to run down your spine.

Like fingers pointing to the moon, these essence words are whispers guiding you toward the particular gift(s) that is/are yours to give to the world. Once you have your words, carry them in your wallet, etch them on your heart, and speak them in public so that they might guide you to engage wholeheartedly with your life.

And what might all this look like? Well, anything, really. My friend Tsultrim told me that her life has constellated around the single word "gratitude." As a result, Tsultrim now understands her "job"—her core mission—in life as giving thanks for everything that is. It's important work. Tsultrim is the one who gives thanks! What about you? You are the one who…?

(v) A Medicine Walk: In many cultures, both today and in the past, humans have sought refuge in nature so that they might deepen their quest for meaning and purpose. Moses went to Mount Sinai in search of a vision, Jesus to the desert, Muhammad to the cave, Buddha to the Bodhi tree. "Nature and soul not only depend on each other, but long for each other and are of the same substance, like twins or trees sharing the same roots."[9]

For those of us alive today, the path to awakening could include what is known as a "Medicine Walk." The setting for such a Walk is the natural world. While this might ideally mean a pristine wilderness—like a desert, remote forest, or a mountaintop—any nearby natural area that offers quiet and solitude would also work.

Typically, a Medicine Walk begins at sunrise and ends at sunset, during which time the wisdom-seeker abstains from food.[10] Place yourself, now, in the position of someone embarking on a Medicine Walk. You have with you all that you will need for the day: appropriate clothing and a pack with essential items, including water and a journal to record the Story of your Walk. In your heart, you carry a specific question—perhaps around discerning your life's calling—in hopes that this time in nature will offer you guidance in some form.[11]

When you arrive in the setting for your Walk, you look first for a Threshold which will serve as your gateway to an alternative way of being in the world. Once you step through the Threshold (which might simply be a space between two trees), your mission will be to pay careful attention to the natural world around you, opening to the possibility that the particular things that attract your attention have revelations and teachings to offer you.[12]

As a seeker, constant motion and particular end goals or tasks are not the point—opening, trusting, and receiving are. This means wandering without aim with your senses open and alert, allowing your intuition to lead you right or left, upstream or downstream, sun-wise or earth-wise. You might be moved to crawl into a cave, dance on a knoll, swim to the center of a lake, rub your cheeks against a tree, roll in tall grass, gurgle back to a babbling brook or sing a duet with a songbird. Just as likely, you might enter into conversation with the energies that you encounter in a flower, a lizard, a rock, a wisp of wind, or a crescent moon.[13] Anything you feel called to do or which seems to call out to you, will become part of the Story of your Walk, to be analyzed later for the Medicine it might contain.

Melissa's Medicine Walk: Not too long ago, I entered into the sacred space/time of a Medicine Walk when I stepped through my Threshold—a gap in a low stone wall—at a state park near my house. In so doing, it wasn't that the world was different, but that I was. Recalling my question—my reason for journeying to the land—I readied myself to listen, to look, to ask, and to receive.

Of the many adventures and encounters I had that day—whether following deer paths or searching for stones in quiet groves—the most significant symbol was that of Bumblebee. Everywhere I wandered, Bumblebee was present, whether it be in the branches of trees, buzzing through the grass, or hovering near the many flowering bushes. Just after I arrived and just as I was about to leave, Bumblebee appeared and circled me three times.

I recorded all of this, knowing that it was possible that my interactions with Bumblebee could have been a coincidence or a psychological projection, but it felt like more than that. It felt like the natural world was calling out to me, pointing me in the direction of the answer to the question I was holding and the larger lessons I needed to learn. I still trust that this is true.

Before any attempt at meaning-making, however, I concluded my Medicine Walk by crossing back through the stone wall Threshold and back into my community. I returned, not to tell others of my Medicine Walk, but to metabolize and make sense of what I saw, felt, heard, and learned during my time on the land. As ecopsychologist John Davis explains: "Medicine is guidance toward wholeness. Sometimes it is bitter to taste; sometimes sweet. Either way, it is growthful if we are able to take it in … [insofar as it] is both a gift from outside and a quality of our inner nature."[14]

Wrap-Up

We are all called to awaken to the miracle of life, which, of course, includes the miracle of ourselves and the miracle of each other. But to hear this call requires that we slow down, become curious, and listen deeply. So, if you haven't already done so, take a break from reading so that you can give your attention to one or more of the above practices. See this as a means of attending to your shy soul, for the purpose of awakening, ever more fully, to the gift that is your one precious life.

From Breakdown to Breakthrough

> We must be willing to get rid of the life we've planned, so as
> to have the life that is waiting for us.
> —Joseph Campbell[1]

So, here we are at the end of Part II, having, so far, explored:

i. Breakdown as a catalyst for your self-discovery
ii. The role of rites of passage in fomenting your awakening
iii. The importance of defining success on your own terms
iv. The benefits of seeing yourself as a generative *acorn* rather than a *blank slate*
v. Practices you can pursue to discern your *calling*

We tie these pieces together, now, with three true stories, each illustrating how a willingness to embrace Breakdown can awaken us to "the life that is waiting for us."

Story 1—Sam Polk: Former hedge fund trader Sam Polk's Breakdown unfolded slowly, with the realization that he was a wealth addict. In a 2014 *New York Times* article, Polk wrote:

> In my last year on Wall Street my bonus was $3.6 million—and I was angry because it wasn't big enough. I was thirty years old, had no children to raise, no debts to pay, no philanthropic goal in mind. I wanted more money for exactly the same reason an alcoholic needs another drink: I was addicted.[2]

How does someone get to a place where a $3.6 million bonus is even an option, let alone a letdown? Well, as the child of a kitchen cabinet salesman who dreamed of making a million dollars, Polk came to believe from a young age that "money would solve all of [his] problems." So, when he made it to the trading room floor at Credit Suisse First Boston, at the age of 22, he knew he was on his way:

> When I ... saw the glowing flat-screen TVs, high-tech computer monitors and phone turrets with enough dials, knobs and buttons to make it seem like the cockpit of a fighter plane, I knew exactly what I wanted to do with the rest of my life. It looked as if the traders were playing a video game inside a spaceship; if you won this video game, you became what I most wanted to be—rich.[3]

Sounds pretty fantastic, right? I mean, what young person straight out of college wouldn't want to play a video game in a spaceship and make millions of dollars?

Though the internship at Credit Suisse didn't result in a full-time position, Polk kept trying, finally getting a job at Bank of America "by the grace of a manager willing to take a chance on a kid who had called him every day for three weeks."[4]

Over the course of the next several years, Polk dedicated himself to his work, moving steadily up the Wall Street ladder. After only four years, he was offered something called "1.75 by 2," which means $1.75 million per year for two years. Understandably, it went straight to his head. He says, "I started dating a pretty blonde and rented a loft apartment on Bond Street for $6,000 a month. I felt so important."[5]

A special restaurant in Manhattan where he wanted to eat? No problem! A broker would ingratiate himself to Polk by arranging the reservation and paying for the whole meal. Feeling like a Knicks-Lakers game? Sure thing! Second row seats and again, a broker to pay the tab.

But Polk was still dogged by envy! After all, there was always someone else making more. Compared to ten million, Polk says, one million looked way less impressive. So, he was constantly pushing, trying to make more and more money. He says, "Now, working elbow to elbow with billionaires, I was a giant fireball of greed. I'd think about how my colleagues could buy Micronesia if they wanted to, or become mayor of New York City. They didn't just have money; they had power. Senators came to their offices. They were royalty."[6]

Interestingly, though, it was these self-same billionaires who showed Polk that something was terribly wrong with his dogged pursuit of unlimited wealth. The longer he worked with them, the more he came to see how much control the dogged pursuit of wealth exercised over their lives. For example, one day at a meeting, he and several of his bosses were talking about new regulations, which would benefit Wall Street, as a whole, but potentially set their company back slightly. The bosses were furious. Despite all the wealth they had accumulated, they were still afraid of losing even a little bit of it!

For Polk, this was like a punch in the gut. Having been addicted to drugs and alcohol in college, he recognized the signs of addiction in both his colleagues and himself. Though (potentially) clean as far as substance abuse goes, Polk observed that these men and women would do anything and everything to get their "fixes," which could only be achieved through accumulating more and more wealth.

For the first time, Polk began to be embarrassed by his own greed and the antics of people around him, caught in the throes of their own money cravings. He began to question why he made so much money—more in a single year than his mother had made in her entire life. He said, "Yes, I was sharp, good with numbers. I had marketable talents. But I didn't really <u>do</u> anything. I was a derivatives trader, and it occurred to me that the world would hardly change at all if derivatives traders ceased to exist. Not so with nurse practitioners. What had seemed normal now seemed deeply distorted."[7]

Added to this understanding were the facts that the world was full of problems and that he wasn't doing a single thing to help. Instead, Polk was profiting from many of them! For example, he said that in the 2008 stock market crash, he'd made a huge profit by anticipating the crash—instead of warning others that it was coming and/or using his personal wealth to help the less fortunate. A day came when Polk realized that he didn't like the person he had become.

With this disturbing awareness, Polk finally knew that it was time to leave Wall Street. He felt it and knew it, but he was terrified of doing it. It's pretty easy to imagine his anxiety: How would he adjust to living on a tiny fraction of his previous salary? If he couldn't and ran out of money, what would he do? And what if in the course of several years, he looked back and saw the moment he left Wall Street as the biggest mistake he had ever made? How could he live with himself then? Besides, what would everyone think of him for leaving his incredibly lucrative job for, well, what…?

He didn't really have a plan, but he knew that he had to get out, so despite his fear and misgivings, he made the break:

The first year was really hard. I went through what I can only describe as withdrawal—waking up at nights panicked about running out of money, scouring the headlines to see which of my old co-workers had gotten promoted. Over time it got easier—I started to realize that I had enough money, and if I needed to make more, I could. But my wealth addiction still hasn't gone completely away. Sometimes I still buy lottery tickets.[8]

And yet, since leaving Wall Street, things have opened up for Polk. He describes himself as happier and more fulfilled. For example, he's spoken to people in prisons and juvenile detention centers about overcoming addiction, taught a writing class to foster children, and started a nonprofit (Groceryships) aimed at helping poor families eat nutritious food. He feels like he's finally making a positive difference, and he considers himself lucky to have escaped the trap of Wall Street and his terribly unhealthy relationship to wealth. But, really, he didn't so much escape as heed the call to awaken. In effect, Polk left a soulless job for a soulful life, transforming his Breakdown into a Breakthrough.

Story 2—John Francis: Unlike Sam Polk's slow Breakdown that led to his eventual awakening, for John Francis, Breakdown came suddenly—like the pounding of a fist at one's door. Raised in Philadelphia in the 1950s, Francis decided to leave Philly behind and try his hand at farming in California. However, before he got very far, an environmental catastrophe that changed the course of his life erupted.

It occurred on an early morning in January 1971, when two oil tankers, the *Arizona Standard* and the *Oregon Standard*, collided near the Golden Gate Bridge. The collision resulted in 800,000 gallons of oil spilling into the delicate ecosystem that is the San Francisco Bay. The water, which was once beautiful to behold, was transformed into black iridescent slime. This gunk covered the beaches and shorelines, while the ebb and flow of the waves pushed dead bodies of thousands of fish and birds up onto the land. Biologists estimated that over 10,000 birds were killed, along with millions of other marine creatures.[9]

For Francis, something deep within him was stirred as he watched a young woman's vain attempt to rescue an oil-soaked seagull. Suddenly, the oil spill was no longer an abstract event. Francis experienced it personally, as he considered his own part in the catastrophe. After all, didn't his use of a car implicate him in this spill? He recalls, "I decided I wanted to do something, but I didn't know exactly what. I mentioned to a friend that I wanted to stop riding in cars, and she laughed at me and I laughed at myself and that was the end of it."[10]

But then, Francis was touched by a second tragedy; his neighbor, a young man with a wife and young kids, died when his boat capsized in a storm. This death, striking so close to home, prompted Francis to realize that there were no guarantees in life and that if he was to make something of his life, now was the time. But the time for what exactly?

Francis commemorated the life of his recently deceased friend by taking a 20-mile memorial walk. Though he didn't realize it at the time, this walk marked the beginning of a 22-year period, during which he would rely only on his two legs for transportation. His decision to eschew motorized transport grew from a question that had been haunting him since the oil spill, namely: Are there other, gentler and less harmful, ways to live on this planet? One possibility that surfaced powerfully for Francis during his memorial walk was, "I could say 'no' to fossil fuel-based transit." And this is what he resolved to do![11]

Looking back, Francis acknowledges that in the beginning, he was pretty smug and self-righteous about rejecting fossil fuel-based transit. The ego is a powerful thing, and when a calling grabs someone, the ego sometimes wants to shout, "Hallelujah! Look at me!" from the mountaintop. But folks in Inverness, California, where Francis lived, felt a bit annoyed by this guy who was openly and self-righteously disparaging the use of cars.

Eventually Francis grew tired of arguing his cause, and on his 27th birthday, he decided to give his jaws and head a rest by observing a day of silence. He thought this day of silence would be a gift to the community, insofar as they would be relieved of his argumentations for a day. Little did he know that he would not speak again for 17 years! One day extended to a week and a week to a month, and then silence became a lifestyle. The larger gift, he was to discover, was to himself, for in the act of quieting his jaws, he had the opportunity to really listen to others for the first time in his life. In describing this decision to stop speaking, Francis wrote: "Most of my adult life I [had] not been listening fully. I only listened long enough to determine whether the speaker's ideas matched my own. If they didn't, I would stop listening, and my mind would race ahead to compose an argument against what I believed the speaker's idea or position to be."[12]

While abstaining from both speech and fossil fuel–based travel, Francis was still able to communicate. He simply carried a typewritten note explaining that he walked without words but was happy to communicate through written exchanges using a notepad that he carried. His other belongings were a sleeping bag, a banjo, a sketchpad, and a palette of watercolors, plus a few other odds and ends.

Starting along the west coast of the U.S., his walking eventually extended throughout the U.S. In describing his experience, Francis—a scraggily dressed black man walking with a banjo—comments, "When I walked across the country, there were no red states, there were no blue states; it was just America. People you might think would not bring me into their home brought me into their home and put me down at the table with their family, with their children, and invited me to stay."[13]

During the many years that Francis maintained his vow of silence and his commitment to travel on foot, he continued to be guided by what had come to be his central life question: "Are there other ways to live on this planet?" In the pursuit of answers to this question, he stopped in his journey to study ecology and environmental policy, earning a bachelor's degree at Southern Oregon State, a master's at the University of Montana, and a Ph.D. at the University of Wisconsin—and yes, he did this absent the spoken word.

When it came time to choose a topic for his Ph.D. dissertation, he came full circle by focusing on the impacts and politics of oil spills. He was, in effect, taking a fuller measure of personal responsibility for the oil spill that he had witnessed years earlier. Later, with Ph.D. in hand, he finally broke his vow of silence and went to work for the U.S. government, helping to write oil spill regulations following the *Exxon Valdez* disaster in March 1989. Though he could have stayed on at this well-paying government post, after a year he had accomplished what he had set out to do and returned to the road.

Now in his early seventies, Francis continues to pursue his calling. Appointed as a goodwill ambassador by the UN, he continues to walk the world. Why? To show respect and to extend the hand of brotherhood.

Regarding the value of silence, he says: "I still practice being silent every morning and sometimes don't speak for several days at a time. It reminds me to listen properly; not to judge what I think I'm hearing, but to try to understand what people are really saying."[14]

Story 3—Christy Carfagno: Sometimes even a small Breakdown can trigger a significant Breakthrough, provided we act. For example, several years back, one of my Teaching Assistants at Penn State, Christy Carfagno, found herself feeling increasingly upset because her social interactions had become scripted and lifeless. Her first impulse was to blame other people. Then it occurred to her that maybe it was her own tendency to always be talking that was getting in the way of the authentic connections that she longed for. This prompted her to wonder what would happen if she, like John Francis, devoted herself to listening rather than talking. This idea both frightened and excited her—a good sign that she was on a path to self-discovery. So, without further deliberation, Christy resolved to take an oath of silence for three days.

She hung a sign around her neck explaining that she was ready to listen to what anybody had to say. This sign even included some open-ended questions (e.g., What makes you feel most alive? What's something that you have been pondering? What do you love about yourself? What is creating anxiety in your life these days?). Here is Christy's account of what happened:

> What I experienced over those three days was so much bigger than I imagined. I listened to stories of heartbreak and love and excitement and wonder. I said nothing, yet I felt so much....
>
> In the days following my experiment, a number of people reached out to thank me for reminding them that their voices deserved to be heard. And as someone who had, herself, once felt entirely voiceless in an abusive relationship, this touched me deeply.
>
> In retrospect, this entire experiment was like an enormous and victorious exhale that left me feeling more whole than I had in years. In the bliss of that fullness, everything around me, including myself, truly felt like enough.[15]

Wrap-Up

> Often our deepest fear is that we might become who we are intended to be, who we already are at our core. For becoming who we truly are requires the greatest amount of change....
> The real risk in this life has always been that of becoming oneself amidst the uncertainties of existence.
> —Michael Meade[16]

These three stories provide palpable examples of how Breakdowns, both large and small, can lead to Breakthroughs. For all three individuals, shifts became possible as they began to let go of their patterned ways of being. For you, the challenge might not have anything to do with leaving behind an extravagant lifestyle for something more modest, yet meaningful, as was the case for Polk; nor might you feel called to take a vow of silence that lasts for many years, like Francis did (or even for three days, like Carfagno). The particulars don't matter so much. What does matter is that we come to experience our Breakdowns not as problems, but as invitations—i.e., soul calls to let go of ways of being that have become limiting and spiritless.

Coda

Breakdown

We are here to AWAKEN. This is our shared mission. It's often the pain of Breakdown that prods us to discover our life's true purpose. How? Jamie Reaser's poem (below) offers wise counsel.

Note to Self[1]

Cry.
Expand.
Let the longings
that tug at your heart
be the strings of your
Sun Dance.

Kneel.
Pray.
Surrender to your Destiny—
the glory of who you
are meant to be.

Listen.
Speak.
The Truth chimes
in your ears.
It has always done so.
Now you must give it resonance
in your lungs and across
your vocal chords.

Remove your shoes
and your limiting beliefs
Make love to the Earth
with every footfall.
Hers is the most intimate relationship
available to a human.

Look.
See.
Your purpose vision
dwells within your eyes.
All three.

Extend.
Hold.
The hand, the body
that you embrace
is the Other's salvation
and your own.
We are physical beings because
Spirit knows what it takes
to birth a miracle.

Love.
Because that's what you
were born to do.
        —Jamie Reaser

Cry.... Expand.... Kneel.... Pray.... Surrender.... Listen....
Look.... Extend.... Hold.... Love.... These are our touchstones
on the journey to Awakening. We have the equipment. Do we
have the will?

A Curriculum for Waking Up

Introduction

In today's conventional school settings, the curriculum is mostly centered on providing young people with the cognitive tools deemed necessary to meet the needs of our economy. Meanwhile, what often goes missing is the set of skills, attitudes, dispositions, and sensibilities that contribute to self-knowledge, wholeness, and human flourishing. The seven stepping stones in Part III address this void by offering perspectives and tools for becoming more open-minded, imaginative, embodied, and soulful.

There is a myth from Ancient Babylonian culture that illustrates the role that surrendering plays for those who are committed to awakening. Though you may have negative associations with *surrendering*, open, now, to the possibility that it is through acts of surrender—i.e., acts of letting go—that we might awaken.

As this ancient myth goes, Ishtar, Queen of Heaven, arrived at the first gate to the Underworld and demanded entrance. The gatekeeper of the first gate was terrified by her presence and sent word to his queen, Ereshkigal, goddess of the Underworld.

Queen Ereshkigal was enraged by Ishtar's intrusion, but Ishtar assured her that she would obey the laws of the Underworld. Because of her submission to Ereshkigal's rules, Ishtar was granted entry. So it was that she began to descend.

As she passed through the first gate, the crown was removed from her head.

"Why have you taken my crown?" she asked the gatekeeper.

"To enter, my lady, such is the law of the Underworld," was the gatekeeper's only response.

Passing beyond the first gate, Ishtar eventually descended to a second gate. There, the gatekeeper told her that, to gain admittance, she must remove her earrings. Again, Ishtar asked, "Why?" and again the reply came: "Such is the law of the Underworld."

At the third gate, Ishtar's necklaces were stripped from her; and at

100

the fourth the ornaments at her breast were taken. Her belt was removed at the fifth gate. The bracelets on her arms and legs were stripped away at the sixth gate. And at the seventh and final gate, the gatekeeper took her waistcloth. Only then, naked and utterly vulnerable, did Ishtar gain full entrance to the Underworld and, because of this, the opportunity to awaken.[1]

Now, Dear Reader, as you begin Part III, imagine the Gatekeeper of the Underworld calling up to you, inviting you to descend. Will you surrender? Are you willing to let go of all that you have understood yourself to be—stripped of all your armor, all your hubris, all your egoistic trappings? For it will only be then—released from whom we once believed ourselves to be—that we might truly awaken.

When you are ready, come and knock at the first gate. Demand entrance. And then surrender!

Transcending Dualism

The only thing worth learning is to unlearn. The way to do this is to question everything you think you know. As long as we're stuck in what we think we know, the world remains small…

—Byron Katie[1]

Dualism is a deeply ingrained Western habit of mind that predisposes us to divide things into either this or that—e.g., either good versus bad, fast versus slow, attractive versus unattractive. In this black versus white world, we either believe in God or we don't, we are either conservative or liberal, male or female, right or wrong, guilty or innocent. While this way of seeing can make our lives simpler, it also limits us by locking us into singular perspectives.

For example, I recall a time two decades ago when I was in the wilds of the Amazon Basin identifying trees with the help of two native men. When the time came for lunch, on our first day, the men set out a mixture of cassava meal, hot peppers, and canned sardines on a banana leaf. After lunch, as we prepared to move on, I watched as my companions tossed their empty sardine cans on the ground. This bugged me because leaving behind trash in a pristine forest was just plain wrong by my standards, but I refrained from commenting.

Three days further along on our journey, it happened that my companions came upon the remains of a rusty can that someone else had discarded in the forest. To my astonishment, they examined that can as if it were an archeological find. It was only then that I realized that what I had earlier regarded as "trash" was, for them, a source of information, offering clues to unfamiliar foods and unknown humans.

On that first day, had I not been stuck in my dualistic—either/or—mindset, I would not have judged the men's behavior as "wrong." But dualistic thinking results in dualistic seeing as underscored in this story from psychologist and author Martha Beck:

> When I was in college, every few weeks I'd join this or that group of artists and we'd all pitch in a few bucks to rent a studio and hire a model. Most of the people we got to pose were college students with bodies that matched the social ideal—slender, fit, perfectly proportioned.... And then, one day, we got somebody really different.
>
> She looked well over sixty, with a deeply lined face and a body that was probably fifty pounds heavier than her doctors would have liked.... Shining purple welts from a cesarean section and knee surgery cut deep rifts in the rippled adipose fat of her lower body. Another scar ran across one side of her chest where her left breast had once been. When she first limped onto the dais to pose, I felt so much pity and unease that I physically flinched. But we were there to draw her, so I picked up a pencil.
>
> The thing about drawing is that you can't do it well with your social self. You have to bring out your essential self, which doesn't know anything about social stereotypes. And so, as I began to draw this maimed old woman, the most amazing thing happened. Within five minutes, she became a person of absolutely wondrous beauty. She didn't look like a supermodel; she didn't have to. Her body, in and of itself, was as beautiful as a piece of polished driftwood, or a wind-carved rock, or a waterfall. My essential self didn't know that I was supposed to compare the woman to various movie stars, any more than it would have evaluated the Andes mountains by judging how much they looked like an Iowa cornfield. It simply saw her as she was: an exquisite sculptural form.
>
> When this perceptual shift happened, I was so surprised that I stopped drawing and simply stared. The model seemed to notice this, and without turning her head, looked straight into my eyes. Then I saw the ghost of a smile flicker across her face, and I realized something else: She knew she was beautiful ... and she knew that I'd seen it.... Knowing that a roomful of artists couldn't draw her without seeing her—I mean really seeing her—she may have decided to give us a gentle education about our perceptions.[2]

For the young Beck, it was dualism—her mental separation of human bodies into young versus old and attractive versus unattractive—that initially blocked her from truly seeing the woman on the dais. But once she set aside her social self and picked up her pencil to draw, she was able to see the uniqueness, the beauty, and the completeness of that woman.

Recognizing Dualism: How does dualism show up in your life? How attached are you to either/or thinking? You can explore this now by examining the word pairs below, deciding which word in each pairing belongs to the "Superior" column and which to the "Inferior" column.[3]

Word Pairs	Superior	Inferior
Up—Down	_____	_____
Rich—Poor	_____	_____
Human—Earthworm	_____	_____
Young—Old	_____	_____
Teacher—Student	_____	_____
Fast—Slow	_____	_____
Mind—Body	_____	_____
Clean—Dirty	_____	_____
Success—Failure	_____	_____
More—Less	_____	_____
Good—Bad	_____	_____
Mental—Physical	_____	_____
Reason—Emotion	_____	_____
Generous—Selfish	_____	_____
Happy—Sad	_____	_____

Are these superior versus inferior decisions easy for you to make? Or do you struggle? Take the first pair, "up versus down." If you marked "up" as superior and "down" as inferior, you are not alone. But is "up" really superior? The fact that we often use phrases like, "things are looking up," "the music is upbeat," "I'm up for it," "she brightens up the room," leads us to associate "up" with good and desirable. But, really, this is just a cultural overlay. "Up" is not superior to "down." In fact, these concepts need each other; without "up" there is no "down," no way of distinguishing upstairs from downstairs, uptown from downtown, uphill from downhill.

What about, "rich versus poor?" I understand if you are inclined to regard "rich" as superior to "poor." However, if you were to live among the "poor" of this world, you just might be surprised to discover (as I have been) that so-called "poor people" are often far superior to those classified as "rich" in terms of common sense, patience, generosity, and compassion.

Now, how about: "Human versus earthworm?" It's easy to assume that humans are superior to earthworms. But consider: Earthworms are masters at aerating soil as they go about their business of transforming decaying plant matter into the nutrient-rich castings that enable plants of all kinds to flourish. Through this ecological lens, earthworms are far more important to the health and well-being of the biosphere than are humans. Gulp!

With a bit of thought and an appetite for devil's advocacy, you could make a case that the second category, in each of the above pairings, is superior to the first. None of this is meant to say that dualistic thinking is wrong or bad. That would be ironic. But when dualism carries over to our beliefs, edging us toward fundamentalism (my religion is right, so yours must be wrong), dogmatism (the only solution for crime is incarceration), or narrow-mindedness (I only see one option here), we compromise our freedom of thought, crippling our capacity for creativity as well as compassion.

Transcending dualism calls on us to practice metacognition—i.e., to reflect on why we think, believe, and act as we do. This requires a willingness to critique our thoughts and opinions by asking open-ended questions like:

- Why do I think or believe as I do on this issue?
- How did I come to see this as I do?
- How does my stance on this issue blind me to other ways of knowing?

It is questions like these that ventilate our thinking, awakening us to new ways of seeing and being.

The Limitations of Dualism: When I was in first grade, I was taught that $1 + 1 = 2$ because when I answered "2," I got the problem "right." If I answered with any other number, I was told that I was "wrong." Right versus wrong, true versus false; this is dualism in action.

In fact, I can't recall a single time during my schooling when I was invited to step beyond dualism. For example, there was never an instance when someone invited me to consider a case where the sum of $1 + 1$ could equal 1. Yet, when two people marry, their two previously separate existences coalesce into a singular union. It's the same when algae and fungi join in symbiosis to create a lichen (again: $1 + 1 = 1$). Nor was I ever challenged to consider that $1 + 1$ could equal 3. But what about water? It is composed of two elements, hydrogen and oxygen, but depending on the temperature, three results are possible—(i) solid, (ii) liquid, and (iii) vapor ($1 + 1 = 3!$).

Not all cultures are as deeply steeped in dualism as is ours. For example, Buddhist monks-in-training are given knotty questions, called "koans," to ponder. A classic koan is "What is the sound of one hand clapping?" There is no logical solution to this question. It can only be resolved by side-stepping rational thought and adopting what is sometimes referred to as "beginner's mind." By way of illustration, here is a koan for your consideration:

> When Banzan was walking through the market, he overheard a conversation between a butcher and a customer. "Give me the best piece of meat you have," said the customer. "But everything here is the best," replied the butcher. "You cannot find here any piece of meat that is not the best." At these words Banzan became enlightened.[4]

If, as a Buddhist monk in training, you were given this koan and a year to ponder it, how might you make sense of it? Could you? Surely some cuts of meat are better than others, just as some apples are better than other apples. They can't all be the best. So, what is this butcher thinking? And why did his words lead Banzan to become enlightened? Your first thought might be that the butcher is just a con artist hawking his goods. But if that were the case, why wouldn't he single out one cut of meat, extol its greatness, and ask the highest price for it? But, remember, there are no logical answers to koans.

So, put yourself in the place of a young monk, "living" this koan, day after day. Eventually, you exhaust all mental attempts to fit your square pegged answers into the round hole presented by the koan. Only then, in a state of mental surrender, do you open yourself to the possibility that the butcher is simply telling the truth, that each cut is the best. With this breakthrough, you might be ready to leave behind your dualistic world of good versus bad and best versus worst, and step into the butcher's world where each cut of meat, each element of existence, truly is excellent, complete, and good, just as it is. And what if the same were true of that sardine can in the jungle and that old woman on the dais? Each just right, perfectly placed and formed? By acknowledging this, you too might experience a measure of awakening.

From Tree to Me: By now it should be apparent that to awaken we must learn to let go of rigid ways of thinking, seeing, and being. Many past cultures and some still today have rites of passage expressly designed to trigger awakenings. For example, imagine yourself as a sixteen-year-old boy, living in an African village. One evening an elder knocks on your door. You have been anticipating this day. The man gestures for you to follow and you obey. Eventually, you arrive at a clearing in the forest where other young men have gathered, each accompanied by an elder. You know why you are there; your rites of passage are about to begin.

The elder who fetched you shaves off your hair with a razor, symbolically cutting away your old identity. He then rubs ashes into your head, all the while praying and chanting. You know that in the coming weeks you will undergo many tests, each an invitation to let go of your social self so that you might awaken to your essential self.

Just before sunrise the next day, you follow the elder into the forest. He tells you to wander until you feel called by a tree and then to stay with that tree until something is revealed to you. Though you have no idea what that "something" might be, you wander until you have the subtle sense of being *called* by a gently swaying tree with deeply fissured bark. Respectfully, you approach the tree and settle down before it. You begin by slowly taking in all the tree's parts—the colors, textures and distribution of its foliage; the layout and delicacy of its twigs and branches; the thickness and curvature of its trunk; the fragile, winged nature of its seeds, and more. An hour passes and then another. The temperature changes from cool to warm and then to hot. You begin to sweat.

"Is this some kind of stupid game?" you wonder. In the midst of your angst, you notice that the elder is watching you from a distance. His face is placid. Nonetheless, you experience a surge of alarm at the specter of failure. "I can't do this; I'm no good," you think.

More hours pass. Now it's dusk. You have all but given up; the tree will never be anything but a stupid tree.

In the waning light, the elder approaches, nods and says, "Sleep now and resume at first light."

Hungry and broken, you make a bed of leaves and shiver your way through a restless night. At first light, you resume your position. Focusing on the tree, you remind yourself that your task is to discover something that is at once tree and more than tree, something that is unmediated, pure. Hours pass; it is midday. Sweat drips from your body, and again you are filled with despair and frustration.

You begin to cry. Then, in the midst of your tears, you start speaking to the tree, recognizing for the first time that this tree has a life of her own. At first you just blubber about how forlorn and pathetic you are, but then a moment comes when you confide in the tree that it is not her fault that you cannot see her essence. It is the result of your own ignorance, your own blindness. Between sobs, you apologize, asking her for forgiveness. Then, you go quiet.

As dusk approaches, you are overcome by an exhaustion greater than any you have ever known. At the same time, you are buzzing with sensations of aliveness, beyond what you have ever imagined possible. Suspended on the transformative edge between breakdown and rapture, you realize that the tree you have been sitting with is not a "tree" at all—not a category, not an "it"; but instead, just like you, that "tree" is a unique manifestation of Earth's generative energies. Yes, for a brief moment, you have transcended dualism; the notions of inferior and superior have dissolved. You are one with life.

Wrap-Up

> All the big problems of the world today are rooted in the philosophy of separateness and dualism.
> —Satish Kumar[5]

Rather than living in an either/or world, imagine choosing to live in one that is both/and. One way to imagine this is to call to mind the ancient Chinese yin-yang symbol. You know the one, with a circular image that swirls—black into white into black again, with a dot of black at the center of the white and a dot of white at the heart of the black [☯]. This iconic symbol reminds us that things which appear to be in separate categories are often more similar than we imagine.

Upshot: Just as the gatekeeper at the first gate demanded that Ishtar surrender her crown (the mark of her identity as Queen-Goddess), so, too, must we be open to letting go of aspects of our identity that block us from experiencing the interconnectivity of all life.[6]

Recovering Imagination and Play

Alice laughed. "There's no use trying," she said. "One can't believe impossible things."

"I daresay you haven't had much practice," said the Queen. "When I was your age, I always did it for half-an-hour a day. Why, sometimes I've believed as many as six impossible things before breakfast."

—Lewis Carroll[1]

A willingness to playfully imagine the seemingly impossible is an important disposition for those seeking to awaken fully to the gift of a human life. How is it with you? Can you call to mind a recent instance when you allowed yourself to believe "impossible things?" This falls into the realm of what Melissa calls "half-beliefs"—a world where playfulness abounds, facts are fluid, and beliefs are bendable.

Growing up, one of Melissa's half-beliefs involved a giant oak tree growing on the banks of a creek, where she often played. She recounts: "One day I noticed a large crack in the back of that enormous oak, revealing that the entire inside was hollow. Seeming to defy all logic, the tree was still alive, its leaves green and healthy. In my amazement, I recall asking my friend how this hollow tree could still be living? She looked at me, rolled her eyes, and said, 'It's a fairy tree, Melissa. The fairies hollowed it out to live inside, and their magic keeps it from dying.' From then on, we sang fairy songs and built little tea tables and houses for the fairies at the base of that oak. As years passed, I lost my belief in fairies, but it has recently been half-revived. For example, now I will blame them for causing something to fall that I thought was stable or for the mysterious reappearance of something I desperately needed, like my car keys. You never can tell, because fairies like to play tricks, you know. At least, I half-believe that this is true."

Aerating our Lives with Silliness: Our culture conditions us to view silliness as fine for children but not OK for adults. Perhaps you remember times, as a child, when you were chastised for being a "silly boy" or a "silly girl." It turns out, though, that giving ourselves freedom to be just plain silly can be tremendously enlivening. It was with the intent of celebrating silliness that I recently invited the students in one of my classes to write stories about an adult who was not afraid to be silly. One student, Jamie Quail, wrote:

> My experiences with silliness, growing up, came largely from my goofy, lovable, and caring mother. For example, she used to have all these "Confucius Say" jokes, such as, "Confucius say, man who farts in church sits in his own pew." She also knew the *Gilligan's Island* theme song in French, but she would only sing it on long car rides, out of the blue. We'd beg her to sing it, but she wouldn't budge. Just when we had given up asking, she'd do it, and we'd all burst with laughter.
>
> There was also this time, riding with a friend to the midnight premiere of one of the Twilight series movies about love and vampires. Just as my mom began to drive us to the theater, she switched on the inside car light. Then, turning to us in the back seat, she smiled and revealed her fangs—you know, those fake plastic ones you get for Halloween. We couldn't help but crack up at that. It was these little moments that could turn a bad day and a bad mood into a humorous and lighthearted one.

By forthrightly choosing to be silly, Jamie's mom was bucking a social norm and, in so doing, giving her daughter permission to jettison her fear of how others might judge her if she, too, were to take a plunge into silliness.

Turning Failure Inside Out: Just as letting go of the fear of being judged as "silly" can lead to fun and freedom, the same could be said for letting go of the fear of failure. I grant you that pairing failure with fun and freedom might seem like a stretch. However, consider this story from one of my students, Hayly Hoch, who described how she and some of her friends had the crazy idea to turn failure inside out to see what they might learn. That's right; instead of fearing failure, they would embrace it, believe in it, and seek it out with as much earnestness as they might seek, you know, success. Here, in Hayly's words, is what happened:

> We were all so jazzed just thinking about the benefits of [earnestly pursuing failure] that someone proposed that we actually test out this idea right then

and there. There were eight of us, so we split into two teams of four. Then, we gave ourselves an hour to go around town and to fail as outrageously and creatively and frequently as possible. My group, although we didn't win the competition for most failures, sure had a lot of delightful surprises. By the end of the hour we had received free ice cream from an ice cream vendor, a hand-drawn portrait of our group, multiple phone numbers for future dating escapades, pictures with strangers to remember our night, and more than one piggyback ride.[2]

Amidst all the shenanigans, Hayly's whole concept of failure evaporated—poof! Yes, many of her group's requests were refused, but it no longer mattered. The larger story was that failure ceased being a terrifying monster. It no longer controlled the steps and risks that Hayly and her friends were willing to take. Instead, failure became a gateway into fun and freedom.

Laughter as Elixir: Seriousness is way overrated. Think about it. When your jaw is set and your brow is furrowed, how open, spontaneous, creative, and alive are you?

The good news is that, as humans, we each possess a kind of elixir that combats seriousness while promoting freedom, goodwill, and health. This elixir is laughter. Yes, laughter, especially the ability to laugh at ourselves, is good medicine. For example, imagine it's a beautiful day; the sun is shining, and you are on a walk, happy as can be. Everything is perfect, but then you remember that you might not have enough money to pay for your rent this month. In an instant, you are pulled from bliss to stress.

Now, run this scenario again, but this time when that anxiety-producing thought about not having enough money arises, imagine yourself simply beginning to laugh. Of course, on the surface, there is nothing funny about your predicament, but what *is* funny is that you allowed yourself to become suddenly hooked by anxiety when just a minute earlier you had been walking along in a state of relative bliss. Now, that's funny! And it's doubly funny, because stressing over your rent in this moment won't fix anything.

Still, it can be really difficult to shift to laughter when we are overtaken by stress. But imagine this: Rather than continuing to walk when you are suddenly overcome by rent anxiety, you come to a full stop. Then, you raise your arms to the sky and inhale deeply; and on the outbreath, you allow your arms to flop down to your sides, while simultaneously expelling a big audible "HAH!" That "HAH" is incipient laughter. Though there is still nothing to laugh about, this audible release of energy leaves you feeling a tiny bit better, and so you repeat that big in-breath/arm flop/ release routine three more times: (1) HAH, (2) HAH, (3) HAH. By now you are almost smiling.

Next, you bring your hands to the sides of your head and enact a pull-ing motion as you yank your stress-causing thoughts from your mind—all the while, vocalizing HAH... HAH... HAH... HAH... HAH-HAH-HAH. Yes, at first, you will be faking the laughter, but soon, if you persist, you will be truly laughing at the absurdity of it all—your absurdity, life's absurdity, human absurdity.

Recent research shows that laughter is a kind of natural medicine that boosts the human immune system, triggering the release of endorphins (the body's natural feel-good chemicals) and protecting the heart by increasing blood flow and lowering blood pressure. Amazingly, research also reveals that these laughter benefits accrue even when people engage in fake or simulated laugher (as in the above example). No wonder, then, that "laugh yoga" and "laugh therapy" groups are proliferating around the world![3]

Life as Play: Cultivating a lightness of being can act as a stepping stone toward awakening. And what better way to lighten up than by en-gaging, on a daily basis, in full-fledged, spontaneous play? This is not to say that play doesn't exist within our culture, like in competitive sports or in card or board games, but such "play" is largely circumscribed by rules and protocols.

This contrasts with genuine play, which is always an invitation into spontaneity, authenticity, and self-discovery, insofar as it is never orches-trated. And, of course, this is why genuine play is so enlivening and, yes, scary. For example, imagine yourself sharing a bottle of wine with three friends, when spontaneously one of your buddies starts tapping out a beat on his knee. Then, to your surprise, a second friend picks up two spoons and adds a backbeat, and before you know it, your third friend blends in a regular low-pitched clicking sound. You want to participate, but you don't know how. Then, you take a big swallow of wine and a deep breath, and you give yourself permission to just soak in the rhythms; and the next thing you know, you are spontaneously adding in a staccato snap/clap.

None of this was planned; none of your friends are musicians. So, what happened? Well, apparently, all four of you were able to trust enough in yourselves and each other to set self-consciousness aside, letting go of your need to look good or to get it right! Here are three more vignettes that illustrate how genuine play might erupt.

    i. You are walking in the woods with those same three friends. You ask everyone, including yourself, to pick up a natural object. Then, together, you begin to create a game using the four gathered objects. After a time, the initial version of your game morphs into another game, and then another.

    ii. Feeling light and free, you begin to skip through the forest; your friends join in. You add a whistle to your skip, and they follow suit. Next, one of your friends begins skipping backwards, and then all three join in. Soon, you are spinning each other around, laughing, releasing, opening. A woman walking a dog joins in—each of you, creating, playing, and expressing—with the dog, a bona fide play master, at the center of the fun.

    iii. Now, it's twilight. There's a chill in the air. You and your three buddies gather sticks and make a small fire. Warmed by the flames, you are filled with gratitude and share the sources of your gratitude with each other. From this simple beginning, a gratitude ceremony unfolds. It is unscripted, heartfelt, born out of the fecund present moment.

In these and numerous other ways, play foments awakening, inviting us to let go of the need to control events by surrendering to what each present moment might offer.

Wrap-Up

> It is paradoxical that many educators and parents still differentiate between a time for learning and a time for play without seeing the vital connection between them.
>
> —Leo F. Buscaglia[4]

In our everyday, business-as-usual world, there really are no fairies or vampires with fangs, nor is there much active encouragement to be silly or playful, or to allow our imagination to be stretched by half-beliefs. As often as not, adults in our culture tend to frown upon magic, shun mystery, and discourage silliness. But just as Ishtar freed herself of her earrings at the second gate to the Underworld, we, too, can release ourselves from cultural dictates that stifle our generative imagination and innate playfulness. And what might we gain? How about the experience of becoming ever more fully human!

Reclaiming Wildness

I confess that I do hug trees in my backyard and any place else where I happen to meet impressive ones. I hum beside creeks, hoot back at owls, lick rocks, smell flowers, rub my hands over the grain in wood. I'm well aware that such behavior makes me seem weird in the eyes of people who've become disconnected from the earth. But in the long evolutionary perspective, they're the anomaly. Our bodies were made for this glorious planet, tuned to its every sound and shape.

—Scott Russell Sanders[1]

What do you make of Sanders' confession (above)? Does he sound a bit wild? If so, is that a good thing or a bad thing? What are your associations with wildness? Find out, right now, by using your journal to write down and complete the following open sentences:

To be wild is to be _____
_____.

What scares me about wildness is _____
_____.

The last time I freely expressed my wildness was _____
_____.

If I were to give myself permission to be more wild, I would ____
_____.

As you consider your responses, note what, if anything, surprises you.

Now go a step further by considering how you would respond if you saw someone acting wild in public—e.g., laughing hysterically or rolling in the grass or dancing ecstatically? Would you feel uncomfortable? Indifferent? Worried? Or might witnessing unabashed, uncensored wild behavior actually delight you?[2] Indeed, what if being able to express wildness is an essential component of what makes us human? And what if by suppressing our innate wildness, we sacrifice our aliveness, inhibiting our own awakening?

Discovering Your Innate Wildness: Today we live in a machine culture surrounded by all manner of contraptions, devices, gadgets, and technologies, with new inventions appearing every day. And yet we are really no different, biologically, from our human ancestors who inhabited Earth tens of thousands of years ago. Sure, we have evolved in technological terms since those distant times, but our biology is still rooted in that long-ago world when our survival depended on being attuned to the sounds, movements, rhythms, and behaviors of Earth's inhabitants. This means that, at our core, we each still possess a wild indigenous self—i.e., a self that possesses ancestral wisdom and knows that we are a part of Earth, composed of Earth.

Ecopsychologist Bill Plotkin writes that when we connect to our innate wildness:

> "...we are in communion with the world through our eyes, ears, nose, tongue and skin, as well as through our indigenous heart and wild mind.... We delight in playful contact with the flesh and fur of fellow living animals, with bark and seed, husk and fruit, wind and water.... We are thrilled by the scent of jasmine, the taste of honey, the spectacle of elk or eagle, the roar of thunder, or the buzz of bees, or by full-bodied immersions in ocean, storm or the final dazzling rays of sunset.... Our sensuous communion with the world sends shivers of seductive appreciation through our limbs."[3]

Plotkin's words challenge us to expand our understanding of what it means to be fully human. Caught in the rhythms of modern life, it is easy to forget that each of us was born wild, with the potential for an open, sensuous, intimate relationship with Earth.

One way to recover our innate wildness is to apprentice oneself to a child on a summer afternoon, observing how that child responds to a stick, a worm, a flower, a clump of mud, a sudden blast of wind, or the shadows cast by trembling leaves. Then, follow the child's lead and give yourself permission to have a full-on encounter with another life form—e.g., crow, cat, cricket, cactus—allowing the child within you to behold this other—not as object, but as subject—i.e., as if you have never seen such a miracle before. Then, continue to bring all your senses to bear until you begin to sense your profound kinship with this other. It might even happen—as it sometimes does with children—that you begin to merge with, or even shape shift into, this other being, the veil of separation momentarily dissolving.

By way of example, take in this story, recounted by psychologist and author Tobin Hart, about a father (Mark) and his child (Miranda) spending a summer day at the beach. Miranda, at age eight, was drawn toward the gentle surf and was soon standing in the cool water up to her waist. For fifteen minutes, she stood there, moving slightly with the ebb and flow of the tide. Thirty minutes passed and then an hour. All the while, Miranda remained stationary, swaying back and forth in the surf. As Mark watched, worries arose (e.g., does she have enough sunscreen?), but he was able to rein in his anxiety and simply let Miranda be.

After an hour and a half, Miranda finally turned from the water and ambled back to join her father. It was then that Mark noticed that Miranda's whole being was radiating peace and joy. When he was unable to contain his curiosity any longer, he asked Miranda what it was like being in the water.

"I was the water," Miranda replied softly.

"The water?" Mark echoed.

"Yes," she confirmed, "It was amazing. I was the water. I love it, and it loves me."[4]

Miranda didn't reach this profound understanding through rational analysis. More likely, it emerged as an intuitive knowing, triggered by the prolonged encounter between her own watery body and the watery body that is Ocean.

Hugging a Tree: One way, near at hand, to experience a measure of wild communion with nature—as Miranda did—is to hug a tree. If it helps, imagine that the tree you hug is like a relative who you are encountering after a long separation. This isn't so farfetched! After all, trees have played a significant role in influencing human evolution over millions of years. In times long past, our hominid ancestors lived in trees, meaning that the current design of our bodies is, in part, the result of adaptations our ancestors underwent to sustain arboreal life. For example, they developed strong, flexible limbs for swinging and climbing, as well as paws (hands), replete with opposable thumbs for grasping.

These attributes live on in us today. Further, trees helped to shelter and feed our primate ancestors, just as they continue to do for us, in some measure, today. This alone could be cause for offering a hug to a tree now and again!

But maybe you are thinking that a hug is a bit much? For example, when I asked some of my students about tree-hugging recently, one responded, "Why would I hug a tree? It can't hug me back." At first, I didn't know how to respond, but later, it occurred to me that the trees living around me produce a portion of the oxygen that I breathe in each day. When this tree oxygen enters my lungs, the hemoglobin molecules in my blood grab onto it (i.e., hug it). In a reciprocal fashion, each time I breathe out, I offer nearby trees my carbon dioxide—a crucial ingredient for photosynthesis. So, while a tree may not be able to hug us back in the traditional way, maybe this deep interdependency could be sufficient motivation for hugging a tree anyway! Even sitting and breathing with a tree, now and again, might engender both appreciation and awakening.

If it is still your way to see trees more as objects than as wild, animate beings, I understand—I really do. I was in your camp until I was challenged by one of my college professors to enumerate three things that humans have in common with trees. At first, this question made no sense to me, but slowly I came to see similarities.

For example, do you know that trees—just like humans and other mammals—have a circulatory system? Instead of carrying blood, tree circulatory systems transport water and minerals from the roots to the leaves, while also carrying sugars and other nutrients down from the leaves to the roots.

And get this: Trees, like us, have a sex life. Believe it or not, the real purpose of the flowers festooning trees in Spring is not to delight us, but to attract insects that feed on flower nectar. In the process, insects pick up pollen (think sperm) that they transport to other trees of the same species, ensuring fertilization and eventually seed production.[5]

Another fascinating similarity is that some tree species—e.g., Red Maple—have evolved the ability to warn each other when there is danger afoot. In the case of humans, if there is peril in the neighborhood, we sound an alarm. Trees sound their alarms using chemicals. For example, if insects begin to attack the leaves of a certain red maple, that tree will send out airborne messenger molecules, *telling* nearby maples to protect themselves. When the neighboring maples receive the airborne message, they escape defoliation by producing insect-repellent chemicals within their own foliage.

The more I have come to learn about the life of trees, the more I find myself filled with awe and respect when I am in their presence. Whereas, as a young man, I sometimes, absentmindedly, plucked leaves from tree branches, now I repent by exchanging breath with tree leaves.

So, if you still aren't inclined to hug a tree, what's holding you back? Is it because you are concerned that people might see you in the midst of a hug and judge you as weird? They very well might, but, as Scott Russell Sanders reminded us at the beginning of this piece: "Our bodies were made for this glorious planet, tuned to its every sound and shape."

An Encounter with the Wild Other: We each have the choice to either conform to the cultural dictates that limit us or open ourselves to the call of the wild. If it's a taste of wildness that you seek, don't wait! All that is required is that you make a date with yourself to visit a wild patch of forest. Any patch will do. Then, once you arrive, simply wander about, going where your feet take you. Don't try to find anything; instead, allow yourself to be found. How? Just trust that, eventually, something will attract you … will call to you. It might be a delicate tree seedling, or a scurrying beetle, or a tuft of moss, or a butterfly or a salamander.

Whatever it is, ask for permission to spend time together. I grant you that it may seem odd to ask for permission, but think about how you would feel if someone came barging into your house and swaggered around as if s/he owned the place! Now, consider that when you walk into a patch of wild forest, you are literally walking into the home of other beings. Viewed from this perspective, asking permission is a way of extending the same respect to the denizens of the wild that you, presumably, would expect others to extend to you in your home.

As you settle in with the wild being who has captured your attention, consider the connections between the two of you. After all, the fact that you are both living creatures means that you share things in common. Finally, from a place of humility, open to what this other might have to teach you. Go slow. Breathe. And when the time finally comes to end your encounter, express your gratitude.

Unleashing the Wild Within: Have you ever seen a horse standing peacefully in a meadow and then been surprised to witness that same horse suddenly erupt in raucous, unbridled movement, racing around as if on fire? This is actually a common occurrence with adolescent horses. These rambunctious beings don't censor themselves out of fear that other horses might judge their antics as inappropriate. Instead, they simply surrender to the energy rising and falling within them.

Just as with horses, our bodies are also filled with energy—energy that is capable of moving us into ecstatic aliveness provided that we are willing to give ourselves permission to express this. If you'd like to explore what I am talking about, locate a place outside—e.g., a meadow, a patch of forest, a sandy beach—and simply allow your body to move in whatever ways it wants. You are not performing a dance; rather, you are surrendering, giving your body permission to move in any way that it wants, spontaneously, without any interference or direction from your head.

It is important to be patient with this activity because it may take a while to release all the layers of body prohibition, accumulated over a lifetime, that tend to keep us in a kind of harness, holding our spontaneity and wildness in check.

Begin by standing in a relaxed posture, receiving life energy on your in-breath and releasing on your out-breath. Then, allow your hand to move in any way that it wants to move. At first it might remain limp. That's okay; be patient. As you surrender to your body's impulses, sooner or later, your hand will begin to move, spontaneously, along with the other parts of your body. Eventually, you may even find yourself down on the ground, crawling or pawing about. Just surrender to whatever impulses arise. You are, by nature, a wild animal, after all!

This exercise is about throwing off the harness of our conditioning; it's about removing all those body shackles, accumulated over a lifetime, that routinely hold us in check; it's about expressing and celebrating our innate freedom in the most radical of ways. There are no rules, no *shoulds*, no rights, no wrongs. All that's required is creating a space wherein your life energy is free to express itself, moving you into generative relationship with yourself and the world.[6]

Wrap-Up

> In wildness is the preservation of the world.
> —Henry David Thoreau[7]

If this call to recover and cultivate your innate wildness feels scary, this is probably because you, like most of the rest of us, have been raised in a culture that teaches you to keep yourself under control at all times. But if it is awakening that you truly seek, you can do as Ishtar did at the third gate and remove the choker from around your neck and—thus unbridled—begin to awaken to your innate wildness.

Discovering Full-Body Intelligence

It is amazing how many hints and guides and intuitions for living come to the sensitive person who has ears to hear what his body is saying.

—Rollo May[1]

Have you ever heard the expression, "Human beings are just brains on a stick?" In this formulation, our bodies are like cars that our brains drive around. This head-centric view of identity conjures the often-quoted words of 17th century philosopher René Descartes: "I think, therefore I am." For Descartes, our core identity as humans resided in our heads. But today, this "brains on a stick" view is a hard sell in light of recent studies revealing that in addition to a cranial brain, we possess dense neural networks both in our heart (the so-called heart brain) and in our gut (the belly or enteric brain).[2]

These body brains are especially attuned to relationships and feelings, as evidenced in expressions like: "My heart is breaking," or "I have a gut feeling." While it is true that our cranial brain is adept at dealing with abstractions and providing perspective, it is our body-based intelligences that play a critical role in sensitizing us to the world around us. Said differently, our head brain specializes in analyzing and controlling the world, while our body-brain complex helps us to make sense of, and harmonize with, the world. Control (head) and harmony (body) can be seen as complementary, insofar as control imposes top-down order, while harmony, arising from the body, creates wholeness, unity, and balance.

As author and body intelligence coach Phillip Shepherd points out in *New Self, New World*, many past cultures had ready access to the sensitivities and sensibilities delivered through their body's intelligence. This is revealed through language. For example, in Japanese the word for belly, "hara," signifies the center of one's being—i.e., the place where one's deepest truth resides. Even today in Japan, one might say, "She has a well-developed belly," to denote a person with common sense, whereas we, in the West, would say, "She is level-headed."[3]

While our cranial brain is good at reasoning, we easily forget that reason alone is of little use when it comes to some of the most important things in life. For example, you can't reason your way into love, nor can you use reason to coax yourself to live in the present moment. Likewise, reason will be of little use to you if you wish to gain access to your body's innate intelligence.

Intelligence as Sensitivity: Our body intelligence manifests as sensitivity. This sensitivity comes in many forms. For example, perhaps you are sensitive to musical rhythms. You have never studied music, yet you are always tapping out complex syncopating beats. Your friends are amazed by this, but for you it just comes naturally. Or maybe you are super-sensitive to colors and patterns and have been creating spellbinding paintings ever since you were a child. Or perhaps you are sensitive to birds and are able to identify literally hundreds of bird species simply by their songs. Indeed, there are countless ways that intelligence, understood as heightened sensitivity, can be expressed, and none are confined to the brain.[4]

But, hold on! Surely something like solving a mathematical problem happens purely within the confines of the cranial brain. Not so! Our body-based sensitivities play a part there, too. For example, feelings of confidence and satisfaction that arise in your body as you work through the problem, inform you that you are on the right track. Even the body-based feeling of triumph at having the numbers align as you check your work, tells you that you have successfully solved the problem!

Similarly, body-based intuition is often an under-appreciated facet of our intelligence. Explore this now by asking yourself a question that you know you will answer Yes to, like, "Do I want to spend time with my best friend?" or "Do I like playing my favorite game?" Ask your question and then simply notice how your body *feels* as you experience an unequivocal Yes to your question. Do you feel light or heavy? How does your chest-heart region feel: Open? Contracted? Tingly? Numb? Now, go a step further and ask yourself a question that you know you will say No to, like, "Do I want to spend the afternoon sitting in a dumpster filled with garbage?" or "Do I want to bang my head against a concrete wall?" And, then register how your *No* feels in your body, with special attention to your chest and gut.

Once you have established baselines for how your body registers your Yes's and No's, you will be ready to begin to employ your body-based sensitivity—i.e., body intelligence—as a helper when you are unable to make a clear decision relying solely on your cranial brain. For example, imagine being faced with a question like: Should I quit my job? You could proceed by using the logical, head-based, approach of listing pros and cons and then choosing the option with the most support, but you probably know that following this path can be unsatisfying, especially when the outcome doesn't *feel* right. In cases like this, it can help to break the question—e.g., Should I quit my job?—down into smaller questions, like: (i) Do I like what I do at work? (ii) Do I feel appreciated at work? (iii) Am I getting paid enough at work? Paying attention to how your body responds to these smaller questions will reveal to you whether you should stick with your job or leave it behind.

The point here is that our body-based sensitivities, when used in concert with our head-based, rational intelligence, can help ensure wise choices regarding both the big and small things in our lives.

A Body Awareness Exercise: Another way to explore body-based intelligence is to move your awareness from place to place within your body. This takes a bit of practice, but once you get the hang of it, you will be in for some surprises.

Give it a try now by bringing your awareness—your attention—to your feet. This is not a request to think about your feet or to create an image of your feet. I am asking you to actually experience the physical sensations present in your feet, right now. Start with the toes of your right foot, noting any sensations there—e.g., coldness, itching, warmth, tingling. Be patient ... curious ... attentive. Next, move your attention to the bottom of your right foot. There is a lot of territory here, so go slowly. Note the sensations associated with your heel, sole, instep, and the ball of your right foot. Then, bring your attention to your left foot, similarly, exploring all of its dimensions. As you do this, you might come to see your feet in new ways, appreciating their remarkable ability to ground and balance you as they move and pivot you throughout your day.

Finally, consider listening to your feet! After all, your feet are a part of you, and they are imbued with nerve endings that experience the world in ways that are unique to them. So, it is not farfetched to consider that your feet might have things to say to you, provided you give them your attention and are sensitive to their messages. Do this now by completing the open sentence: I am your feet and I _____. Then, pay attention to what arises. If words don't come, that's OK. Just the act of bringing awareness to your feet is a step toward wholeness, integration, and body intimacy.

Use this same procedure to come into relationship with other parts of your body. From your feet, move your attention to your ankles, then to your calves, your knees, your thighs, your spine, your arms, your hands, and your shoulders, all the way up to your neck and head, noticing the sensations in each body region and giving voice to the intelligences—i.e., sensitivities—embedded therein.

Receiving the World: Once you get the hang of shifting your awareness from place to place within your body, consider exploring the unique intelligence housed within the core of your body. Philip Shepherd (mentioned above) has developed a nifty technique for this that he's dubbed the "elevator exercise." It's easy to do. Begin by picturing a hollow tube (think elevator shaft), extending from the top of your head, along the front of your spine, all the way down to the very bottom of your pelvic bowl. Place the elevator on the top floor, up in your head. Then, as a warm-up, move your awareness around in your head—i.e., from side to side and front to back, just as you did earlier, with your feet. As you do this, note the sensations, if any, that you experience in your skull. Perhaps, like many people, you will experience your cranial space as airy, light, or spacey. But if your experience is different, that's fine, too.

When you are ready, slowly drop your attention from your head, down along the front of your spine—in effect, riding the "elevator" down—until, eventually, your awareness comes to rest in your pelvic bowl. Again, don't imagine this elevator ride. Instead, literally move your attention—your awareness—from your head, gradually down the front of your spine until it is firmly rooted way down there, at the base of your pelvic bowl. This may take a while; there is no rush.

With your awareness anchored at your core, notice any sensations there. How does it feel to have your awareness centered in your pelvic bowl? Light and airy, like up in your head, or perhaps more grounded, rooted, alive? Just notice.[5]

You can take this elevator exercise further by going outside and standing before a tree. If you are dwelling in the familiar head-centric consciousness of our culture, you will likely see the tree as an object, and if you are able to assign a name to it (e.g., identifying it as an oak tree), you might assume that you know it. But, of course, all you would really know is the name that your culture assigns to that tree.

As a way to truly know/experience that tree, ride the elevator, again, slowly moving your awareness—your attention—from your head down to your pelvic floor.

Once your awareness is grounded in your pelvic bowl, you will no longer be a spectator, monitoring the world from your head, but, instead, a co-inhabitant, receiving the world into and through your body. As this happens, that tree will be transformed slowly from a concept in your head to a body sensation, a somatic knowing. In other words, it will no longer be an object, but, instead, a subject, available for relationship.

Of course, this won't happen immediately, but it is likely that there will be something qualitatively different about your experience as you behold Oak through the medium of your body, even on your first attempt.

And what might it be like to receive and know the world in this way? Well, recently I was lost in thought (in my head) while riding my bike across town. Noting this, I slowed down and gradually moved my awareness down to my core. As this happened, I was surprised that I was no longer seeing the trees lining the street as background objects. Instead, I experienced each individual tree as brimming with aliveness. And this was no less true for the road sign and the fire hydrant and the gas station, each one broadcasting a unique energetic signature that I was able to sense as I pedaled along. Later, I gained insight on my experience when I read these words from Shepherd:

> When we clear the body of its rigid presumptions and consolidations and open ... then the vibrations of Being become our vibrations.... In its essence, the body is a vibratory medium—but only our receptivity to ... the present makes us aware of that....[6]

The world around us is waiting and available for relationship in every moment, but we miss out when we are stuck up in our heads.

Saying "no" to Headism: Living predominantly in our heads, as so many of us have been conditioned to do, creates separation. Our culture frames this separation as independence, teaching us to believe that the more independence we achieve—through the pursuit of wealth, status, power, control etc.—the more secure and successful we will become. But the so-called "independence" that is made possible by wealth and power and control is premised on a lie—namely, that independence is actually possible. It is not! We are part of a universe that is governed, from the atomic to the cosmic, by relationship. It is interdependence that is at the foundation of existence. It is impossible to separate ourselves from the whole. When we try, the result is not independence, but alienation.

Genuine awakening becomes possible as we summon the courage to question the assumptions that have been handed down to us by our culture, rejecting the ones that feel limiting, deadening, soul-crushing. This means saying "no" to *headism*, "no" to control-based consciousness, and "no" to the frenetic machinations of the fearful mind, while saying "yes" to receiving the world just as it is, minute by minute. This surrendering becomes possible as we attune ourselves to—and harmonize with—the subtle intelligences that imbue and unify the world.[7]

In this vein, Albert Einstein sagely advised, "The most important question you can ever ask is if the world is a friendly place."[8] Certainly, to declare that the world is a friendly place is an act of faith—an act of submission, and it can also be a source of solace, reminding us that we don't need to spend our lives attempting to control and fix everything. Instead, when faced with a misfortune, we can simply respond with, "All is as it should be," trusting that through the alchemy of surrender, our every misfortune provides us with opportunities for awakening.

To make this last point more concrete, imagine the misfortune of being in a fight with a close friend. There is an issue that the two of you can't agree on, and the more you both talk about it, the more frustrated you each become. I was caught in precisely this unfortunate place not long ago with my life partner. Minute by minute, we were becoming more exasperated with each other. My thoughts went something like this, "Why is she being so stubborn? What is wrong with her? This is driving me crazy."

Though I didn't realize it at the time, I was hopelessly trapped in my head, judging, complaining, feeling like a victim…. When I was unable to bear the tension any longer, I went outside for some fresh air. Eventually, after a half hour of walking, I managed to calm down enough to remember to ride that "elevator" from my upset head—that had become a kind of courtroom—down to my core. As I gained access to the harmonizing intelligence of my body, things were no longer personal. Instead, I simply saw our "fight" as energy expressing itself—life unfolding, no right, no wrong.[9]

Wrap-Up

> The downside of living in your head, of course, is that taking up residence between your ears can make you crazy.... We become solitary souls, even if we do not live alone. Our skulls can become echo chambers, our notions of our lives and the world self-reinforcing. That can get scary.
> —Richard Cohen[10]

Our society tells us that the more head-centric knowledge we accumulate, the more progress we make and the more successful we become. But consider that although we humans have used our heads to accumulate massive amounts of information and knowledge over many thousands of years, we have not necessarily become wiser or kinder, nor have we become more sensitive or honest or peaceful or compassionate. Instead, many of our head-centric decisions and actions have rendered our society, and our planetary home, less healthy and less whole.

Awakening happens as we harness our full-body intelligence, learning to live in harmony with ourselves and the world. There is a parallel here with Ishtar, who, upon arriving at the fourth gate, was commanded to strip away the ornaments that covered her breast. For all of us, this points to the importance of stripping away barriers that separate us from our unique and fecund body intelligence.

Opening to Love

The 20th century poet William Butler Yeats said, "There are no strangers here; only friends you haven't yet met."[1] This may have been true for Yeats, but what about for you? If you're not sure, the next time you walk into a space filled with strangers (e.g., a crowded market, a busy restaurant, a large auditorium), take in all the people around you and ask yourself: "Am I seeing THEM or am I seeing US?" If it's "them" that you see, you are surrounded—not by fellow humans, but by strangers, and insofar as this is true, your capacity for love is crimped.

But take heart, for to be human is to have the seed of unconditional love and compassion at your core. For example, if by chance, you were to encounter a four-year-old child perilously perched on a wall above a swiftly flowing river, chances are your impulse would be to quickly swoop that child to safety. You wouldn't check to see if the child was a relative of yours. No, without thought, your heart would instinctively open to this stranger, and you would save the child. In other words, you would respond to the child's plight with a combination of compassion and unconditional love, and in so doing, you would be seeing the child as *us*, not *them*.

Religion studies scholar Karen Armstrong reminds us that love and compassion are at the very heart of the world's major religions and moral codes. For example:

- Confucius (500 BCE), the founder of Confucianism, taught that to become a mature human being, it was necessary to be oriented toward others' perspectives and needs, not one's own narrow self-interests.

129

- Gautama Buddha (470–390 BCE) taught his followers to love all beings equally.
- Rabbinic Judaism (grounded in the Torah) and Christianity (anchored in the Bible) teach the importance of loving one's neighbor as oneself.
- The Qur'an, divinely transmitted to the prophet Muhammad in the 6th century CE, stresses the importance of sharing one's wealth with those less fortunate.[2]

This emphasis on extending kindness, love, and compassion toward others is also found within many indigenous cultures. For example, the Mayan people of Central America greet each other with the words, "In Lak'ech Ala K'in," which translate to "I am another of yourself." This echoes the Hindu "Namaste" greeting, which translates to "I bow to the divine (to the light) in you." It also parallels the sentiment in the words, "Mitakuye Oyasin," of the North American Sioux Nation, which translate to "We are all related" where "we" refers, not just to other humans, but to the entirety of creation.

All of these calls for connection and love are concordant with recent discoveries from science, validating that there is no such thing as separation. We live in a Universe where "everything relies on everything else in the cosmos in order to manifest—whether a star, a cloud, a flower, a tree, or you and me."[3] Again, this means that there is no such thing as independence. Instead as Buddhist monk, Thich Nhat Hanh, points out: "Because of our deep interconnection … we *inter-are* with each other and with all of life."[4]

> **This is another place to consider pausing to reflect on how what you are reading here relates to your life…**

Love as Both a Choice and a Practice: Bring your awareness to your breath. Soften and open with each in-breath and release any tension you might be holding with each out-breath. When you feel grounded, direct your attention to your heart region and ask: In this moment is my heart mostly closed and constricted or more open and spacious … or is it somewhere in between?

By paying attention in this way, you may discover that over the course of a day your heart vacillates between open and closed and everything in between. This matters because when our heart closes—e.g., because of anxiety, fear, judgment, anger, or any number of other things—our life force is diminished, compromising our ability to both express love and receive it. By contrast, when our heart is wide open—vibrating with acceptance, gratitude, and compassion—we are fully alive. And the people around us can't help but be touched by our awakened presence.

The good news is that love is a way of being that we can actively cultivate by choosing to open as love. David Deida describes it this way:

> As openness you open as every being. Walking down the street, you pass an old man in a wheelchair. Can you feel his shape? Can you breathe his raspy squeak of a breath? Can you feel death nearby, youth behind, and stretched-out days of gurgle, pain, and disintegration? Feeling his entire pattern of being, can you open as this old man? Can you open as love, feeling every nuance of his decrepit form as the basis of your opening.... Living each moment open, you bless the world. Your openness begets openness.[5]

We can practice love by cultivating compassion for ourselves and for those around us. For example, when someone says or does something that upsets you and triggers your heart to close, you can replace your upset with compassion. It's not easy. Our patterned response is to shut down in the face of unkind treatment, but we can begin to undo this conditioning by considering that the other person's behavior is born of her past pain, just as our own "shutting-down" is triggered by our own wounds.

Healing is a choice and so is love. In this context, my friend Richard Chadek asks: "What if being 'in-love' is merely the threshold of being love? What if it's this precision—I see you, and I'm not asking you to be something else—that is actually love? … What if being love is … better understood as a spiritual practice? The slow diminishment of me, me, me and its replacement with Thou, Thou, Thou? What demands, what requirements, of ours have to die for that to take place?"[6]

Love Without Conditions: Love, in its highest expression, is not something that we are duty-bound to give to another, nor is it something that we need someone else to give to us! For example, if you are in a romantic relationship, you might imagine that you *need* your beloved to express his/her love to you. But imagine saying, as you hold this beloved in your mind's eye: "I don't <u>need</u> your love to be OK. I can be OK without your love." Could you do this and really mean it?

This may seem like an odd scenario, but a big step on the path to awakening is freeing ourselves from mindsets that keep us from loving unconditionally. So, when I declare that I don't *need* my partner's love to be happy, this doesn't mean that I withdraw from her. In fact, when I realize that I don't *need* her love, I discover, paradoxically, that I am able to love her, free of my own stipulations and needs, because my openness to love is no longer predicated on receiving her love in return. Stated differently: If I really cherish my beloved, my heart is open to her. I enact this openness by giving her space to grow so that she might nurture the seed of life and love that is uniquely hers. This includes supporting and celebrating her, even if this means that, one day, her life journey might lead her away from me.

Wrap Up

> Love is your true identity; it is who you really are and what you exist for. Love connects you with all other human beings and with all of creation…. We are created by love, to live in love, for the sake of love. Love is expressing itself not only through us but as us.
>
> —Gerald May[7]

Love is the experience of unity, of oneness with the world. It is the great connector, and when we open to it, we are opening to and surrendering to whatever life brings. To grasp this concept is relatively easy, but to live it is the challenge of a lifetime. There is no definitive map to take us there. And there is, arguably, no more important practice than noticing when our hearts are closed and then choosing to open them. If you commit to doing this again and again and again—surrendering and opening, gate by gate, as Ishtar did—you will be on the journey toward your truest identity.

Living Life Now

How we spend our days is, of course, how we spend our lives.
—Annie Dillard[1]

On an early morning in January 2007, amidst the morning rush-hour crowds in a Washington, D.C., subway station, a young violinist began to play. Who was he? The world-renowned violin virtuoso, Joshua Bell.

As commuters streamed past, Bell, on his $3.5 million Stradivarius violin, filled the metro station with "masterpieces that have endured for centuries on their brilliance alone, soaring music befitting the grandeur of cathedrals and concert halls."[2] And was this famous performer mobbed by crowds, as was feared when this social experiment was first proposed by *Washington Post* journalist Gene Weingarten? Hardly. In fact, as Weingarten later related in his Pulitzer Prize winning article:

> 63 people passed by before anyone even paused to listen. After 45 minutes, 1,070 people had paid no attention at all to the glorious music, and just seven had actually stopped to listen. Accustomed to earning up to a thousand dollars per minute, Bell made a total of 32 dollars and said he felt "oddly grateful" when someone threw in a bill instead of change.[3]

Can you believe it? This incredibly talented performer, playing some of the most gorgeous violin music ever written, earned a scant seven admirers!

But, honestly, consider: Had you been in that crowded D.C. metro station on that January morning, would you have spared an unknown violin player more than a passing glance? The question is a big one in that it gets to the heart of Annie Dillard's declaration: "How we spend our days is how we spend our lives." To the extent that we mechanically enact our daily routines, we will sleepwalk right past daily opportunities for awakening.

A Question of Time: Surely you are familiar with expressions like: making time, finding time, spending time, wasting time, and sparing time. But what is time, really? Is it simply seconds, minutes, watches, clock faces, digital beeps?

If humans didn't exist, questions like "What time is it?" and "What's the date today?" would be quite meaningless. Oak or Eagle would be surprised by such questions. "What time?" they would say, "Well, of course, it's now. What else is there?"[4]

When I really think about it, I realize that all there is to experience is now. The past is over. Sure, I have memories of it, but the past truly is passed. Similarly, the future will never exist until it arrives, at which point it will be now—the present.

This understanding is beautifully transmitted in a story about a Buddhist monk who was being pursued by a ravenous tiger. The monk was able to momentarily escape to safety by climbing down a steep cliff and then easing himself out onto a thick tree branch. But as the monk looked below to plan the rest of his escape, he saw a second tiger poised on a ledge, immediately below him, and in that moment he understood, like never before, that all he had was NOW—i.e., his past was over and his future, not yet arrived. It was only then that he noticed a wild strawberry plant, bearing a solitary berry, just within reach. After beholding the exquisite beauty of the strawberry, he reached out and carefully plucked it. Then, after gently feeling its subtle contours—top, bottom, and sides—he savored its aroma. Finally, he slowly bit into the strawberry, ecstatically aware of the sounds and the subtle release of flavors, enjoying every dimension of the strawberry for the miracle that it was.

In recounting this story, Stephan Rechtschaffen writes: "If we are aware of the now, if we experience it, we are in the flow of time. The rush of the past and the pressure of the future—those twin tigers—are cast aside. There is only the present.... No matter what has just happened or will come in the future, why miss the full experience of the present? Even if you're about to slip into the void, why miss the strawberries?"[5]

The Cult of Busyness: Between 1973 and 2000, U.S. citizens added approximately 200 hours to their annual work schedule, and this trend of more work and less play continues today.[6] This may partially explain why dual-income couples only carve out about 15 minutes a day to talk with each other and why, for many people, weekends have become as hectic as weekdays. This go-go-go beat is hammered out in the form of societal messages to do more, produce more, possess more, be more. There is, it seems, always more to be done and never enough time to do it. So it is that instead of participating in open-ended, leisurely conversations, we increasingly engage in skim talk via texting and tweeting. Rather than enjoying home-cooked dinners with family and friends, we often skim eat—gobbling down processed foods while glued to our screens. This skim even extends to sex, as evidenced in the book *Five Minutes to Orgasm Every Time You Make Love*, as well as to parenting, as reflected in the Disney book series *5-Minute Snuggle Stories*.[7]

Destination Addiction: Amidst the myriad addictions that now plague us, there is a common one that is often overlooked. It's called "destination addiction." If you find yourself living your days to get to the end of them, or if a good day for you is one where you get everything checked off your to-do list, you know about destination addiction! I think of it as the belief that the purpose of our days and lives is to get somewhere other than where we are right NOW. For example, imagine that you are walking down the street, on your way to your favorite restaurant. If you are in "destination" mode, your thoughts and concerns will be focused on the restaurant—e.g., Will I arrive on time? Will the restaurant be crowded? Did I remember my credit card? and so forth. But now, imagine that you are able to let go of all of that. You are still heading to the restaurant, but this time you are living in the now, present to your surroundings—e.g., noticing the pink hue of the evening sky, appreciating the song of a street musician, delighting in the kinesthetic sensations of walking. And when you arrive at the restaurant, you are right there, opening the door, experiencing the feel of the door handle, registering the sensations of muscles tightening in your arm … your doing and your being as one.

If you are still struggling to grasp the far-reaching effects of destination addiction, consider this counsel from spiritual teacher Thich Nhat Hanh: "If I am incapable of washing dishes joyfully, if I want to finish them quickly so I can go and have dessert, I will be equally incapable of enjoying my dessert. With the fork in my hand I will be thinking about what to do next, and the texture and flavor of the dessert, together with the pleasure of eating it, will be lost. I will always be dragged into the future, never able to live in the present moment."[8]

The Challenge of Slowing Down: Could it be that the reason that we (both as individuals and as a society) have such a difficult time slowing down is because if we were to do so, we might be overwhelmed with anxiety? You can gauge the extent that this might be true for you by engaging in a simple experiment. All that's required is that you find a quiet place inside and settle down in a comfortable chair for a half hour. Arrange it so that there are no distractions—no phone, no TV or screen of any kind, no books or magazines, no food—just you in a comfortable chair, alone with your thoughts, feelings, and body sensations.

Be forewarned that attempting this experiment may be more challenging than you expect. For example, absent your normal routines, you might start thinking about all the things that you should be doing. This, in turn, may cause you to feel anxious and perhaps even guilty because, like the rest of us, you have been conditioned to believe that to succeed in life you should spend your time hustling and competing, not sitting around doing nothing.

But imagine that there is someone else, sitting on another comfortable chair on the other side of the room from you. Rather than being mired in impatience and agitation, this person is radiating calmness, contentment, and well-being. She's not fidgeting or checking her phone; instead, she's simply dwelling in the present moment, relishing every second.

Such an open, tranquil way of being becomes possible when we choose to live within a new story of what it means to be a human being. This new story reminds us that we are, first and foremost, Human Beings, not Human Doings. In other words, we are here to connect with life, and in so doing, to experience and manifest wonder, curiosity, creativity, love and much more.

Time-shifting: When we treat time as a commodity, we fall into the trap of thinking that by speeding up, we will eventually earn the right to slow down. But rather than viewing time as a scarce resource, we could choose to believe that time is abundant. Instead of thinking of it as tick, tick, ticking away, we could accept that time is, truly, a present-moment phenomenon. Each moment blooms fresh; there is no passage, only now and now and now.

Consider, too, that when we are fully present, it is impossible to experience time scarcity. What am I talking about? You can find out by trying another simple experiment: The next time you find yourself rushing to do something or to get somewhere, take a deep breath, leave your head—

i.e., your thoughts and concerns—behind, and drop your awareness down into the core of your being, so that you might experience the world passing through you.[9] You will know that you have been successful when the world around you abruptly shifts from background to foreground, as if the lights were suddenly turned on—and BAM!—you are no longer apart from the world, but a part of it. Here is how my friend Johanna Jackson described one of her "BAM" moments:

> The other day I had time at my house, and I was deciding how to spend it. I was puttering at one thing and then another—fixing lunch, checking emails, washing dishes—when I realized that my time had already begun to slip away. What was I doing? Everything! And for that I was doing nothing. I sat down in a chair. I stopped my hands from moving. I closed my eyes. And in that pause, some questions arose: "What is essential for now? How do I want to use this moment?" In this simple act of pausing, I discovered that time was abundant, not scarce. I didn't need to be doing this and doing that. Being present to the beam of light coming through the kitchen window, the beating of my heart, the rise and fall of my breath—was not a waste of my time. No, I was living in time, in awareness, and, oh my, the gratitude and wonder and awe that arose from this simple blessed awareness.

Johanna's story suggests that by slowing down we don't fall behind; instead, we fall ahead, insofar as our lives become more spacious.

A Healthier Relationship with Time: There is hope. Recall that it wasn't so very long ago that many Americans set aside one day each week—the Sabbath—as a "day of rest." Today, as Rabbi Michael Lerner points out, "You don't have to think of yourself as religious or a believer in God to get the benefits of the Bible's most brilliant spiritual practice"—Shabbat or the Sabbath.[10] This practice calls us to take one day each week to celebrate the wonder of being. This means removing ourselves completely from worldly concerns. To this end, Lerner offers this list of things to avoid:

- Don't use or even touch money.
- Don't work or even think about work.
- Don't cook or clean or sew or iron or do housework.
- Don't write or use the computer, e-mail, telephone, or other electronic devices.
- Don't fix things up or tear things down. Leave the world the way it is.
- Don't organize things, straighten things up, or take care of errands. Put your "to do list" away for the day.

And what should you do? Lerner responds: "Focus on pleasure. Good food ... singing, dancing, walking, playing, joking or laughing, looking at the magnificence of creation, studying spiritual texts, communing with one's inner voice, or whatever else really generates pleasure."[11] In short: Dedicate this one day each week to joy, celebration, and expressions of gratitude.

To take this idea of celebration and joy and gratitude further, Linda Goodhew and David Loy propose substituting our present understanding of life as work—in terms of the commodification of time that this connotes—with the radical notion of life as play. The rationale is that when we play for play's sake, we are completely present and without the need for gain or want of more. And "when we do not need to extract something more from this time and place, we will not devalue it by contrasting here-and-now with some other location or time. Then, there will be time to join in the children's games, to enjoy the flowers, and to do our jobs with loving care."[12]

Imagine, if you will, how it would be if this idea—life understood through the cultivation of presence and play—was to assume a central place in our culture. How different this would be from our future-oriented story of Economism that conditions us to believe that we must always be destination-oriented, always doing, always profiting!

Inhabiting this new story, we could begin to live a life where: Here is better, less is better, slower is better, *being* is better, letting go is better, now is better. In sum, we could live a story that invites us to consider that success isn't some future thing that we need to spend our lives running toward. Instead, success only exists right now, in the form of successful present moments.

Wrap-Up

> In order to be present, you have to appreciate that the present is an unknown—it has never been here before, and neither have you.
> —Phillip Shepherd[13]

Taking Shepherd's words to heart, what would happen if you chose to believe that each moment is filled with unknowable possibilities?

As you ponder this, recall that when the Gatekeeper, at the fifth gate to the Underworld, commanded Ishtar to surrender her belt, she courageously complied. The parallel for us is to dare to remove our own belts—the ones that bind us to habitual, speed-based, ways of living—so that we might awaken to the potential gifts enfolded within each present moment.

Befriending Our Shadow

If we flee from the evil in ourselves, we do it at our hazard. All evil is potential vitality in need of transformation. To live without the creative potential of our own destructiveness is to be a cardboard angel.

—S.B. Kopp[1]

In seeking to awaken, there comes a time when we must learn to accept, and even to love, aspects of ourselves that our culture teaches us to regard as undesirable or even shameful. I am referring to our human capacity to be greedy, hateful, petty, cowardly, deceitful, boisterous, rude, moody, and mean, along with a hundred other things. Psychologists use the word "shadow" to refer to these seemingly unsavory human qualities.[2]

The American poet Robert Bly likened the shadow to a big black bag that we spend the first several decades of our lives stuffing with things about ourselves that we have been conditioned to see as unacceptable. Then, we drag our bag around behind us for the rest of our days, afraid to reveal its contents.[3] Each of us has our own unique black bag, stuffed with all our self-alienating beliefs and fears that are the product of our self-judgments. But the fact that this darkness is stuffed inside of a bag does not make it disappear. And that's a good thing because embracing our shadow is fundamental to our awakening.

As a starting point for exploring your shadow, take up your journal and complete the following sentence three times:

I am not _____ enough.

I am not _____ enough.

I am not _____ enough.

Then, reflect on the possible sources for your three not enough beliefs.

Origins of the Human Shadow: Psychologist John Wellwood explains the origins of the human shadow by likening a human being to a beautiful castle. At birth, the castle, that was you, had thousands of rooms. As a very young child, you began to explore those rooms, each one representing a feeling, sensation, thought, or way of being. At that tender stage, the concepts of good and bad did not yet exist for you. This being so, you experienced each room of your castle as acceptable. In other words, you experienced yourself as "enough" in every respect, and, therefore, you were able to dwell comfortably within every room of your castle.

But then one day, when you were still at the toddler stage, someone—say, your mother or father—transmitted with a mere facial expression that one of your castle rooms (i.e., one of your modes of being) was unacceptable; and, so, you locked the door to that room. With time, others also passed judgments on certain rooms. For example, some found rooms in your castle that were too noisy or too confrontational. Others complained of rooms that were too shy or too serious; still others complained that certain rooms in your castle were weird because they were not seen in other castles, and so on.

Wanting to belong and to be loved, you naturally began to close off all of those unacceptable castle rooms, until, eventually, the expression of your life was confined to just a small part of your castle.[4] In other words, you pruned away all those parts of yourself that were not socially sanctioned or deemed acceptable by others.[5]

Today, your acceptable castle rooms—the ones you endeavor to occupy—probably have titles like loving, honest, patient, diligent, kind, smart, obedient, and so on. Each of these rooms represents personality traits and behaviors that you have been conditioned to see as praiseworthy, right, and good.

Meanwhile, your so-called *shadow* attributes reside in all those rooms that you locked up long ago. In fact, for every one of your rooms that contains a quality that you deem as good, there is a corresponding room—probably locked—that contains its opposite. This means that there are probably rooms in your castle that represent your capacity for hatred, deception, selfishness, timidity, anger, ignorance, and so forth.[6]

You may be wondering why anyone would ever want to acknowledge the presence of such negative qualities within themselves? One reason is that in accepting our seemingly unsavory aspects, we become more fully and authentically ourselves. For instance, when I recognize and fully accept that I make a lot of mistakes that others might judge as stupid, I, in effect, give myself the freedom to be stupid. This means I can jump into the turbulent waters of life, trying out new things, making outrageous mistakes, failing, and then failing again. If, on the other hand, I block myself off from the possibility of doing things that others might judge as "stupid" (i.e., by keeping my "stupid" castle room locked), my life may become safer, but it will also be rendered more uptight, more fearful, and more boring.

And there is a second reason for fully accepting the shadow sides of ourselves—namely: What we refuse to see and accept in ourselves, we will, inevitably, project onto others, often in the form of harsh judgments and intolerance. For example, imagine opening the newspaper to a story about someone who has committed an act of vandalism by setting fire to a public school. "How ignorant and thoughtless!" you think to yourself. You might even believe that this person should be locked away for a time. But then you pause and ask yourself: "What kind of person would do such a thing?"

As I reflect on this, I realize that it would probably be someone who is insecure, angry, confused, and lonely among other things. And though I have never committed an act of outright vandalism, I can easily call to mind times in my life when my behavior has been the result of feeling insecure, angry, confused, and lonely....

If you are thinking that by owning up to our shadow energies, we might run the risk of becoming thieves, rapists, tyrants, bigots, or worse, it doesn't work that way. In fact, it is precisely when we suppress our shadow qualities that these dark energies build, sometimes bursting forth in violent, even horrendous, acts. Indeed, "the greater the repression, the louder our shadow has to yell to be heard—like a pressure cooker that you are holding the lid down on—and the greater its chance to become demonic."[7]

In sum, our shadow elements are like neglected children. The more we ignore them, the more they/we act out. But by embracing these neglected parts of ourselves—these locked castle rooms—we reclaim their instinctual energies, and, in so doing, we awaken to the potential gifts— YES, GIFTS—contained in our shadow energies.

Shining Light on Your Shadow: Full awakening is only possible to the extent that we are able to recognize and befriend our shadow. A good way to begin is to simply pay attention to the things other people do that tend to "push your buttons." Psychologist and author Debbie Ford suggests imagining that you have hundreds of different electrical outlets affixed to your chest, with each outlet representing a distinct personality trait—e.g., one outlet for boisterousness, another outlet for sullenness, another for kindness, another for aggressiveness, and on and on. There are covers over the outlets that correspond to aspects of yourself that you fully recognize and accept. So, when someone you know manifests one of these "acceptable" qualities, there is no charge—i.e., you don't react. By contrast, behaviors in other people that carry a charge for you—that "push your buttons"—denote aspects of yourself that you have not fully acknowledged, much less accepted.[8]

For example, it used to be that when I encountered someone who forthrightly expressed their feelings and emotions, my buttons were pushed. I knew this was happening because I became uncomfortable and sought to escape. Sitting with this realization, I came to recognize that my reactivity was the result of having been discouraged from sharing my feelings and emotions, when I was growing up. Because of this, I had, without knowing it, locked up the "vulnerability" room in my "castle." As a result, when I was placed in situations that called me to be vulnerable, I tended to tense up and go silent.

In recent years, I have been gradually opening the door to my vulnerability room by becoming more open and transparent with others, especially when it comes to sharing my feelings and emotions. What might become possible for you if you were to cultivate, rather than shun, one of your shadow qualities?

The Golden Shadow: Just as our shadow is constituted of aspects of ourselves that we may struggle to appreciate and manifest, our shadow also harbors potential gifts that we may be slow to recognize and acknowledge. I am referring here to what Swiss psychiatrist and psychoanalyst Carl Jung called the "Golden Shadow." Have a peek at your own Golden Shadow by bringing to mind someone who you admire. It could be a person you know personally or a someone you have read about and come to hold in high esteem. Once you have picked someone, turn to your journal and write down three qualities that you most admire in this person:

Quality 1: _____.

Quality 2: _____.

Quality 3: _____.

Then, entertain the possibility that these same praiseworthy qualities also lie dormant within you.[9] How could this be? Well, say the admirable qualities that you list include curiosity, open-mindedness, and bravery. Now, consider that as a child you may have been criticized when you displayed these very same attributes. For example, the adults in your world may have censored you, in subtle or not so subtle ways, for being too curious (e.g., asking too many questions) or too open-minded (e.g., being attracted to weird ideas) or too brave (e.g., taking unnecessary risks); and, as a result of this, you have come to believe that you are lacking in these qualities and potentials. But they lie dormant within you. All that's required is that you give yourself permission to express them. Once you understand this and choose to believe it to be so, you can begin to unlock the potentials lying dormant within your Golden Shadow.

A Collective Wound: It's time to return to those three "not enough" statements that you wrote down earlier. Consider that each one is rooted in a reluctance to give yourself permission to be yourself! Yes, the antidote to the scourge of "not enoughness" is awakening to the simple truth that we don't have to PROVE ourselves. We just have to BE ourselves; and we do this by opening to, and accepting, the totality of who we are, moment by moment. This can be excruciatingly difficult, as revealed in this personal testimony from one of my students, Antonia Bartolomeo:

> Fat. Ugly. Unwanted. This was my truth as a fifth grader, struggling with puberty and the strenuous, competitive culture of middle school. I even recall one day noting in my diary how surprised I was when a popular boy gave me attention. Why me? I was unpopular, fat, and ugly. Why not one of the "pretty girls"? But as puberty reached its end, I slowly learned to accept my appearance. There were even moments when I was able to say to myself: I am beautiful.
>
> But this acceptance changed abruptly when, at age twenty, I fell off a horse and split my head open. After ten stitches, I was left with a swollen face and a broken heart. Worse still, I was marked with a four-inch vertical scar right in the middle of my forehead. "How will anyone ever love me like this?" I cried. The confidence and self-love I had worked to achieve was suddenly stripped from me, gone! I lay in bed for two days crippled with depression, with a hideous scar right in the middle of my face.
>
> I was once beautiful, but no more. Wallowing in my depression, I reached out to loved ones, and with their encouragement and kind words, I came to realize that I was actually lucky. If I had landed in a slightly different way when I fell, or if the horse's powerful hoofs had hit me straight on rather than only graze my forehead, I may have lost my life.

Nevertheless, the question, "How will anyone love me like this?" festered in my mind. And then … and then … I got it: Anyone—indeed everyone—will love me provided I have the courage to love myself, forehead scar and all!

So, today, rather than a story of my victimhood and heartbreak, my story is one of extreme gratitude for the life that is still mine to live. And I have gratitude, as well, for my sweet scar that reminds me to love myself unconditionally.

I am a warrior. I am a lover. I was beautiful. I am beautiful. I will always be beautiful.[10]

If you are still thinking that you are deficient when it comes to your looks or your social skills or your intelligence or your creativity or your emotional expression or who knows what else, you can choose, as Antonia did, to end the war with yourself by remembering that you are a uniquely configured human being. Using the person next to you as your standard for enoughness is a recipe for insanity, just as it would be crazy for someone else to use you as their benchmark.

Bottom line: To believe that you are *not* enough is to argue with reality. You are who you are, just as you are; you are your own standard. Given what we each have available to us, we are all doing the best that we can. And as we each open to life, in all its many facets, we fulfill our destiny of enoughness, in our own unique way.

Wrap-Up

You don't have to prove yourself. You just need to be yourself.

We each have a shadow self. This shadow is, to a significant degree, the result of being conditioned to believe that there are parts of ourselves that are unacceptable and that, in order to be acceptable, we must hide these parts. But this is a mistake.

Recall that as Ishtar travelled deeper and deeper into the Underworld, she reached a point, at the seventh gate, where she surrendered her very waistcloth and was left naked![11] It was only then, absent the hubris of all her earthly trappings, that she fully awakened. Both for Ishtar and for each of us, our willingness to accept ourselves just as we are—without hubris, adornments, or masks—is essential if we are to grow into the totality of who we are meant to be, precious shadow and all.

Coda

A Curriculum for Waking Up

> Some of us think holding on makes us strong; but sometimes it is letting go.
>
> —Hermann Hesse[1]

Part III opened with the myth of Queen Ishtar. In this story, Ishtar descended to the Underworld, passing through seven gates. At each gate she was ordered to let go one of her earthly attachments. Just as with Ishtar, we, too, are called to let go of life-denying beliefs and dispositions so that we might awaken to our life's deeper meaning and purpose. Among the many realms where this "letting go" is called for, we chose to focus on seven:

- Gate 1—Letting go of *either/or* thinking so that we might create space for more expansive *both/and* consciousness.
- Gate 2—Letting go of rigid cultural dictates that stunt our imagination and playfulness.
- Gate 3—Letting go of the inhibitions that shackle us so that we might discover and fully express the generative wildness that lies at the core of our being.
- Gate 4—Letting go of *headism* so that we might actively cultivate our body's sensitivity-based intelligences.
- Gate 5—Letting go of our fear of intimacy so that we might courageously open to one another as love.
- Gate 6—Letting go of incessant doing so that we might learn to dwell peacefully in the fecund present moment.
- Gate 7—Letting go of self-alienation so that we might come to accept ourselves just as we are, precious shadow and all.

So, Fellow Traveler, now that you have, metaphorically, passed through the Seven Gates of the Underworld, you, too, have the opportunity to name and let go of what might be keeping you small, silent and fearful. Will you surrender in this way in order to manifest the full beingness that is you?

It's a choice, and it begins as we each learn to love ourselves enough to let go of what no longer serves life. Of course, it won't happen all at once. It's a process, a journey; we slip, we fall, we get back up; and in the process, our hearts crack open and our consciousness expands.

PART IV

Awakening in Action

Introduction

Welcome to Part IV. The six stepping stones in this section will invite you to explore awakening in the context of your daily life. In so doing, we will present you with new possibilities for living life more fully and fearlessly. Begin by taking inspiration from Jamie Reaser's poem, "No Fear."

No Fear[1]

I don't want to live in fear

To give credence to the voices
of other people
that have been circling me

with warnings of
loneliness,
suffering,
poverty,
and annihilation

since the moment
of my conception.

In so many combinations
of words and accents they all say:

"Stay small."

"Don't take risks."

"Never let yourSelf be seen."

Like cages,
Like ropes,

Their beliefs about the world
entrap and suffocate.

"Life is dangerous,"
say the so-called living.

No more.

No more!

I want to roam and breathe.

I want to dance naked in
a public square
until everyone there
has counted all
of the moles on
my body,
twice.—

I want to warble my
True Name
from a branch of
the oldest tree on Earth,

and then I want to ask it
what it has to say
about standing up
straight and tall,

about unabashedly offering its
services to the multiple generations
of frightened humans
who have sat in the
shade it has gifted.

Homo sapiens:

The most self-terrified species.

Ah,

What is this the bold wind
offers?

It is the sound of leaves
rustling in a far off
land.

And in the way that the words
of the wise always out-travel
and out-live their speaker,

I hear the Elder tree say,

"Just keep reaching
for the Light."

—Jamie Reaser (with permission)

In this poem, Reaser reminds us of the fear-filled voices that seek to entrap and suffocate us with their messages that life is dangerous … and that to survive we must stay small and never let Ourselves be seen. At the same time, Reaser highlights the freedom, beauty and awakening that become possible when we muster the courage to fiercely embrace our lives.

Each Day as a Call to Presence

I think that what we're seeking [in life] is an experience of
being alive ... the rapture of being alive.
                                        —Joseph Campbell[1]

Awakening requires that we bring presence to the things that make
up our lives; it means having the "experience of being alive ... the rapture
of being alive."

How do your experience your aliveness? How awake are you to the
sensations, rhythms, and movements that comprise your everyday life?
Our potential for experiencing the "rapture of being alive" depends, it
seems, on our capacity to transform ordinary life moments into opportunities for awakened presence.

These possibilities begin the moment we wake up each day. What's
that moment like for you? Do you wake naturally of your own accord,
or does an alarm jolt you into action? How do you feel as you open your
eyes? What about your first thoughts upon waking?

Asking myself these questions led me to create a morning wake-up
ritual. I begin by placing my attention on my breath: Receiving the breath
of life and returning it ... in and out, back and forth, my lungs like an
accordion, being played by the biosphere. After a time, I begin to move
my fingers and toes, marveling at the miracle of human hands and human
feet. Then, I bring my attention to my heart, assured by, and grateful for,
its steady beat. My sense of gratitude expands as I acknowledge my arms
and legs, eyes and ears, muscles and organs and bones.

Morning Bathroom Practice: It is common practice to launch our
days in the bathroom with mirror-gazing, showering, toileting, and grooming. If you are like most people, you probably perform these activities on

153

autopilot, missing opportunities to awaken to the miracle that is your body, but this need not be! You could transform your time in the bathroom by experimenting with this four-step practice.

Step 1—Beholding Yourself in the Mirror: Upon entering the bathroom each morning, it's common practice to look in the mirror and then to frown at our bedraggled appearance; but what if we were to greet ourselves with an open, easy smile and then proceed to lovingly accept *all* our features, from head to toe—e.g., the pointy nose as well as the bright eyes, the soft hair as well as the stubborn cowlick, the mole on the chin as well as the endearing dimple, the fleshy thighs as well as the graceful fingers. All good, all wonderful, all us.

Granted, this is easier said than done because for many of us, accepting our bodies—just as they are—can be challenging. If you feel this way, you might begin by focusing on just one part of your body, maybe your feet! Then, express your gratitude by calling to mind the things that your feet do for you. For example, they support and balance you every day, carrying you where you need to go. That's surely a reason for acceptance and gratitude! Then, perhaps the next time you behold yourself in the mirror, consider focusing on another part of your body, again, extending acceptance and gratitude.[2] In so doing, you will be rewriting your body story, taking tender steps toward greater self-acceptance and, ultimately, self-love.

Step 2—Washing: Turning from the mirror you slowly open the shower faucet, and viola—water! The miracle of it! Like a child standing awestruck by a waterfall, you take in the symphony of sounds, as water rushes, streams, splashes, patters, and puddles. Stepping into the shower, you are attentive to the rush of sensations, marveling at how the water bathing your outside skin is the same stuff that comprises your organs and tissues and that leaks from your eyes when you cry. Opening further, you consider how the water, escaping down the drain, will eventually find its way to the ocean and then to clouds and rain and, one day, back to you—as shower water!

Step 3—Toileting: Out of the shower, now, and on to the toilet. Every day, each of us deposits roughly a pound of solid and liquid materials into bathroom toilets. These are the organic leftovers after our bodies have digested our food.

As you settle in on the commode, consider how odd it is that we, modern humans, are often delighted, in one moment, by the colors, textures, and tastes of the food that we place in our mouths, but repulsed, hours later, by our poop, when it lands in the toilet. We could choose, however, to be grateful for, and impressed by, the extraordinary work our bodies do in service to our life. For example, our body converts our food into energy, giving us the power to breathe, think, talk, smile, walk, play, love, and much more. So, what if we were to use our time on the commode as an opportunity to offer gratitude? How? By giving thanks to your magnificent kidneys for filtering, flushing, and balancing your body fluids, day and night; thanks to your faithful heart that animates and invigorates your body, minute by minute; thanks to your industrious digestive organs, working to transform Earth's nourishment into new skin, new hair, new blood, new bone, new you; and thanks to the tens of trillions of microbes living in your gut, helping to digest your food and maintain your vitality. Reframed in this way, time on the commode provides opportunities to practice both gratitude and humility.

Step 4—Sprucing up: Before leaving the bathroom, most of us devote some time to putting on our game face. Depending on your style, sprucing up could mean applying deodorants, gels, lotions, makeup, concealers, perfumes, colognes, and so forth. Yet, only a few generations back, the grooming items found in American bathrooms were limited to toothbrushes, razors, and soap. Today, by contrast, our bathrooms are often packed with all manner of appearance enhancers and body cleansers. Women apply, on average, a dozen different products to their bodies each day, while men average a half a dozen. Each of these products contains an average of twelve different chemical ingredients, many of which have not been adequately tested for safety.[3] No surprise then that so-called "body-care products" can, and sometimes do, jeopardize our health and well-being. This realization prompted one of my students, Kaitlyn Spangler, to question the wisdom of applying makeup to her skin each morning, as revealed in the following disclosure:

> I began applying makeup in eighth grade—as soon as my parents let me— and I welcomed this as a part of womanhood. Now, four years later, I have begun to see the ridiculousness of applying makeup every day, as it is used to create an alternate identity.... I mean, makeup is meant to make the face look "better," while at the same time masking it....
> So, I have decided to shun it from my routine. This has meant convinc-

ing myself not to go to my makeup bag if I feel like my face is particularly unimpressive on a given day. Instead, I stand in front of the mirror and look myself in the eyes to take in what is actually my face. I tell myself that this face holds heritage, history, genetics, and individuality. If I, along with others, cannot accept it at "face value," then I am failing to appreciate the woman I am.

Walking around every day, without makeup, has been an enlightening experience.... I can comfort myself in knowing that my current appearance is all me, with no help.

I force myself to maintain solid, confident eye contact with others so that they, too, can embrace an unenhanced face. Most of the time, they accept this....

It turns out my face does not need black lines and red accents ... that was all a socially imposed theory.[4]

By bringing presence to her makeup routine, Kaitlyn was able to question it and then let it go. As her mentor, it was remarkable for me to witness how Kaitlyn—after shunning her makeup bag—became more alive, more herself, more radiant.[5]

Stepping Outside: Just as it's easy to sleepwalk through a morning bathroom routine, the same is possible as we enact our days. For example, when I walk through the Penn State campus, I note that most of the people around me are plugged into their music and/or tethered to their phones, separated, to a considerable degree, from the real world surrounding them.

A while back, in an effort to nudge myself and those around me beyond our scripted daily routines, I decided to declare the first day of the Spring Semester, "What's Alive Day?" It began with me making a poster with the question: "What's Alive for you today?" and then strolling around campus. Each time someone approached me, I smiled and held up my sign.

The first person I encountered (a student) looked at my sign in bewilderment, so I explained: "Here we both are. It's a fresh day on planet Earth. What's alive for you today?" He stopped to consider and then remarked that he sensed a lot of energy on campus because it was the first day of a new semester. I thanked him, pleased that he had taken time to share this with me. Next came a professor, toting an armload of books. He took in my sign and asked, "Is this some sort of pedagogical inquiry or experiment?" I explained that I was simply curious to know what was alive for him. He smiled, looked up at the clear sky and told me he was enlivened by the brisk air and early morning light. We walked together in amicable conversation until he arrived at his destination. Then, I extended my hand and told him my name. Rather than shake, my new friend bowed and left me with his card. And so it went for an hour, me presenting my sign and others responding with a mix of amusement, humor, and warmth—all of us taking the time to eschew our routine for a genuine moment of aliveness!

Wrap Up

> The little moments? The little things? They aren't little.
> —John Kabat-Zinn[6]

On the surface, this stepping stone has been about the most ordinary of human acts: awakening, washing, excreting, grooming, and stepping outside and into the world. It would be easy to regard these things as simply background elements to your life. But, beginnings matter! Presence matters! For without presence and the gratitude it evokes, we might be stuck in slumber, never to truly experience the rapture of being alive!

Stuff

Living Within the Story of Enoughness

Abundance is not a number or acquisition. It is a simple recognition of enoughness.

—Alan Cohen[1]

You've probably heard of "inadequacy marketing." The psychology is simple: An advertiser attempts to convince the consumer—e.g., us!—that we are lacking—i.e., not enough—in some way, but if we buy what they are trying to sell, we will feel better. For example, perhaps our apparel is not sharp enough, but a new jacket would fix that; or we're not sexy enough, but buying a fancy sportscar would turn eyes. So, we purchase the product to discover that it only brings us temporary relief. Why? Because it fails to address what we are truly needing.

The Primacy of Money: In the society in which we find ourselves, we all need money to live, but how much is enough? Ask this question to a class of college students, as I sometimes do, and most say that they need to make somewhere between $80,000 and $150,000/year to be OK. Some weigh in higher, some lower, but few believe that they could be OK earning less than $40,000/year.

But, in the spirit of self-exploration, consider the possibility that reducing your income expectations could actually translate to more well-being, more happiness, and more opportunities for awakening.

As a way into this inquiry, imagine that you were actually able to lower your projected income needs by half (say from $80,000/year to $40,000/year). This would significantly reduce the hours you would have to work, freeing you for other pursuits. For example, if you had been working a full five-day week, now you might only need to be working a two-and-a-half to three day week. Can you imagine the freedom you would have, the discoveries you might make, the new relationships that you might cultivate, the things you might learn?

If you hesitate to seriously entertain this scenario, that's normal. After all, it brings up fear-generating questions, like: (i) If my income was reduced by half, how would I even survive? (ii) Wouldn't other people judge me as lazy if I were only working 2–3 days/week? (iii) What would I even do with myself if I wasn't working all the time? Rather than shying away from these questions, you could see them as opportunities for self-discovery—i.e., as steps toward awakening.

Solving for Enoughness: When it comes to figuring out how much income is enough, you could begin by assessing your essential needs. As a warm-up, consider your clothing needs. Unless you've been wearing the same couple of outfits for months, you probably own more clothing than you need. But how much more? Twenty-five percent more? Fifty percent? Two hundred percent? You could find out within an hour or two by conducting a thorough inventory of your wardrobe.

But before starting, let's be clear: This is not about creating guilt by beating up on ourselves; rather, it's about promoting freedom and exercising creativity. So, now, in the spirit of self-discovery, make four columns on a sheet of paper. Put "Clothing Categories" as the heading for the first column. In the second column write down the actual number of items you possess in each of your clothing categories (e.g., 6 sweaters, 8 pairs of shoes, 4 pairs of pajamas, etc.). In the third column consider, for each category, the minimum number that you would need just to get by. For example, in the case of sweaters, let's say that you own six sweaters, but determine that three sweaters would be enough—a lightweight one, a heavy one, and a dressy one.

Finally, in the fourth column, enter the *overrun* for each clothing category by subtracting your minimum number (Column 3) from the number you possess (Column 2). In the sweater example, if you possess 6 and only need 3, your *overrun* (Column 4) would be 3 sweaters.

After completing your four-column chart for all of your clothing categories, you could create a similar chart for your kitchen possessions using categories like plates, bowls, silverware, cooking utensils, pots, pans, mixers, cutlery, and so forth. As you conduct your inventory, take special note of any new kitchen items that you have purchased within the last two years and ask yourself: Did I really need to buy that new kitchen thing, or would I have been OK without it? Again, the overall idea is to take an inventory of all of your kitchen stuff, all your wardrobe stuff, all your bathroom stuff, all your closet stuff, all your bedroom stuff, and so on. In this way, you can determine the degree to which your possessions exceed what is necessary—what is enough!

A fair question before embarking on such a seemingly tedious and time-consuming endeavor might be: Why bother? Really, why would you want to pare down your belongings to only that which is essential? One possible answer is that having to buy and maintain less stuff would significantly reduce your living expenses. To see why, return to the sweater example, where the hypothetical results revealed that you owned twice as many sweaters as you deemed necessary. The financial implication of this is that you could reduce your future sweater expenditures by as much as half. If similar levels of saving held for other clothing and household categories, you wouldn't need to spend as much money on *stuff*, meaning that you wouldn't need to devote as many hours of your life energy working a job and shopping for non-essential materials.

In a related vein, it's worth noting that people who engage, whole-heartedly, in this inventory become motivated, of their own accord, to purge themselves of their non-essential stuff. For example, Melissa experiences a measure of catharsis when she gets rid of the things in her life that she no longer needs. She describes it this way:

> In deciding what to keep and what to pass on, I ask: Does this article of clothing or this book or this mug still hold energy for me in the form of fond memories, beautiful aesthetics or essential utility? If not, then that object can become a weight, a guilt-maker, a space-taker. In letting it go, I can be grateful for whatever pleasure it brought or practical need it filled, and then send it back out into the world so that it might bring fulfillment to someone else. In this way, I am left with only the things that move me and speak to who I am right now, leaving me the space to awaken to who I am becoming.

Upshot: Needing less stuff means needing less money, means having to spend less time working a job and therefore having more time to devote to the things that truly enrich your life![2]

Housing: How Much is Enough? Trimming back on personal possessions could lead to some savings, but, let's face it, the big-ticket item, when it comes to living expenses, is housing.

Today, the average size of a new house in the U.S. is 2,400 square feet, and the average sale price is in the $300,000 range.[3] This means that if you are a recent college graduate and hope to purchase a new house, you'd best be prepared to shell out at least $2,000/month in mortgage payments over a thirty-year period. But what if you don't actually need a house with 2,400 square feet, and what if—no matter how unskilled you might be— you could play a part in the design and construction of your dwelling? To make this more tangible, imagine that, on the occasion of your 21st birthday, you inherited $10,000 and decided to use this money to design and build your very own house.

Given your limited budget, you know that you won't be able to afford the materials to build the typical 2,000-plus square foot U.S. house. But that's OK; you don't need a ten-room house. Maybe just one or two rooms would be enough. Indeed, this is the core principle behind the Tiny House Movement where dwellings range in size, from 100 to 400 square feet.

In addition to being a whole lot cheaper to build, Tiny Houses are also cheaper to live in. For example, Jess Belhumeur and Dan Sullivan, a couple living in Rhode Island, built a 128-square-foot Tiny House for almost exactly $10,000. Instead of hiring a professional to design their home, they designed it themselves, using a free software program at Sketchup.com. Their building materials were either purchased second-hand via Craigslist or scavenged in abandoned lots. Now that their house is completed their only significant operating expense is the $120/month they pay for electricity.[4]

When asked about her motivation for building a Tiny House, Belhumeur said, "I had already owned a home before this, and I realized that I only used two rooms—the kitchen and the living room. I felt ridiculous. I was in a stressful financial situation, and I wasn't even making use of the house I had." She added: "I'm a very environmentally conscious person [and] I was driven to live in a way that reduces my impact on the planet."[5]

What I find inspiring about this decision to live modestly is that Belhumeur was honest about her needs and her environmental concerns, and she made bold choices to live in accord with them, in spite of what others might think.

Even whole families are choosing to dramatically downsize their homes. For example, Kim Kasl, along with her partner, two kids, and dog, moved out of a standard 2,000-square-foot home and into a tiny house, measuring just 267 square feet. Their house, positioned next to a lake, has two lofts and a catwalk. As a result of their "tiny lifestyle," the Kasls are now able to live on just one income, allowing time to homeschool their kids while engaging in all manner of adventures. Asked to contrast their new lifestyle to their previous one, Kasl wrote, "We're more content. More colorful. More outdoorsy. More rooted. More united. More adventurous. More resourceful. More ridiculous. More creative. More experienced. More trusting. More delighted. More fulfilled."[6] That's a lot of "mores"!

Thinking Outside the Box: There are lots of other options for creating a home on a minimalist budget. Consider how people created dwellings before the Industrial Age. What did the early Americans do? How about the Europeans in the Middle Ages or the ancient Chinese?

The Plains Indians created tepees, cone-shaped wooden structures covered with buffalo hides. The Sami people of Northern Scandinavia used something similar to the tepee, a squat structure called a lavvu, covered by reindeer hide.[7] While buffalo and reindeer hide might be hard to come by today, other covering options can be accessed through internet-based exchange forums like FreeCycle. Another possibility is to make a yurt, a round shelter that has been used on the Asian steppes for over 3,000 years. Or, how about something modeled on traditional Irish stone huts? After all, few things are more readily available than stones![8]

Yet another option is to create a cob house, similar to European earthen houses and the adobe shelters of the Pueblo Indians. Cob is essentially sand and mud, often with straw or grass mixed in. Brian Liloia, a member of the Dancing Rabbit eco-village in Arkansas, built his own cob house over a nine-month period. The end product was a charming 200-square-foot dwelling, costing less than $3,000 in materials and featuring a terracotta-tiled floor, earthen plasters, a living roof covered in wild grasses, and a foundation made of recycled concrete. Reflecting on his endeavor, Liloia wrote: "It was the most satisfying experience of my life. There's nothing quite like the experience of building your own home with little more than your hands."[9]

Finally, consider this: By building your own house, with your own hands, your building expenses could be easily paid off within a year or two. This means that you wouldn't be stuck paying a $2,000/month mortgage for thirty years, as is typically the case for most of us stuck in the housing narrative of our culture. There is another bonus that comes with tiny houses: Because of their limited space, there is a built-in limit to what will fit inside—e.g., there just might not be enough room for that fourth pair of shoes.

Wrap-Up

> The things you own end up owning you.
> —Tyler Durden[10]

By daring to explore enoughness, as we have invited you to do in this stepping stone, you may discover, like many others, that simplifying your life—i.e., minimizing your needs—might result in maximizing your aliveness, connectivity, creativity, and well-being.[11]

Food

From Passive Consumer to Awakened Participant

> Where did you get that orange juice? Where did it come
> from? McDonalds? Weis? Starkist? Florida? Humans didn't
> produce it. The corporation didn't create it.... Soil did....
> Trees did.
>
> —Derrick Jensen[1]

What does food and farming have to do with awakening? Not
much if we are stuck in the mindset that food is just *fuel* that we need
to ingest to keep our bodies running. But, what if food is so much more
than this? Indeed, how we see and experience our food is determined,
in large part, by the amount of presence we bring to the gathering and
preparing and eating of our food. It was with this in mind that I recently
invited my students to experience their food, from farm to plate, by taking them on a half-day field trip to a family farm. The arrangements
were simple: We would offer our labor in exchange for the opportunity
to harvest fresh vegetables that would comprise the ingredients for a
farm-fresh soup.

Imagine yourself, joining us, walking out into a field of potatoes in
October. The plant tops are brown, signaling that the potatoes are ready
for harvest. We dig into the ground with spading forks and discover loads
of potatoes! After filling six wheelbarrows with potatoes for the farmer,
we set out with two harvest baskets, in search of ingredients for our farm
soup.

Looking to our left, we behold leeks, beets, broccoli, and onions; and
on our right we are greeted by squash, kale, cabbage, and parsnips, along
with parsley, sage, thyme, and garlic—each one calling to us, in its own
way, to touch, pick, smell, and savor!

Then comes fire-making, water-fetching, and vegetable-chopping, along with the simple joy of witnessing the soup warm and bubble.

Later, gathered in a circle, our bowls brimming with goodness, it all seems too good to be true; and it is in this moment that the students begin to voice their amazement that a meal so simple could be so profoundly satisfying. The appreciation runs deep because, on this day, nothing stands between us and the food on our spoons—no corporations, no packagers, no retailers, no processing firms, no food distributors. Rather than being separated, we are palpably connected with the land that we have walked upon, as well as with the food we have harvested that is now filling our bellies.

Our Modern Story of Food: As recently as 150 years ago, almost all of the food that Americans ate came from within a dozen miles of where we had our homes. No more! Today, the average food molecule travels some 1,500 miles before reaching our plates. This is why the food that we consume is often lacking in freshness—i.e., in aliveness. It also explains why much of the food in our grocery carts is not recognizable as *food*. After all, real farm food looks like leaves, roots, tubers, shoots, seeds, fruits. This contrasts sharply with the highly processed foods that line most grocery store shelves. The vast majority of these store offerings are not so much food as "food-like substances"—i.e., they bear little resemblance to anything that exists in nature.[2]

Perhaps this is why it doesn't seem to matter that most of us know very little about where our food comes from, who grows it, the conditions under which it is grown, or even its nutritional qualities. Indeed, as Wendell Berry points out, "People are fed by the Food Industry which pays no attention to health and are treated by the Health Industry, which pays no attention to food."[3] Given this disconnect, it shouldn't come as a surprise that our industrial food system has, for years, been unwittingly promoting eating habits that contribute to a rising incidence of heart disease, diabetes, and obesity.

Just as careless eating habits negatively affect our health, so, too, do our careless industrial farming practices compromise the health of Earth's land, water, and air. For example, more than 80 percent of U.S. farms are steadily losing topsoil—the foundation of human survival. Add to this the fact that the massive Ogallala Aquifer (the single largest groundwater reservoir in the world!), which supplies irrigation water for much of the

U.S. "breadbasket," is being depleted more than a thousand times faster than it is being replenished! This means that irrigation-based agriculture will no longer be possible in much of America's heartland within this century.[4] Finally, and perhaps most disturbingly, the cumulative amount of energy (mostly in the form of fossil fuels) used to grow, process, package, and transport the food that we consume is ten times greater than the nutritional energy actually contained in the food itself.[5] Taking all of this together, it is clear that today's industrial food system is alarmingly unsustainable.

Taking Food into Our Own Hands: Can you even imagine how you would feed yourself if you were cut off from our industrial food system—e.g., if you no longer had access to grocery stores, fast food joints, snack shops, and the like?

Before concluding that you would be doomed, recall the housing challenge from the last stepping stone and how, with a bit of searching and digging, a multitude of frugal, sustainable shelter options were brought to light. It's much the same with food. Exciting alternatives to the industrial food system are now within reach. Examples include: (i) Farmers' Markets, (ii) Community-Supported Agriculture initiatives, (iii) Grow-It-Yourself vegetable gardens, (iv) WWOOFing internships, and v-Slow Food practices. Let's have a look.

(i) Farmers' Markets: There are now over 8,000 farmers' markets in the U.S., and this number continues to rise. Why the surge in popularity? Some obvious reasons are that the food in these markets is fresh, non-processed, and usually sold by local farmers "just down the road." But there is more to the growing popularity of farmers' markets. To find out, some sociologists conducted a study where they observed shoppers in both big-box grocery stores and farmers' markets. One of their discoveries was that the average farmers' market visitor has ten times more human interactions while shopping than the average grocery store shopper.[6] If you have ever shopped at a farmers' market, this is probably not surprising to you. You know what it's like: the smells and the colors and the hustle and bustle; the presence of the food growers, themselves; the generous offerings of food samples; the spontaneous encounters with friends and neighbors. There is an ineffable sense of "rightness" about all of it. Indeed, up until very recently, this is how all people in urban settings did their food shopping. Yes, we came together, as members of a community, in large, public outdoor markets, and this is still how it is for many people throughout the world. Supermarkets, by contrast, are an anomaly, historically speaking, and it is no wonder if you feel a bit lonely shopping in one.

(ii) Community-Supported Agriculture: A second possibility for taking food into your own hands is to become a shareholder at a Community-Supported Agriculture (CSA) farm. Recall the opening story about my students eating food straight from farm to bowl, absent any middlemen. That's what CSAs are all about.

Here's how it works: Families living in the vicinity of a CSA farm purchase a "farm share" at the beginning of the growing season. Then, once the season begins, each shareholder family receives a 5–10 pound basket of farm-fresh food every week. In the spring, these baskets are filled with greens, strawberries, snow peas, and radishes; in the early summer, baskets are laden with kale, garlic, blueberries, and green beans. This is followed by the likes of sweet corn, tomatoes, peaches, onions, and beets, later in the summer, and then, in the fall, other delights such as butternut squash, apples, broccoli, Brussels sprouts, leeks, parsnips, and potatoes. Many CSAs also supply locally raised animal products, including eggs, meat, and honey. And for those not able to afford a food share, there is the option of exchanging several hours of farm labor each week for harvest baskets.

Since the first CSA was established in 1984, this concept has spread like wildfire. At present, there are more than 2,500 CSAs in the U.S.—meaning the chances are good that there is one not far from where you live.[7]

(iii) Grow-It-Yourself Vegetable Gardens: If you'd like an even more intimate relationship with wholesome, fresh food, consider growing it yourself. For example, imagine if everything growing in your yard was edible—from the fruit-bearing shrubs for your smoothies, to the basil, peppers, and tomatoes for your pizza, as well as a range of delicious vegetables for your soups. After all, why grow grass when you can grow vegetables? In fact, fifteen years ago, my partner Dana and I asked ourselves this very question, and since that time we've been gradually replacing grass with raised-bed vegetable plots. The result: Today we get to eat some fresh food from our yard for six months out of the year.[8]

And even if you lack a yard, don't despair! Consider the possibility of growing food with others in a community garden. If that's not possible, you could be bold and knock on the door of a neighbor who has some space and propose to establish a vegetable garden in a sunny section of their yard. What's in it for them? Perhaps the prospect of receiving a portion of the harvest, along with relief from having to mow grass?

(iv) WWOOFing: Maybe you are interested in growing food, but don't know beans about farming. One way to learn is to become a WWOOFer—i.e., a <u>W</u>illing <u>W</u>orker <u>O</u>n <u>O</u>rganic <u>F</u>arms. Many WWOOFing opportunities exist in the U.S., as well as in more than one hundred other countries around the world.

Volunteer as a WWOOFer and you might find yourself helping to build a farm irrigation system in Africa, harvesting olives in Portugal, making cheese in the Swiss Alps, or who knows what else. Here's how past WWOOFer Lindsay Nicholls summed up her experience:

> For my farm experience in central Portugal, there was no electricity, but our British/Dutch combo family was so warm and welcoming and the work so varied and considered that my overall experience was completely fulfilling. I sowed corn, planted trees, milked goats, and made cheese from their milk. I ate with the family, balancing my plate on my lap, while pushing the dogs' noses away. My every question was answered with gusto, all my suggestions taken on board. I discovered what WWOOFing is about, and now I'm hooked![9]

In sum, WWOOFing is a great way to go on an adventure of awakening, not knowing just where you might land, whom you might meet, and what you might learn.[10]

(v) Slow Food: The *new story* around food isn't just about who grows it, or where and how; it's also about the actual act of preparing and eating food. For example, the next time you have a nice home-cooked meal in front of you, try this slow-eating experiment. It starts by picturing the food on your plate, as it occurred in nature just before it was harvested. So, if an apple is part of your meal, picture the apple tree that produced the apple, growing year by year in an orchard: sun streaming down, rain falling, blossoms opening, and bees buzzing/pollinating. Then, visualize the farmer picking the apple, while, at the same time, acknowledging the other human hands that helped to bring the apple to you. Do the same for the other foods on your plate. After all, each item was, just a short time ago, a living part of Earth, brought to you through a constellation of relationships. As you experience this interdependence, consider joining hands with those around the table to voice words of gratitude, like these:

> Earth, water, fire, air, and space combine to make this food.
> Numberless beings gave their lives and labor that we may eat.
> May we be nourished that we may nourish life.
> —Joan Halifax[11]

Then, go ahead and take your first bite, attentive to the crunching sounds, aromas, and taste sensations. And when the impulse to swallow arises, pause. That's right; don't swallow. Instead, continue to savor and chew. In so doing, you will likely discover that you weren't really ready to stop experiencing and enjoying the food that, fortunately, is still in your mouth.

When you have finished eating, turn to those you have gathered with to acknowledge that one of the most powerful attractions of the slow food movement is that it's social and celebratory, not solitary and mechanical.

Wrap-Up

Anna Thomas, author of *Love Soup*, wrote, "We all eat, and it would be a sad waste of opportunity to eat badly."[12] Fortunately, there are food options that can save us money while bringing us health, wholeness, and connection. Maybe, for you, it means trading some of your labor for fresh-grown food at a CSA, or replacing a swatch of lawn with a pea patch, or growing vegetables with others in a community garden, or choosing to make regular visits to your local farmers' market, or, who knows, maybe even spending time WWOOFing in a foreign land. The good news is that as we learn to connect with our food, we can't help but become more connected to our communities and to the good Earth that sustains us.

Transportation

An Exercise in Awakening

> Yes sir, yes madam, I entreat you to get out of those motor-
> ized wheelchairs, get off your foam rubber backsides, stand
> up straight like men! like women! like human beings! And
> walk-walk-WALK upon our sweet and blessed land.
> —Edward Abbey[1]

The year was 1965. I had just turned sixteen and was sitting alone in the driver's seat of my family's old red Studebaker. It was a four-on-the-column stick shift, and I was attempting to teach myself how to shift gears from first gear to second, third, and fourth.

A week later I was seated in the passenger's seat as my dad drove me to a nearby parking lot for my first driving lesson. I can still recall the moment when I turned the key and heard the engine sputter to life: my tight grip on the steering wheel, the butterflies fluttering in my belly, the pounding of my heart.

I looked over at my dad. He gave me the go-ahead with a nod. Tentatively, I pushed down on the clutch pedal with my left foot and set the gear lever to first gear. Then, I lightly feathered the accelerator with my right foot while slowly lifting my left foot off the clutch. When the clutch finally engaged, the car lurched forward. Panic stricken, I pressed on the accelerator and the brake pedal at the same time, caus-ing the Studebaker to shudder to a stop. I apologized to my dad, but he appeared to be unfazed. I tried again, and again, and again. It was as if I was attempting to tame a wild bronco—so much did that Studebaker lurch, buck, and balk.

After a half hour, I had finally begun to establish a kinesthetic rap-port with that Studebaker, which is to say, I was driving.

In retrospect, I see that my father was guiding me through a rite of passage by giving me access to a powerful machine that would serve as a launch pad for greater independence and adventure.

But in the midst of all my excitement around cars and driving, it never occurred to me that there might be a downside to the automobile. Like just about everyone else living in the sixties, I was conditioned to see cars as amazing in every way.

How is it for you, today? Are you 100 percent sold on cars, or do you think they might have a downside? You could begin to articulate your beliefs around car-based transport by using your journal to complete and reflect on the following open sentences:

1. For me having a car means _____

_____

2. Without a car, I might _____

_____

3. The impacts of car-based transit include _____

_____

4. Cars have changed society by _____

_____

If you were to ponder your responses to any one of these questions, you might arrive at insights that could change your relationship with cars. For example, take question number 3, "The impacts of me driving a car are...." Certainly, car driving helps you to move quickly from place to place, with comfort and privacy. However, other possible impacts could include things like lost time stuck in traffic jams and high costs of gas and repair bills, as well as the threat of a disabling accident.

Pondering this a little longer, you might also come up with impacts beyond those that affect you, personally, such as:

- Climate warming due to carbon dioxide emissions from cars—e.g., roughly five metric tons of the greenhouse gas CO_2 are released per year, from each car operating in the U.S.[2]
- The eradication of farmland and forests associated with the construction of the roads and parking lots that cars

necessitate—e.g., for every five cars in operation in the U.S., an area the size of a football field is covered in pavement.[3]
- The killing and maiming of human beings—e.g., approximately 40,000 Americans are killed each year in car crashes, along with more than 6,000 pedestrian fatalities.[4]

I grant you that it can be uncomfortable to take such a critical/negative perspective on cars insofar as we have been conditioned to assume that cars are essential components of modern life. But, unmasking common assumptions regarding the merits of car-based transportation could serve as a catalyst for awakening to alternatives to the automobile.

For example, consider the widely held belief that cars are great because they save us lots of time. Is this really true? How would you react if you were to learn that your average speed while driving is only about 10–15 miles per hour? That's preposterous, right! I mean, really, how could that be? If you are out on the open road, you are probably going 60 or 70 mph, and even in town, speed limits are seldom below 25 mph. So, really, how could our average car speed be only 10–15-mph?

Well, for starters, consider all the time that car users spend stymied by stoplights, traffic congestion, and road construction delays. Consider, too, the time spent searching for parking spots and waiting in repair garages. Take into consideration all these time fragments, and you will discover that you are not going as fast as you think.

But don't stop there: If you want to be thorough, consider all the hours you have to spend working each year to earn the money to cover car payments, fuel costs, insurance fees, and maintenance/repair costs. Then—and here is the clincher—take your total car mileage for a given year (the average in the U.S. is roughly 15,000 miles/car/year) and divide that number by the total number of hours you spend in your car (either driving or stalled in traffic), PLUS all the hours you need to spend working in order to earn the money necessary to own and operate and maintain your car. Do this more comprehensive, full-cost accounting, and you will discover that your average speed is in the 10–15 mph range—i.e., not much different from someone pedaling a bicycle![5]

Alternatives to Car Culture: Most of us believe that the only way to meet our daily transportation needs is to own a car, but what if you were to challenge this widely held assumption? How? Easy: Just assume that starting right now, you no longer own a car; you are now carless and will be carless for the rest of your life! Is this the end for you? Or might it be a new beginning? Here are three possibilities that could serve as springboards for reducing car dependency.

(i) Car Libraries: We've all heard of book libraries, but how about a car library, where you simply borrow a car now and again, as necessary? This option is ideal for people who require the use of a car for only a couple of hours a week, and, given that the average car in the U.S. is used for only about one hour a day, there are millions of car owners in the U.S. who might benefit from this car-library alternative. If this sounds like you, you could ditch your private car and join a community-oriented car sharing company. Zipcar, for example, now operates in hundreds of cities all over the U.S. Just as a library maintains a supply of books that it lends to users, Zipcar has a supply of cars that it provides to its members. Indeed, in Boston there are more than 20,000 Zipcar members serviced by a fleet of 1,500 Zipcars.[6]

How does it work? Well, if you have a membership, all you need to do is check the Zipcar app on your phone to locate a nearby car. Then, you can reserve that car for a particular stretch of time, use it, and return it to the same designated parking space where you found it. The economics are attractive. Zipcar members save roughly $450/month in car-related transportation expenses, compared to full-time car owners. There are also dividends for the environment, insofar as each Zipcar in operation serves the needs of 13 people who no longer need to own private cars. This means a substantial reduction in the number of cars that would, otherwise, have been manufactured, sold, and operated.[7]

Zipcar is just one of many names for car sharing companies. There are also peer-to-peer car-share options, like GetAround and RelayRides,[8] whereby those with private cars make their vehicles available to others, and, of course, there are taxis, Lyft, and Uber, should you need someone in your community to help you get around.

(ii) Trains and Buses: Suppose you want to give up cars entirely, but you still need a viable option for longer trips. Consider trains. Similar to cars, trains are a means to an end, but they are also good places to get things done because in a train, you don't have to have your hands stuck to a steering wheel and your eyes glued on the road. Instead, you can read a book, surf the Internet, play board games with friends, etc. In cases where trains aren't convenient, buses can be an effective option. Compared to cars, both trains and buses get far better fuel mileage—190 mpg per passenger on trains and 330 mpg per passenger on buses—and both are much safer than cars.[9]

(iii) Walking: Get this: A quarter of all car trips in the U.S. are to destinations that are less than one mile away. It would be easy to walk that! And think of all the ways in which walking might be the better option. First, it's cheaper; second, it's more environmentally friendly; and third, as Edward Abbey pointed out in the opening quote (above), getting out of our "motorized wheelchairs" and off of our "foam rubber backsides" is a great way to maintain our health. Walking also creates opportunities for serendipitous encounters—e.g., meeting a neighbor, being stopped in your tracks by the delicacy of a wildflower, not to mention experiencing the kinesthetic delights of your body moving through space.[10]

(iv) Biking can also be a fine alternative to the car, especially for trips in the one to five-mile range. And guess what: More than 40 percent of all car trips in the U.S. are in this range, and more than half of all Americans live within five miles of their job sites—i.e., within biking distance.[11]

There used to be a tendency to regard bikes as things just for kids, but this attitude has been changing, as today's adults rediscover both the utility and joy of biking. Consider this testimony from a single mom who returned to biking when her car failed inspection and she didn't have the money to fix it:

> I thought I needed a car. I couldn't have been more wrong. I cycle to all my jobs—the furthest away is 6 miles—no matter the weather. I hadn't cycled for over 30 years and never for more than a couple of miles. Now, ten months on, I take the long route home (around 20–25 miles) whenever I can, just for the fun of it. I've lost 3 dress sizes, and I am discovering places that I never knew existed. If I were offered a car as a gift now, I'd say, "Thank you very much for your kindness, but no thank you."[12]

Here's another testimony—this one from a man who moved to a new city and decided to ditch his car in the process:

> I don't miss owning a car…. No financial drain, no parking headaches, no sitting in crammed streets going nowhere, no feeling drained by the morning commute…. It's turned my entire relationship with the street on its head,

and the time spent walking and riding is simply of a higher quality than time spent behind the wheel.[13]

I've personally been commuting by bike to work for several decades and can confirm that it's just downright fun. Yes, feeling the wind and navigating roads, bike paths, bumps, and sharp turns, as well as pedal-pumping up steep inclines and zooming down hills—it's all wonderfully enlivening!

What's more, biking is inexpensive and eco-friendly. For example, the food energy that a person on a bike burns to travel 1,000 miles is equivalent to the amount of energy in one gallon of gasoline. Translation: Ditch your car for a bike, and you will be getting 1,000 mpg, instead of 20–30 mpg driving a car.[14]

What's more, I've discovered that when I travel around town by bike, I usually arrive at my destination in less time than the time it takes to go by car. Don't believe me? Find out for yourself. The next time you need to make a trip to a place that is within a mile or two of your home, determine how long it takes to drive there by noting the time elapsed, from the minute you leave your front door until the minute you arrive at the door of your destination. Then, the next time you go to that same place, hop on your bike, and time yourself again door to door. Conduct this simple time audit, and you will probably discover, as I have, that your biking time is less than your driving time.

Wrap-Up

The bicycle [in contrast to the automobile] is the vehicle of a new mentality. It quietly challenges our [car-based] system of values which condones dependency, waste, inequality and daily carnage.... There is every reason why cycling should be helped to enjoy another Golden Age.

—James McGurn[15]

Before the invention of the internal combustion engine, it was our streets that served as the hub for social life in cities and towns all over the world. Streets were where markets hummed, goods and services were exchanged, and wedding and funeral processions were enacted. Until recently, the city street was a veritable outdoor room for play, enlivened conversations, civic debates, performances, and festivities—in short, for LIFE! But, now, with the advent of the modern automobile, this once precious social sphere has become a noisy, often dangerous place, occupied predominantly by fast-moving cars.

This need not be. Living an awakened life means bringing awareness and presence to our everyday actions and then making choices based on new understandings. This could very well mean replacing the old story— that cars are the only way to go—with a new story that prioritizes simpler, safer, more sane transportation alternatives that can enhance all dimensions of individual and community well-being. The choice is ours!

Community

What Can We Do for Each Other?

> When you don't have community, you are not listened to;
> you don't have a place you can go to and feel that you really
> belong. You don't have people to affirm who you are and to
> support you in bringing forward your gifts.
>
> —Sobonfu Some[1]

The places where we live, and how we live within those places, determine, in large measure, how we each show up in the world. For example, when we have the experience of truly belonging to a place and a community—i.e., belonging to something much greater than ourselves—we become more grounded, more whole, more engaged, and more aware of our gifts and how we can share them.

But few of us today live in such idyllic circumstances. Instead, we often dwell in social settings that are etched with a measure of loneliness and separation. Indeed, recent research reveals that almost half of adults in America feel, in some measure, alone—i.e., like they don't belong.[2]

This begs the question: What does it even mean to belong?[3] This word "belong" holds so many possibilities, from belonging to a physical body, to belonging to a family, to belonging to a job or vocation, to belonging to a religion, or even belonging to an ancestry with its traditions.

Of course, no matter what any one of us might feel, the larger truth is that we already do belong! Not by any action or good deed or adherence to any particular way of being, but simply by virtue of our existence. For example, that we are each alive and breathing is a testimony to our belonging to something greater than ourselves, and the fact that we dwell within bodies that have the capacity to feel joy and love and fear and heartbreak bespeaks of our membership in the human family.

And, yet, many of us don't have the embodied experience of living in an authentic community. What about *you*? Do you live in a community? Sure, there are probably people living near you—e.g., the folks next door or across the street or in a neighboring apartment—but, again: Do you live in a community? How would you know? What does it look like and feel like to live in community? You could explore this right now by reflecting in your journal on the following three questions:

- Do you live in a place where you know the names of your neighbors, including the names of the children and the elderly?
- Do you live in a place where you can count on your neighbors to support you in hard times and where you stand in full readiness to support them too?
- Do you live in a place where you feel seen and affirmed and supported by those living around you and where your gifts are called forth and appreciated?

Few of us, it seems, are able to respond with a resounding "Yes" to these sorts of questions. After all, in today's America we are taught to value our independence, claiming that this makes us free, even free of the need for community![4]

It is the ideology of Economism that teaches us to believe that it is money—not caring relationships with other people—that will ensure our well-being, safety, and happiness.

Upshot: Though we are technologically linked to more people than ever before, we are often less connected to the people close at hand, living in our neighborhoods. Indeed, it seems that the age-old dynamic of caring and sharing within the crucible of community is being replaced by a capital-based system that seeks to commodify just about everything.

Cultivating Interdependence: How might we recover the sense of belonging that is born of having rich, deep connections with those in our neighborhoods and communities? One way might be to consider how we can share what we have with those with whom we live. For example, say you have just moved into a new place and want to hang some pictures, but you don't have any tools: no hammer, no nails, no level, nothing. So, what do you do? Head out to the nearest Home Depot and spend money to buy these things, even though you'll only be using them for a few minutes? Sure, you might have a need for them later, but how often? Imagine instead that there was a tool library in your neighborhood where you could "check out" the tools you needed, use them until you were finished hanging your pictures, and then return them! Such tool libraries are springing up around the country, reminding us that we don't always need to own things. In the case of tools, we only need occasional access to what they allow us to do. And if there's no tool library where you live, rather than feeling like a victim, why not join with others to create one or reach out to friends via social media to see if you might borrow what you, otherwise, would have to purchase?

Perhaps, in addition to wanting access to a tool now and again, you'd also like to gain some home repair skills. You could pay money and sign up for a course, but this overlooks the possibility that there are probably people living right in your neighborhood who might be happy to share their home repair skills. For example, Brooklyn Skillshare, one among many such groups in the U.S., connects neighbors so that they can share and swap skills based on people's needs and/or expertise. Skillshare groups aren't government programs. They emerge spontaneously when one of us sees a need and acts to create community connections.

Another avenue for community sharing is through internet-based exchange forums like FreeCycle. Existing in over 85 countries, FreeCycle—grounded in the philosophy that *what's mine is yours and that there's plenty to go around*—facilitates the gifting of materials among people. So if one of us happens to have more than we need right now—e.g., surplus tools, clothes, books, etc.—we can give the extras to someone who needs them. And in the future, if we happen to find ourselves in need, we could become recipients of FreeCycle materials. Can this system really work? Well, already more than 24,000 items are exchanged every day through FreeCycle—that's nearly 700 tons of goods daily.[5]

The point, not to be missed, is that as we reduce our dependence on money, we have the opportunity to discover another form of wealth that is truly life-sustaining—namely: the social capital that manifests through community bonds and that swells as we forge ever-more creative and expansive responses to the question: "What can we do for each other?"

Eco-Villages: When we choose to live in genuine community, we discover that many of our material and social needs can actually be met outside of the cash economy through relationships of interdependence. This is what people living in so-called "Eco-Villages" are discovering.

Such eco-based communities are now located in nearly every country in the world, with thousands worldwide. Eco-Villagers are united by a desire to co-create sustainable communities. Members often live in their own small, sometimes self-constructed, dwellings, while sharing access to communal spaces like kitchens, workshops, meeting rooms, play areas, laundry rooms, tool sheds, and guest rooms.

Daily routines, such as cooking and maintenance, are often shared. Similarly, many eco-villages make decisions through democratic processes grounded in consensus. Villagers typically grow a portion of their food for communal consumption, with everyone helping out. Furthermore, because of a shared ethic to live lightly, eco-villages are often designed to ensure efficient energy use while minimizing the community's overall ecological footprint.

If you like the idea of living in an eco-village but don't want to move from the place you live right now, you might take inspiration from the Transition Town initiative that sprang into being in England in 2005. This movement is grounded in the belief that to ensure a viable future, humans must now transition to truly sustainable practices, and that this will become possible as *existing* towns, communities, and neighborhoods change the ways they relate to energy, health, food, transportation, waste, shelter, work, and more.

There are now cities and towns in 43 different countries registered in the Transition Town Network. The United States alone hosts over 160 Transition Towns—e.g., Los Angeles, Charlotte, Chicago, Pittsburgh, Milwaukee, and Tulsa, to name just a few. Transition Town participants understand their endeavor as a giant social experiment that could fail. Still, they say, "If we wait for the governments, it'll be too little, too late; if we act as individuals, it'll be too little; but if we act as communities, it might just be enough, just in time."[6]

The call that I hear in all of this is to begin to think of the neighborhoods, towns, and cities where we currently live as Eco-Villages-in-waiting. We only need to change the way we look at our neighborhoods to see that, with some creativity and flexibility, they could become genuine communities where everyone belongs!

This isn't a dream; it's an emerging reality. By way of example, take in this true story from *Yes! Magazine* about two women, Naomi and Jackie, who were walking in their neighborhood one day, bemoaning how stressed and busy they were in their attempts to balance housework, day jobs, and child rearing. During a pause in the conversation, Naomi shared her excitement about how one of her neighbors had volunteered to teach her son practical building skills in his workshop. This prompted both women to wonder if there might be others in their community with skills to share. Holding that seed question, Naomi and Jackie, along with four other neighbors, took on the task of tallying up all the skills and interests of both the adults and kids in their neighborhood. Here's what happened:

> The six neighbors named themselves the "matchmakers" and, as they got more experience, they began to connect neighbors who shared the same interests. The gardeners' team shared tips and showed four families how to create gardens—even on a flat rooftop! Several people who were worried about the bad economy created a website where neighbors who knew about available work could post job openings....
>
> Jolene Cass ... posted one of her poems on the website and asked if there were other poets on the block. It turned out there were three. They began to have coffee, share their writing, and post their poems online. [Similarly,] eleven adults and kids formed the Block Band, and neighborhood singers formed a choir led by Sarah Ensley, an 80-year-old woman who'd been singing all her life....
>
> Three years later, at the annual block party, Jackie Barton summed up what the neighborhood had accomplished: "What we have done is broken all the lines. We broke the lines between the men. We broke the lines between the women. Then the lines were broken between the men and the women. And best of all, the lines were broken between the adults and the children and between all of us and our seniors. All the lines are broken; we're all connected. We're a real community now."[7]

And all of this came into being when one man took the time to teach a boy some building skills and when two women cared enough to share their lives with each other. Indeed, building strong community bonds appears to be our best and final hope—not just for finding fulfillment and happiness, but also for surviving uncertain times.

Wrap-Up

> I don't know, of course, what's going to happen, but it seems to me, imaginable, that a time could come when we will either have to achieve community or die, learn to love one another or die. We're rapidly coming to the time, I think, when the great centralized powers are not going to be able to do for us what we need to have done. Community will

start again when people begin to do necessary things for each other.

—Wendell Berry[8]

In the end, each of these examples of creating and strengthening community bonds came about because of a shift in the way people saw themselves and each other—i.e., not as strangers but as companions, not as consumers but as contributors to the common good, not as independent individuals in an impersonal global economy but as interdependent members of a community. This shift will surely spread as we awaken and muster the vulnerability and empathy to open-heartedly ask: "What can we do for each other?"

Happiness from the Inside Out

Folks are usually about as happy as they make their minds up to be.

—Abraham Lincoln[1]

When I would visit my mother in the years leading up to her death, she would sometimes ask, "Son, are you happy?" I always responded with a simple "Yes," believing that she wanted my assurance more than a muddled discourse on happiness.

Only recently have I come to realize that my mom wasn't asking me if I was in a happy mood; she wanted to know if I was fulfilled and at peace in my life. Framing happiness in this way is an invitation to consider what it means to be truly happy. So, what about you? Are you happy? How do you know? You could begin to sink into these questions by completing the following open sentences in your journal:

1. A time when I was truly happy today was _____

_____.

2. For me, to be genuinely happy means _____

_____.

3. A person I know who epitomizes happiness is _____

_____.

4. What blocks my happiness is _____

_____.

As you fill in your responses, new questions may arise. For example, if you are unable to come up with a time when you experienced happiness today, you might be led to wonder: Do I have a say in my happiness, or

183

does it depend solely on outside circumstances? Or, in the case of question two, if you responded that, for you, being genuinely happy means "performing acts of service," this could lead you to wonder why you don't dedicate more of your life to service. Your response to the third question—a person you know who epitomizes happiness—might motivate you to ask that happy soul for advice on cultivating happiness in your own life. Finally, if you ignored the first three questions, engaging the fourth one—What blocks my happiness?—could be revelatory, insofar as your disinclination to reflect on happiness might point you toward something that interferes with your happiness.

Material Goods as a Source of Happiness? Though most people say they want to be happy, many of us, it seems, fail to achieve this elusive goal. This suggests that, as a culture, we may harbor a lot of confusion regarding the sources of happiness. For example, our culture teaches us to believe—in subtle and not so subtle ways—that having lots of possessions is important for happiness.[2] But is this really true?

Consider this scene: You are alone and lost in the woods on a cold winter night. You haven't eaten all day. It is snowing, and you are shivering uncontrollably. But then up ahead, you see a flickering light, emanating from the window of a small log cabin. A woman opens the door and directs you to a warm spot in front of a hearth. She drapes a blanket over your shoulders and places a cup of hot soup in your hands, with the assurance that you can stay as long as you like. As you experience the warmth of the fire and breathe in the aroma of the savory soup, you are suffused with happiness.[3]

In this vignette, you went from being hungry and miserable on a frigid night to being "suffused with happiness," and it only took four objects—a cabin, a blanket, a fire, and a cup of hot soup—to bring you to a happy state. But does this mean that if you were provided with four more objects—say a phone, a television, a hat, and a salad—your happiness would double? And would an additional four items lead to yet another bump up in your happiness, and so on? Though there is some logic to this, it turns out that beyond a certain point, further increases in one's material goods do not lead to increases in happiness. For example, while Americans, on average, have increased their annual consumption of stuff almost three-fold since the 1950s, our level of happiness has not increased.[4] Nonetheless, many of us continue to believe that more and more income, as well as the stuff that money can buy, will bring us more and more happiness. This is a bit like believing that because drinking one bottle of beer made you feel a little bit happy, drinking 25 beers will leave you feeling 25 times happier. It doesn't work that way.

Happiness as a Destination? In the preamble to the American Declaration of Independence it states that "the pursuit of happiness" is an "inalienable right." This wording—"the pursuit of happiness"—implies that happiness is destination, a future goal, achievable through determination and hard work. But rather than a destination for our lives, what if we understood happiness as a byproduct of a life lived with meaning and purpose, day by day? This distinction between present versus future orientation is illustrated in a parable about an American entrepreneur who took time off from his work as an investment banker to visit a Mexican fishing village.

Strolling along the shore of the village on the morning of his arrival, the American encountered a fisherman with several large fish in his boat. After greeting the Mexican, the American asked how long it had taken to catch the fish.

"Only a couple of hours," replied the fisherman.

"Why didn't you stay out longer to catch more fish?" inquired the American, "That way, you could sell more and make more money."

"I have enough fish here to support my family's needs," responded the fisherman.

The American then wanted to know how the fisherman spent the rest of his time.

"It's like this," replied the Mexican, "I wake up late, catch two or three fish—enough to feed my family, with one left over to sell at the market. Then, I play with my children and take a siesta with my wife. In the evening, I walk into the village, drink some wine, and play my guitar with my amigos. It's a full and happy life."

"That sounds pretty good, but it could be better," countered the American. "For instance, if you spent more time out fishing, you could make enough money to buy a bigger and faster boat, and with your new boat, you could catch more fish and, eventually, earn enough to buy a whole fleet of boats. That way you would be able to sell your fish directly to processors and, heck, maybe even open your own cannery. Imagine: You could control every part of the business from production to processing to distribution. You might even make enough money to move to Mexico City and then to LA!"

The Mexican thought about all that the American had said and asked, "How long would all that take?"

The American shrugged, "If you worked really hard you could probably do it in twenty years."

"Then, what would I do?" queried the fisherman.

A big grin spread across the American's face, "Well, that's the best part! When your business is booming, you could sell it and make millions of dollars!"

The Mexican nodded, "Okay, and then what?"

"Then you could retire! Move to a small fishing village, sleep late, fish a little, play with your grandkids, take siestas with your wife, and in the evening, walk into town, drink wine, and play your guitar with your amigos. It would be a full and happy life!"[5]

The lesson in this parable is easy to decode: The American—coming from a culture caught up in Economism—would have the Mexican spend the bulk of his life in the pursuit of happiness, failing to consider that, perhaps, the fisherman was already content.

Solving the Happiness Riddle? If happiness isn't about accumulating lots of material goods and isn't a destination to be pursued, then what is it that brings genuine happiness? The answer, I have come to believe, has to do with accepting life just as it presents itself, day by day—i.e., by living in the mindset of enoughness. This becomes possible, in my experience, as we learn to cultivate virtues like gratitude, compassion, and acceptance.

(i) Gratitude: Monk and interfaith scholar David Steindl-Rast contends that happiness comes from living in a state of gratitude.[6] Could this be true? You could experiment with this, on a small scale, by resolving to fill the next day of your life with gratitude. Begin in the morning with your breath. Feel it filling you, animating you, and be grateful. Then, as you rise from bed, appreciate the miracle of standing upright. How amazing that our bodies can stand and walk and see and smell and touch and think and hear! None of us earned our wondrous bodies. They are truly gifts from the Universe.

Continue to open in gratitude as you prepare your breakfast. The water that is heated on your stovetop and that combines with tea leaves, milk, and sugar in a porcelain cup—each have their own story of origins, involving hundreds of processes and innumerable lives. Experience the wonder of this, opening in gratitude as you engage all of your senses, savoring each miracle that is manifested in your breakfast.

And when you step outside, call out in gratitude to the trees for the oxygen they are offering you. Feel gratitude, too, for the wonder of the dandelion that is blooming in the sidewalk crack, for the cloud that shape-shifts before your very eyes, for Father Sun warming your back.

As you continue to open in gratitude, notice how you cannot help but feel just the slightest bit happier—maybe even lots happier. This is the inevitable outcome of expressing gratitude for all that is given to each of us moment by moment. In fact, research on the human brain, using MRI scanners, shows that the region of our frontal lobes associated with happiness "lights up" when we express gratitude. This makes sense: Gratitude brings us into relationship with the world.[7]

(ii) Compassion: As social animals, we have an innate longing to connect with one another. This longing is often expressed through sharing, as revealed in a vignette about an anthropologist who was conducting a study in Africa among the Xhosa people. One day he put a basket filled with fruit under a tree far out in the savannah. Then, he pointed out the tree to a group of children and told them that whoever ran fastest and reached the tree first could take all of the sweet fruits in the basket for him/herself.

The kids took off running, but they did not race. Instead, they joyfully frolicked their way to the tree, and when they found the basket, they sat together and shared the fruits.

When the anthropologist asked the children why they didn't race each other so that the winner could get all the fruit, they replied with the word "Ubuntu"—meaning, in the Xhosa language, "I am because we are." In effect, they were saying, "How could one of us be happy if the rest of us were not?"[8]

It's so obvious, right? How can I be happy if you're not happy? All of this is to suggest that compassion for each other is a fundamental source of well-being and happiness. Just imagine how happy we would be if we all learned to live by the "Ubuntu" principle!

(iii) Acceptance: It's been said that our happiness is determined, to a large extent, by the difference between what we *have* in any given moment and what we *want*. Could it be this simple? By way of example, in this moment, what you have—i.e., what you are doing—is reading the words on this page. If this is what you want to be doing, then you are on the happy side of life. You can visualize this by putting a dot in the box (below) to symbolize your reality—what you are doing right now. Then, place a second dot in the box to represent what you most want to be doing in this moment.

Your Two Dots

If reading this essay is exactly what you want to be doing, then your second dot will be placed directly on top of your first dot. This represents contentment—a moment when what you *want* is perfectly aligned with what you *have*. But maybe you are not really interested in reading this piece. You know this because you are a bit bored and distracted. In this case, your second dot would be separate from your first dot.

In any life moment, the distance between your two dots—far apart or close together—is a good indicator of your happiness or lack thereof. Seen in this light, it is our desire to have things be other than what they are that often creates our unhappiness, our suffering. But, is it even possible to live life with no separation between our dots—a life where we simply resolve that what we have is precisely what we want? Yes, but this would mean accepting how life presents itself, moment by moment, and this is not always easy. For example, there was a time recently when my two dots were far apart. I had made a date to meet a friend on a street corner, but he failed to show up at the appointed hour. After waiting ten minutes, I became impatient, my mind chatter sounding something like: "Where is he? He should be on time! Why doesn't he at least call to say he's running late?" I was agitated because what I wanted (my friend's presence) and what I had (the absence of my friend) didn't align.

Eventually, I caught myself, and rather than being in an argument with reality, I told myself to accept what I had. But issuing this order from my brain wasn't enough. So, I called on my full-body intelligence by bringing my attention to my breath. On each in-breath I noticed the tension caused by the disconnect between what I had and what I wanted, and on each out-breath I gradually released my need to have things be any different than what they were. Grounding in this way, I was eventually able to simply say "yes" to my situation and, in so doing, to align my dots.

As my mind quieted, I began to inhabit the present moment, feeling the crisp autumn air and seeing the delicate dance of shadow and light in the treetops. Eventually, when my friend arrived, I could barely remember what my internal ruckus had been all about.

Wrap-Up

> The goal of life is to make your heartbeat match the beat of
> the universe, to match your nature with Nature.
> —Joseph Campbell[9]

True happiness doesn't come from outside of ourselves. It's not the result of making lots of money or accumulating power and prestige; it's not something that is attained through dogged pursuit. Instead, happiness, it seems, is something that manifests, almost serendipitously, as we cultivate our innate capacity to experience gratitude and compassion, along with our ability to surrender to what is—i.e., to accept life just as it shows up, moment by moment—recognizing that just this moment, just this breath, is enough.

Coda

Awakening in Action

As revealed in the Part IV stepping stones, we can each choose to awaken each moment of every day. It doesn't matter if you are in the bathroom looking in the mirror, on a street corner waiting for a friend, or washing the dishes—opportunities for awakening are always available! It is our capacity to "be here now"—open and porous to life just as it presents itself—that is our portal to awakening. We become skillful in stepping through this portal as we learn to stop holding our breath.

Stop Holding Your Breath[1]

Stop holding your breath.

The one laying there next to you,
back at your side,
hogging all the covers,

that one doesn't have to offer
what you are looking for,

doesn't even understand that
you are looking,

Seeking.

That one prefers to remain asleep,
eyes closed.

Stop holding your breath.

That unmet longing that has you ceiling-staring has nothing
    to do with being completed by another.

Nothing.

That unmet longing is the yet-to-be-had,
never-to-be-ended conversation between your Soul and the
    Spirit that unites us all.

And, Why yet unmet? You ask.

Because you cannot truly engage in any dialogue while holding your
    breath!

Part your lips, open your mouth
And release your inflated cheeks and fears

Breathe.

Inhale Life. Exhale Love.

Inhale Life. Exhale Love.

It's time to do what you've known
it's time to do.

With utmost intent,

it's time to enter into The Sacred Marriage.

With utmost compassion,

it's time to love yourSelf enough…

Breathe.
    —Jamie Reaser

Yes, it's time: Time to let go of the crippling stories that have shuddered
our hearts. Time to live within the generative story of *enoughness*. Time
to Inhale Life, and Exhale Love. Time to fearlessly speak what we know
to be true. Time to stop holding our breath!

PART V

Personal and Cultural Transformation

Introduction

Whether we know it or not, we have each been born into a culturally mediated story that shapes our understanding of our life's meaning and purpose. Ideally, this narrative would call forth our best, or highest, selves; but today our dominant narrative sometimes does just the opposite, by engendering fear, greed, loneliness and alienation. This book's final stepping stones demonstrate how those choosing to awaken can act as pioneers by giving birth to a new cultural story—one that showcases what it means to be in open-hearted relationship with Self, Other and World—i.e., what it means to be fully human.

There was once a powerful wizard who had been wronged in the past and instead of facing his pain and anger, he concocted a magic potion with the power to drive all who drank it mad. Then, under the cover of darkness, the wizard introduced this sinister potion into the kingdom's well.

The next morning everyone in the kingdom drank from the well, as was their custom, and they all went crazy. The only people who were spared from insanity were the King and Queen because they had access to a private well from which they, alone, drank.

When the King realized that his subjects were not in their right mind, he began to issue edicts to keep them safe, but his edicts were of no avail. You see, everyone was truly insane. Therefore, the very people whom the King wished to protect saw his efforts as crazy and ignored them.

The more the people ignored the King's new laws, the more he issued them. This led the people to conclude that their King was no longer fit to rule. So, they marched on his castle, demanding that he step down. Watching the people approach, the King was deeply troubled and began preparations to give up his crown. His wife, the Queen, however, caught his arm and said, "Let us also go and drink from the poisoned well. Then, you can retain your crown, because you and I will be no different from them." And this is precisely what they did, and upon drinking the poisoned water, they too became mad and, as such, were able to communicate in ways that made sense to their subjects. Indeed, believing that their King had finally come to his senses, the people allowed him to remain on the throne until the end of his days.[1]

This story has relevance for our times, especially if we choose to see the potion that the wizard put in the kingdom's well as analogous to our culture's dominant story—the story that tells us what's normal, what's OK, and not OK, to do and say and be. It is this dominant story that tells us that our meaning and purpose in life is to be found in amassing status, wealth and power through work, consumption, competition, and endless doing.

Similar to the potion that the wizard put in the well, our story is mostly invisible to us, though we often experience its subtle, and not-so-subtle, effects in the form of anxiety, confusion, separation, and fear.

If ever there was a time when the human odyssey called for both personal and cultural transformation, now is that time. Welcome to Part V!

A New Story of Self

Ninety percent of the world's woe comes from people not knowing themselves, their abilities, their frailties, and even their real virtues. Most of us go almost all the way through life as complete strangers to ourselves.

—Sydney J. Harris[1]

Could it be that most of us are "complete strangers to ourselves" as suggested in the above quote? Or to use this book's language: Could it be that most of us are *asleep* to who we truly are?

Growing up, I was warned that dwelling on these kinds of questions regarding identity was self-indulgent, and, perhaps, even a bit dangerous. This continues to be a common sentiment today. But imagine living in a culture where engaging, in a sustained fashion, with the great questions of existence—e.g., Who am I? Why am I here? How can I be of service to life?—was both encouraged and celebrated. After all, who we understand ourselves to be determines, to a significant degree, the trajectory of our lives.

So, what is the story that you tell yourself about who you are and why you are here? And where did your story come from? Is it true? Who would you be without this story?

This stepping stone is premised on the idea that genuine self-discovery becomes possible as we learn to identify, and then let go of, the story that our culture transmits to us regarding our life's meaning and purpose. As we do this, we gain the freedom to set sail onto a sea of unknowing, and discover there, peaking out beyond the waves, fresh understandings of who we are.

We invite you to engage in this process of self-discovery right now by completing, ten times, the sentence: I am _____. Just grab a pencil and jot down the first things that come to mind in your journal.

- I am _____.
- I am _____.
- I am _____.
- I am _____.
- I am _____.
- I am _____.
- I am _____.
- I am _____.
- I am _____.
- I am _____.

Now, look over what you have written and consider if your responses capture your *true* identity. For example, suppose the first thing you wrote was, "I am a New Yorker." This sentence might describe the name of your home state/city, but if you lived somewhere else, wouldn't you still, deep down, be you? Or perhaps you wrote, "I am a student majoring in finance." Fine, but again, does what you spend your time studying define the essence of who you are?

This exercise isn't only about questioning the elements of your identity. That's a starting place, but if you have the courage to persist, you may also come to question what you've, heretofore, regarded as core elements of your identity. For example, you might discover that you are really not your religious or political beliefs because even absent these aspects of your identity, the deeper truth of who you are might remain intact. The same is true for your ethnicity, your sexual orientation, your biggest failure, your greatest achievement. Change any of these things and it is very likely that you still won't change the deep essence of who you are.

Loosening the Ego's Grip: Each of your "I am" statements (above) is a product of what psychologists call the "ego." Your ego began to take form when, as a young child, you discovered that a certain sequence of sounds, produced by your caregivers, signified your name. In your young mind, these sounds were connected to the concept "me." As you began to associate things with your name—e.g., a doll or a ball—your "me" expanded so that the doll became "my doll" and the ball, "my ball." Gradually, all sorts of other things relating to your body, your beliefs, your profession, your family roles and your likes and dislikes, congealed around your notion of "me," becoming the story of who you understand yourself to be today.

As each of us persists in using words like "my" and "mine," we inevitably strengthen our ego, and this contributes to the illusion that we exist as separate from everything and everyone else. But what if all of your things aren't actually yours? The shoes on your feet, for instance, aren't really yours. After all, ownership and property are merely ideas that we have been conditioned to accept, not essential truths. As Eckhart Tolle points out, "Many people don't realize until they are on their deathbed, and everything external falls away, that <u>no</u> <u>thing</u> ever had anything to do with who they are. In the proximity of death, the whole concept of ownership stands revealed as ultimately meaningless."[2]

But it's not necessary to wait until your dying day to absorb this lesson. You can grasp it right now by imagining what it would be like if you were born into a culture whose language had absolutely no way of expressing the notion of me, my or mine. In this hypothetical culture it would be nonsensical to declare anything as *yours*—i.e., nonsensical to say things like "my house," "my child," or "my shoes." The closest you could come to expressing ownership would be to speak of "that which I am now with." So, for example, your home would be spoken of as "the place I am now with," your child as "the child I am now with," and so forth. When it came to your own life, there would be no way to say "my life." Instead, you would be left to say, "the life I am now in the presence of." Can you sense how this might lead you to depersonalize your existence and, in so doing, to connect with, rather than separate from, the totality of life—the totality of beingness—that we all dwell within? Try it right now by looking down at your hands and seeing them, not as *your* hands, but as the hands you are now with, or now in the presence of.

You Are Not Your Thoughts: Our culture conditions us to see our identity—our self—in terms of our occupation, our physical body, our race, our nationality, our possessions and so on. All of this information comes to us in the form of thoughts. But what if we are not really the author of our thoughts? After all, they just come and go, here one moment, gone the next. You can confirm this by becoming the observer of your thoughts. For example, the next time you are walking along a city street pay attention to your thoughts. If you are like most of us, your mind chatter may sound something like this:

> Darn, it's really hot. I should have worn shorts. Ooooh…. Who is that guy over there? His name…. What's his name? I hate it when I forget names. Shoot, the <u>Walk</u> signal just changed to <u>Wait</u> … but if I run, I can make it. No, maybe I shouldn't. What will that woman on the other side think of me? Fine, I'll wait. But now I'm going to be late. Why am I always late?

With a little attention, you may be surprised to discover that this "self-talk" is always there in the background. If you saw a friend walking down the street, talking out loud to himself, you'd think he was nuts! But this is what is happening for most of us, inside our heads, much of the time. More amazing still is that we believe that this self-talk, this inner chatter, is who we are. But as author Michael Singer points out, "If you are hearing it talk, it is obviously not you. You are the one who hears the voice. You are the one who notices that it's talking."[3]

Singer suggests treating that voice in your head as your "inner roommate." This roommate is always there, reacting and responding, supervising and controlling. You can depersonalize this inner roommate by giving him/her a name and an imaginary body. Then, when you sit down for breakfast, you can imagine that your inner roommate is sitting across the table from you. You'll still hear this roommate's ceaseless monologue, but it won't be coming from inside of you, instead it will be coming from that "person" sitting over there.

This exploration suggests another answer to the question, Who am I? Namely: I am the witness, the one who is aware. I hear the voice in my head, fully aware that this voice, these thoughts, are not who I am.

What's Left? Once our constructed ego is stripped away, what's left is awareness—and this is no small thing! As a final mini-exercise, pause now, and attend to your breath. I don't mean "think" about your breath. Leave thinking behind. Instead, try to experience the sensations associated with your breathing. Be patient with yourself; this may take a few minutes. When you are ready, ask yourself: "Who is it that is experiencing this moment?"

As you sit with this question, take particular note of any sensations in your belly. As you exhale, let go of any tensions you might be holding, so that your belly softens. Then, do a body scan, deliberately bringing your attention—your awareness—to your feet, then to your legs, your chest, your spine, your arms, your neck and your head. Pause in each place to note the feelings and sensations that are present.

As you continue to drop into your body, becoming ever-more present, ask: "Who is feeling and sensing all of this? Who am I? Who is the one in relationship with this body and its sensations?"

Find out for real, in a way that satisfies you more than spiritual ideas, more than anything you have ever read or thought or heard or understood.[4] If you come up with something like "I am spirit," or "I am energy," ask yourself, "Where did this answer come from?" And, in so doing, muster the humility to recognize that it's just a thought, a cultural hand-me-down, not an essential truth.[5]

Our true Self can never reside in any definition. In trying to define ourselves through thought, we ultimately limit who and what we are. Tolle observes, "If you can be absolutely comfortable with not knowing who you are, then what's left is who you are—the Being(ness) behind the human, a field of pure potentiality rather than something that is already defined."[6]

The revelation here is that there is something essential that, as humans, we share with all that exists. That "something" is relationship! To have a human life or a plant life or an insect life or a molecular life or an atomic life is to exist in a Universe that is rife with relationship. Yes, relationship, is the primordial truth of all that exists; and learning to live in harmony with this essential truth hastens our awakening.[7]

Wrap-Up

> How can we be so poor as to define ourselves as an ego tied in a sack of skin? ... We are, whether we like it or not, permeable—physically, emotionally, spiritually, experientially—to our surroundings. I am the bluebirds and nuthatches that nest here each spring, and they, too, are me. Not metaphorically, but in all physical truth I am no more than the bond between us. I am only so beautiful as the character of my relationships, only so rich as I enrich those around me, only so alive as I enliven those I greet.
>
> —Derrick Jensen[8]

The essence of who we are has little to do with how our culture conditions us to see ourselves. We are not our names, not our possessions, not our beliefs, not our occupations, not our thoughts. These are certainly aspects of our social self but they have little to do with our essential self. Instead of living mostly as static "nouns," with names, genders and job titles, we have the potential to live more as active "verbs"—i.e., as energetic constellations continuously creating, relating, questioning, evolving, becoming!

A New Story of the Human Other

I am you and you are me.
—Thich Nhat Hanh[1]

Picture this: It's early morning and you are walking along a sidewalk, head down, lost in thought. Then, you look up and see a man walking toward you. He's about a hundred feet away. When you glance up a second time, he's just fifty feet away, close enough for you to confirm that you do not know him. Still, you could say "Hi," or at least offer a smile.

As the stranger gets closer, how do you feel? Peaceful? Curious? Anxious? And how do your feelings, whatever they might be, lead you to act? Do you make eye contact or not? Smile or not? Say "Good morning" or not?

In this common, every-day scenario, your feelings and responses will be linked to your beliefs—i.e., to your story—about the human "other." So, what is that story? You can dig into it right now by completing the open sentence "Other people are_____." Do this ten times, jotting down the first thing that come to mind in your journal.

Other people are _____. Other people are _____.

Other people are _____. Other people are _____.

Other people are _____. Other people are _____.

Other people are _____. Other people are _____.

Other people are _____. Other people are _____.

Your responses will reflect your beliefs about *other* people. As you read over them, put the letter "S" next to statements that create Separation between you and other people—e.g., statements that carry a judgment or that are fear-related.

Next, take all of your "S" statements and turn them inside out. For example, if you have a statement that reads "Other people are <u>greedy</u>," reverse it to read: "Other people are <u>generous</u>." Then open to the possibility that this opposite way of seeing other people could actually be as true or truer than your original statement. You could explore this alternative story by simply noting ways that "other people" have extended generosity, however small, to you within the past week.

Then, go a step further and call to mind a person who, in your experience, is just plain greedy through and through, and then challenge yourself to think of just one instance when you experienced that greedy person's generosity. Be patient. It may take a while for your heart to soften and open. As you persist, you may be surprised (as I have been) to uncover instances where you, yourself, have actually displayed the same unsavory behavior that you find so irksome in this other. Ahhh, the bittersweet joys of awakening!

One Human Family: I sometimes offer a challenge to my students by placing an assortment of snacks—e.g., grapes, nuts, carrots, chips, cookies, etc.—down the center of a long picnic table. Then, I give everyone a straight stick and two thick rubber bands, with the instruction to use the rubber bands to attach the stick to their right arm so that it remains rigid. Then, when everyone is ready, I invite them all to sit down at the picnic table and partake in the snacks, with the proviso that they can only use their right arm (the one they can't bend) to eat. Their other arm must be held behind their back at all times. Place yourself in this scenario. It's 4:30 in the afternoon and you are really hungry. What would you do? How would you feed yourself?

Upon hearing my instructions, some students groan, some laugh, others sit quietly, pondering. Everyone, in their own way, experiences the discomfort of being surrounded by enticing food without a socially acceptable way of enjoying it. Eventually, a few experiment by throwing bits of food into the air using their straight arm, hoping that something will land in their gaping mouths; others sheepishly put their lips to the table in attempts to vacuum up pieces of food.

What would you do? How might breaking a social norm transform this situation? Actually, it's pretty simple. All that's required is for somebody to extend their right (rigid) arm across the table and place a morsel of food in the mouth of the person across from them. Once this taboo is broken, everyone becomes free to feed one another! In this way, what is initially a hellish experience is transformed into a kind of "heaven on earth" with everyone experiencing the fun and joy that naturally arises when we extend a helping hand to each other.

Of course, this is a safe experiment with an expected result. So, perhaps you are thinking that while it's a nice and uplifting story, it isn't really a good reflection of the world at large. After all, rather than spontaneously extending kindness to each another, aren't most of us more concerned with taking care of ourselves? I was undecided on this question until I met Satish Kumar and heard his story of how he invited a group of people to join him on a two-year walk through a dozen countries, starting in India and continuing into Pakistan and beyond. They called their sojourn a "peace walk." Trekking from village to village, they took no money, nor did they carry any food, and yet they were walking through some of the most poverty-stricken regions of the world.

According to Kumar, the first thing they did upon arriving in a village was to give the villagers what they had—namely: their compassionate presence, their stories, their songs, and, perhaps most importantly, their genuine interest in the villagers' lives. It was natural—you might even say instinctual—for the villagers, upon receiving these gifts, to open up, offering generosity and hospitality in their own ways. In reflecting on his experience, Kumar wrote: "After walking through a dozen countries for over two years we have found that people are people everywhere. The natural instinct of people in all countries, cultures and religions is to be helpful. Hospitality is normal, hostility is exceptional."[2]

Wherever you happen to live, you could test Satish Kumar's thesis that people are *helpful* by nature. How? Just ask a friend to drop you off in a town close to where you live—but make it a town where everyone is a stranger to you. Before getting out of the car, give your phone and any money you might be carrying to your friend and ask him to come back to get you in two days.

Picture yourself there with no money, no phone and no clothes beyond what you are wearing. It's 10:00 in the morning. What would you do? What would you eat? Where would you sleep?

Though you lack money, you are able-bodied and alert; and your innate curiosity leads you to consider how you might be helpful to those around you. Are there doors you might open for people, bags you might carry, town flower beds you might weed, songs you might sing, trash you might pick up, compliments you might offer, children you might play with, good cheer you might extend to an elderly person, a compassionate ear that you might offer to a homeless person. As you consider all the possibilities, you become excited. And then for two wonderful days you trust in the goodness of the universe and become the one who gives—The Town Giver.

Our common calling as human beings is to become fully human, fully ourselves, fully one family. We are wired, evolutionarily, to look out for and care for one another. But, today, caught up in the narratives of Separation, Economism and Scarcity, we often miss out on the deep satisfaction that comes from extending helping hands to one another.

Designed for Relationship: Have you ever noticed how your body is biologically designed for relationship? Think about it: You are two-legged, standing upright with your heart exposed. Rather than being covered with a thick hide or a protective shell, you are soft-bodied, sensitive, designed to feel, experience and take in the world. Indeed, the more we humans have evolved, over hundreds of thousands of years, the more upright, open and available for relationship we have become.

You can experience this right now by spending some time gazing at a photograph that depicts family members in a moment of happiness. As you take in the faces of your smiling loved ones, notice how you too begin to smile and how this corresponds to a slight rise in your sense of well-being.

Psychologist and author Daniel Goldman reports that when we see a person expressing a strong emotion in a photograph, our own facial muscles and emotions begin to mirror that person's emotions, whatever they happen to be. This response is linked to a group of cells within our brains, dubbed "mirror neurons." Basically, when someone in your presence (or in a photograph) displays a certain emotion, your mirror neurons light up, leading you to experience—to a degree—that same emotion. For example, if I were to look at a scan of your brain while someone pricked your finger with a pin, I would see certain neurons lighting up in response to the pain you were feeling in your finger. What's truly extraordinary, though, is that if my own brain activity was being simultaneously displayed on another monitor, my mirror neurons would be lighting up in the same brain region as yours, even though I was only observing the pin prick!

Goldman describes this phenomenon saying: "Mirror neurons ensure that the moment someone sees an emotion expressed on your face, they will, at once, sense that same feeling within themselves. Our emotions are experienced, not merely by ourselves in isolation, but also by those around us—both covertly and openly."[3]

But perhaps we don't need the latest findings from brain science to tell us this. In this vein, anthropologist Wade Davis discovered that people of the Penan tribe of Borneo don't have any words to distinguish between he, she, or it, but, remarkably, they have six words for "we," the pronoun that reminds us that we are interconnected—that we inter-are.[4]

Greeting the Human Other: Imagine that you lived in a culture where people greeted one another by coming to a full stop, gazing into each other's eyes, and declaring, one at a time: "I am here to be seen," followed by the response, "I see you."

This is how the Zulu people of South Africa are said to greet one another.[5] They don't give a curt "Hi," or say "Whas-up!" Instead, they come to a full stop and declare, "I am here to be seen." Just six short words but consider their implications. Begin with the three words "I am here." That's quite a claim! After all, to declare "I am here" signifies that I am fully present, here, now, with you. Then come the words, "to be seen"—i.e., I am here, free of my masks and my defenses, so that you may see me for who I am. The response to this declaration is the three-word affirmation: "I see you"—i.e., I see you just as you are—breathing, eyes open, standing before me right now, absent any previous judgment or story I might have had about you.

Can you sense both the tenderness and power in this simple exchange? When I first heard about it, I was so intrigued that I invited a friend to try it with me. It felt odd—not bad, just different. The next time we ran into each other, we tried it again and though it continues to feel a bit awkward, we still share this greeting from time to time because we have discovered that by simply slowing down and declaring, "I am here to be seen," we create the conditions for something real and honest to happen between us. This is yet one more example of how awakening can be triggered, provided we break free from culturally scripted behaviors.

The End of Othering: When asked what he thought was the most important thing to teach our children, the Dalai Lama responded, "Teach them to love the insects." Yes, when he might have stressed the importance of compassion, justice, kindness, humility or responsibility, the Dalai Lama focused on loving the insects. Was he joking?

When I explore this with my students, I ask them to call out the first word that comes to mind when they hear the word "insect." Not surprisingly, many respond with things like: pest, gross, annoying, creepy, repellent. These responses echo the story of the entomologist who observed that whenever people brought him insects to identify, they arrived dead, usually with the explanation, "I didn't know what it was, so I killed it." Indeed, for many, it seems that insects are the ultimate "other."

But taking the Dali Lama's suggestion seriously, how might we come to love these beings that we so often fear? Such love may seem out of the question, yet we have all seen how love can transform fear. Think about the Civil Rights Movement or the end of Apartheid in South Africa. In these instances, and many others, somehow love prevailed over fear. And, in each case, it began with small gestures that invited fellowship. At first it seemed impossible, just as it may seem impossible that our world, one day, will be at peace—free of hatred, weapons, fear, greed and abuse. But it is possible. It can happen and it begins as we turn toward, rather than away from, each other and all that which we fear.

By way of example, imagine that I have just invited you (as I do my students) to hold a Madagascar Hissing Cockroach in the palm of your hand. Consider, further, that just the thought of having a cockroach roaming freely on your palm petrifies you. At the same time, you are smart enough to know that you weren't born with this fear; it has its origins in your social conditioning. For example, maybe it's the result of having witnessed as a child, an adult responding hysterically to the sight of a cockroach. But that was a long time ago and now you are determined to let go of this irrational fear.

When you signal that you are ready to finally confront your fear, I sit beside you, holding a female Madagascar Cockroach in my open palm. Gently touching her, I assure you that these beautiful creatures, encased in their lustrous bronze carapaces, don't bite or sting but, instead behave in ways that are gentle and peaceful.

After a long pause, you place your trembling hand, palm up, next to mine and watch as this amazing creature moves, very tentatively, antennae leading the way, onto your hand. You flinch, at first, but then you remember to breathe, slowly and deeply. In time, your hand stops shaking and your face transforms into a radiant smile. You have replaced fear with connection, separation with kinship.

Wrap Up

> In the Light of interbeing, peace and happiness in your daily
> life means peace and happiness in the world.
> —Thich Nhat Hanh[6]

We are connected, not just to each other, but to all sentient beings. As we each awaken to this story of our interbeingness, I foresee a day when we will greet one another, along with all the other beings that comprise Earth's family of life, with the words: "I am you and you are me," feeling deep in our bones the profound truth of this declaration.

A New Story of Earth

> I believe that a great deal of the lostness we feel as a culture
> is a result of how alienated from the natural world we've
> become. Not only are we disconnected from nature but
> anesthetized to the enormity of that loss. Many people don't
> even realize what is missing because they've never known
> it, but underneath our preoccupations with getting ahead
> and being accepted, there is a deep well of pain [that results
> from] our unbelonging to Earth herself.
>
> —Toko-pa Turner[1]

Our English language conventions condition us, in subtle and not-so-subtle ways, to experience ourselves as mostly separate from Earth. For example, have you ever noticed how, in English, we generally use a lowercase "e" when we write the word "earth"? Similarly, we also tend to insert the article "the" before the word, "earth." This really is a bit strange! After all, we don't refer to Venus as "the venus" or Mars "the mars." Instead, we write "Mars" and "Venus" with a capital M and a capital V, absent "the" in front. Placing "the" before Earth implies that we are here and *the* earth is out there, separate from us. Noting this, former pastor Michael Dowd observed, "To refer to the literal ground of our being, the source and substance of our life, as 'the earth' is to objectify our larger body. Such objectification encourages us to continue seeing earth as a resource for human consumption. On the other hand, by using the planet's proper name, we honor Earth's integrity as a creative, self-organizing system."[2]

Consider further that, in English, among all Earth's millions of life forms, only humans are signaled out for respect. Yes, any life form in the wild that is not human is generally referred to as an "it" in English. But animals and plants are not "it"s! Just like us they reproduce and they are gendered—there are male oaks and female oaks, male robins and female robins.[3]

"The arrogance of English," as college professor and author Robin Kimmerer points out, "is that the only way to be animate, to be worthy of respect and moral concern, is to be human."[4] This is significant, because referring to other beings as "it"s opens the door to disrespect. For example, "if a maple [tree] is an it, we can take up the chain saw. If a maple is a her, we think twice."[5] And it's no different in the case of the caterpillar who is stranded on the sidewalk: If we see an it laying there, we will just pass by, but if we see him or her, we just might be moved to help a fellow being back to safety. In this same vein, imagine going for a stroll in the woods with a friend and coming upon an animal track, and hearing your friend say, "Look! Someone passed this way." Some<u>one</u>, not some<u>thing</u>! I grant you that this might all seem like a bit of a stretch, but consider that this is because our language conventions have lead us to see the world as a collection of objects, rather than as a community of subjects.[6]

Part of awakening to what it means to be fully human means developing new ways of using language that underscore that we are each a part of—not a part from—Earth. Yes, we are all Earthlings—you, me, butterfly, bee, frog, ant, dandelion, spider and fern. This is our shared identity.

As we learn to speak in more inclusive and respectful ways, a day may come when we walk in the forest and realize that we are surrounded by a multitude of sentient beings—each alive, each unique, each an individual, all worthy of our respect. When this day arrives for you, imagine how much more alive and less lonely your world will be![7]

Earth as Mother: OK, it's one thing to be told that our most elemental identity is as *Earthlings*, but how might we cultivate this awareness so that we come to know and feel it in our bones? The obvious answer is that we could use our bodies—our eyes, our noses, our ears, our tongues, our skin—to connect with Earth, up close and visceral. But this "obvious" is not so easy! Indeed, as the following story attests, it takes humility, openness and curiosity to enter into an intimate relationship with Earth.

> Gerry [a white man] was walking down a sidewalk at midday in Washington, D.C., with his Native American friend from the Bureau of Indian Affairs. People were husslin' and busslin' along the sidewalk, and the sounds of honking horns and noisy car engines filled the air. In the middle of all the activity, Gerry's friend stopped and said, "Hey, listen … a cricket!"

"What?" said Gerry.

"Yeah, a cricket," said the Native American as he peered under a bush and located a trilling cricket.

"Wow," said Gerry. "How did you hear that with all this noise and traffic?"

"Oh," said the Native man, "This was the way I was raised ... what I have been taught to listen for." Then, he reached into his pocket and pulled out a handful of coins—nickels, quarters, dimes—and dropped them on the sidewalk. When this happened, all the pedestrians nearby stopped ... to listen.[8]

Because the white man in this story was unable to hear the cricket, the cricket didn't exist for him. It was different for the Native American: The cricket was a part of his world; he heard her calling and connected to her, experiencing her as a fellow Earthling.

How is it with you? Are you awake to Earth's call? Are you aware of how she nurtures you, akin to a human Mother? After all, it was Earth that birthed each of us into being—not metaphorically, but literally. You were born out of her insofar as every element in your body came from her; the water comprising seventy percent of your body is her water. It is her soil that grows the food that will be transformed into your blood, your bones, your muscle, your organs. All that nourishes, shelters and clothes you comes from her.

In this same vein, though we have all been conditioned to believe that we live on Earth, the truth is that we live in Earth. If you doubt this, just place your attention on your breath and then look up. The thin transparent band of air—of atmosphere—above you is the source of your every breath. Yes, Earth is above your head, as well below your feet. You live in Earth. We all do! And, just as Earth is our ever-giving Mother, so, too, we might recognize the Sun as our generative Father, endlessly offering us energy, light and warmth.

A Walk on the Wild Side: What might it be like to be deeply connected to Earth in the manner of the Native American man in the above story? To begin to find out, come on a walk with me. Rather than a pretend walk, make it the real thing. Yes, go outside and make your way to a nearby park or patch of forest. When you arrive, remove your shoes—those fabricated contrivances that separate your skin from the skin, the surface, of Earth. Then, step forward, noticing how, with each step, the living Earth is there, meeting the contours of your feet while, simultaneously, your feet press against her. Experience the textures underfoot, the sounds created with each footfall.

Slow down, now, as you consider that there's much more going on than meets your eyes. For example, there are tens of millions of microscopic organisms living in the soil where you are treading, and these beings are sensing you. Yes, wherever you walk, the creatures underfoot "know," with their particular sensitivities, of your presence.[9]

Consider, too, how, with each step, Earth is there to receive you, to hold you; there is nothing you need to do. It is the connecting force of gravity that is securing you to her. Pause to experience gravity for the wonder that it is—the primordial attraction between the body of Earth and the body that is you.

When the time seems right, find a seat on the ground, not on a chair, mind you, but on Earth. By sitting on the ground, you are reenacting what your human ancestors have been doing for thousands of generations. Indeed, sitting in chairs and sleeping in beds is a very new thing for humans, one that, while offering certain comforts, separates us from direct, visceral contact with Earth. With the inquisitiveness of a child, notice what it is like to have the base of your spine in direct contact with Earth—the literal ground of your being.[10] Then, behold all the greenness that surrounds you. You are looking at Earth's most fundamental adornment. Leaves, whether of herb or grass or tree, or alga or seaweed, are the foundation of Earth's fecundity on both land and sea. Without leaves there would be no photosynthesis, no us!

Notice, too, how you are being breathed. Yes, your body breathes you—12 inhalations each minute, 17,000 each day. As you quiet further, experience air "not as random gases ... but as an elixir generated by the numberless organisms that inhabit this world, all of us exchanging ingredients ... as we inhale and exhale ... all of us contributing to the composition of this phantasmagoric brew, circulating it steadily between us and nourishing ourselves on its magic, generating ourselves from its substance."[11]

By encountering Earth in this open, visceral and humble way, we begin to cultivate relationship. This includes coming to feel, in our depths, profound gratitude for all that Earth gives us. And along with this, recognizing that just as we need Earth, so, too, does Earth need us—needs our love, our commitment, and our respect so that she, too, might flourish.

To this last point, one of my past students, Curran Hunter, relates how she was able to come into loving relationship with Earth by befriending a tree. It happened during the Spring of her final semester at Penn State when a lovely oak, growing near her dorm, called to her. Curran picks up the story:

> As winter waned, my new Oak friend was slowly awakening—buds swelling, leaves unfurling, flowers opening.... And I was right there with her, similarly, awakening out of my own winter slumber. Every morning, regardless of the weather, I went to her, and while I had always known that trees change seasonally, I had never witnessed this, close up. Each day I experienced amazement and gratitude in her presence, and, in the end, I couldn't help falling in love with her. Indeed, I uttered some of my most heartfelt prayers under her shade, and I experienced some of my deepest reflections on her grounds. And, low and behold, as I witnessed her life force, I became aware of the growth and opening and softening that was beginning to happen within me.[12]

All Our Relations: It's one thing to accept, intellectually, that we are each a part of Earth, but quite another to live our lives in alignment with this fundamental truth. Here is a Native American teaching story that offers guidance:

> It came to pass one day, many moons ago, that the Great Spirit called together one representative from each of Earth's species. When all the representatives had assembled, the Great Spirit asked each one to step forward so that they might each declare their purpose for being. Deer went first, explaining that she was put on Earth to prune back the shrubs and to run lithely through the forest. Then came Earthworm who declared that his/her purpose was to enrich and aerate Earth's soils. Next, was Songbird who explained that her purpose was to dine on Earth's fruits, and in so doing, to disperse seeds over the land. And so it went, each species having utter clarity regarding their purpose, until at the very end, there was just one creature remaining who had not spoken. It was Human. Timidly he stepped forward, and after stammering for a time, ashamedly confessed that he did not know his purpose. This admission astonished the other creatures. Finally, the Great Spirit addressed Human with these words: "Don't you know, my beloved, that your purpose— the reason you are here—is to glory in the wonder of it all. Your purpose is to see and celebrate the miracle that is life and in so doing to dwell in gratitude and love for all that is!"[13]

The simple fact that we each have been born out of Earth—that we are a part of her—is unequivocal testimony that we each have a right to be here. We belong, we are worthy, and we are enough—just as we are! And how might we reciprocate for the gift of a human life? Just as this native story instructs: With gratitude and with compassion for each other and for all our relations. This is all that the world asks of us. This is what Earth is dreaming through us.

Wrap-Up

> There is nothing of me that is not Earth, no split instant of separateness, no particle that disunites me from my surroundings.... The rivers run through my veins, the winds blow in and out with my breath, the soil makes my flesh, the sun's heat smolders inside me ... the life of the Earth is my own life.
>
> —Richard Nelson[14]

In the end, what is Earth to you? Just scenery—i.e., a backdrop for your life? Or do you perceive Earth mostly as a bundle of resources and/or a depository for your waste? Or might it be that you are slowly awakening to the fact that you are, actually, an extension of Earth—i.e., that she is, in a very real sense, your larger body? The answer you give reflects your story, and as such, affects mightily how you perceive reality and experience the world, including how you experience your very own life.

A New Story of the Universe

> Just as the Milky Way is the universe in the form of a galaxy, and an orchid is the universe in the form of a flower, we are the universe in the form of a human. And every time we are drawn to look up into the night sky and reflect on the awesome beauty of the universe, we are actually the universe reflecting on itself.
>
> —B. Swimme and M.E. Tucker[1]

As highlighted in the preceding three stepping stones, the ways that we have been conditioned to see ourselves, each other, and Earth result in narratives (stories) that determine, in large part, how we live and experience our lives. The same holds true when it comes to our perceptions of the universe.

If you are like many people, the universe may be more of an abstraction, than a reality, to you. But consider that just as you are a part of Earth, so, too, are you a part of the Universe; and as such, your understanding of how the Universe came into being has the potential to expand your story of who you are and why you are here.

Time Traveling: Are you able to harness the power of your imagination to go back 100,000 years in time to the lives of your hunter-gatherer ancestors? These were men and women foraging for wild foods, congregating around nighttime fires, and telling stories of the harvest and the hunt. Now, how about going all the way back to ancient Africa, some seven million years ago, to envision those early ape-like people who are also a part of your lineage?

Incredibly, the story of our ancestry goes back even further. After all, we are mammals, and our mammalian ancestors—those first furry rodents—appeared on Earth more than 200 million years ago. And before that, around 400 million years ago, there were the first fish-like creatures that developed lungs, giving Life the capacity to move on to dry land. And long, long before that, several billion years back in time, the first single-celled organisms came into being, providing a template for the emergence of multi-cellular life in a multitude of forms—including our own human form.

But we're not quite there yet, because before there could be single-cell creatures, there had to be hydrogen and oxygen, the constituents of water—water, of course, being a fundamental necessity for ALL life. Indeed, our human bodies are 70 percent H_2O, making hydrogen the most abundant element, by far, in each of our bodies!

Now get this: All the hydrogen that now exists on Earth (and in the Universe) was created in the so-called Big Bang, 14 billion years ago, when the Universe burst into being out of seemingly nothingness.[2] Only at that time did the conditions exist for the creation of hydrogen! This means that the next time you take a drink of water, you will be taking in billions of hydrogen atoms that were created in the Big Bang and never again since. Upshot: The primary stuff of you—the most abundant element in your body—has been in existence since the beginning of time.

And, what about that atom of oxygen that completes each molecule of water? How did it come into being? The short answer is that Earth's oxygen originated in the alchemy of star death. To understand how this could be, first, note that stars have a finite life span. For example, our star, the Sun, came into being about five billion years ago, and it will continue shining for five billion more years before it fizzles out of existence.

As stars go, our sun is on the small side; but when really large stars die, they don't "fizzle out of existence," they explode, creating so-called supernovas. It is in the core of supernovas—and only there—that oxygen and the other essential elements for life (e.g., calcium, iron, potassium, nitrogen) are forged into being. When these elements are released in supernova explosions, they form nutrient-rich brews that eventually give rise to new stars and planets. This is how our sun and solar system, including Planet Earth, came into existence.

In other words, the hydrogen present in every cell of your body was created in the Big Bang some 14,000,000,000 years ago; and all the other elements in your body, including oxygen and carbon and nitrogen, were produced some 5,000,000,000 years ago in a supernova explosion that gave rise to our solar system.[3] In sum, the stuff of us has, literally, come forth through the generative creativity of the Universe. We are each made of star stuff—star dust! Stars, in a very real sense, form part of our ancestry.

Science and Religion: Though science and religion are often pitted against one another in modern culture, this need not be. Both scientists and theologians are seekers, united in their quest for meaning, understanding and wisdom. In this context, it is worth noting that both the scientific story of the Big Bang (as summarized above) and the story of Genesis in the Christian Bible begin in a similar fashion—i.e., with the flaring forth of light into the world—whether by God's hand (e.g., God said, "Let there be light," and there was light....[4]) or through the inexplicably mysterious flaring forth of light and energy in the Big Bang.

Rather than arguing about which story is right, what if there is truth in both stories? After all, the scientific pronouncement of the "The Big Bang" doesn't necessarily disprove the existence of God. It could just as easily be postulated that The Big Bang offers proof for God's existence. Joyce Keller explains it this way:

> All my life I've wanted to believe in God,
> gone to church, followed every spiritual teacher in town,
> meditated and prayed, attended 12-step programs,
> but still I often felt abandoned and alone in the Universe.
>
> All my life I've wanted to see the face of God.
> Is He really just a mean old man in the sky?
> Perhaps God is a chubby Buddha,
> or maybe the Dalai Lama, always laughing.
> Or is She a woman, the Tara, weeping pearl tears,
> the Virgin of Guadalupe, crowned with roses?
>
> All my life I've tried to solve that old mystery,
> Who are we? Where did we come from? Why are we here?
> Then one day I saw pictures sent back by the Hubble Telescope:
> Hot blue stars born out of the red glow of galaxies,
> a pulsating firestorm of fluorescent clouds,
> the obsidian sky of deep space.
> Spirals of comets, like swirling diamond necklaces.
> Black holes, exploding supernovas,
> a hundred thousand light-years away—endless, unimaginable.
> And I knew that, finally, I had seen the face of God.[5]

In this poem, rather than taking sides, Keller is occupying the fecund space of both/and. In this space, both religion and science can be seen as wisdom traditions with the capacity to expand human consciousness.[6]

One way to begin to bridge this divide is to substitute the word "Mysterium" for "God." This word, Mysterium, refers to something that is ultimately unfathomable, unreachable and beyond description.[7] Substituting Mysterium for God invites a posture of humility, curiosity and awe in the face of that which is, ultimately, unknowable. Rather than being mired in dualism—e.g., my God versus your God, or my God versus no God— the word Mysterium creates space for discovery, growth and common ground while allowing for the possibility that *both* religion *and* science have things to teach us about life's ultimate mysteries. With this expansion of perspective, the nature of God would no longer be something pinned down, static, black and white—but, instead, something dynamic, fluid, generative, soulful and ultimately unknowable.

In the spirit of awakening, I invite you to play with this idea.[8] If you are a Believer, how could the idea of God as Mysterium expand, rather than crimp, your understanding of the nature of the Divine? For example, what kind of God would fashion a Universe, such as ours, organized primarily by gravity, and therefore, grounded in love—i.e., in attraction, bonding, coupling and relationship? Similarly, what kind of Creator would fathom a Cosmos that is wondrous and mysterious beyond our wildest imaginings? Too, what kind of Creator would dream up a universe where destruction and chaos (think supernovas) lead to rebirth and transformation (think emergence of new solar systems)? Finally, what kind of Creator would manifest a universe that is not static but dynamic, in a constant and active process of moving toward more complexity, greater diversity and more intimacy?

Just as exploring the revelations imbued in the scientific story of creation could help Believers expand and deepen their understanding of the nature of God; the same could be true for agnostics or atheists insofar as the science-based story of creation also engenders wonder, awe and mystery.

For example, say you are an agnostic or an atheist at a time of Breakdown in your life—feeling confused and uncertain about how to go forward. You've sought advice from friends, examined the pros and cons and ifs and buts of your circumstances, but still you are lost and forlorn. In exasperation, you wander into the night, eventually making your way to a clearing on a hilltop.

Broken by your psychic burdens, you lie down and look up into the vastness of the night sky. Your familiarity with the scientific story of creation reminds you that you are not really looking up. After all, up is just a human construct; there is no up or down from the perspective of the universe. So, instead of experiencing yourself as looking up, you frame it so that you are looking down at the stars shimmering below you. At first you are surprised that you are not falling down into the dark abyss. You don't fall, of course, because Earth's embrace—her gravitational pull—holds you to her, allowing you to experience, for the first time in your life, gravity as a felt relationship.

As you surrender to Earth's embrace, all the heaviness and pain that you have been carrying lifts as you are momentarily enveloped in gratitude and serenity. Though you do not believe in prayer, you spontaneously enter into a call and response dialogue with the universe. This is certainly not like you, and, yet it feels right. Infused with humility, you have freed yourself from the ego's grip, letting go of your need to know and control your life's circumstances.

Wrap-Up

> The universe is composed of subjects to be communed with, not objects to be exploited. Everything has its own voice. Thunder and lightning and stars and planets, flowers, birds, animals, trees—all have voices, and they constitute a community of existence that is profoundly related.
> —Thomas Berry[9]

We are all Children of the Big Bang, Citizens of the Cosmos, Descendants of Stars. We each belong to the mysteries of swirling galaxies, the fecund forgings of supernovae, and the blazing light of passing comets. We are each a manifestation of the endlessly breathtaking and unfathomable Mysterium. May we each play our part in The Great Work[10] of personal and cultural transformation.

Healing

Breakdown Revisited

> The natural world is the larger sacred community to which we belong. To be alienated from this community is to become destitute in all that makes us human. To damage this community is to diminish our own existence.
> —Thomas Berry[1]

Recall, from Part II, the concept of Breakdown that was used to characterize times when our lives are no longer working—i.e., when we have lost our bearings, along with our sense of meaning and purpose. Now take a moment to bring to mind a time of breakdown in your own life. Maybe it was failing badly at something that was very important to you, or being rejected by a loved one, or suffering some form of debilitation as a result of a severe accident or sickness. Recall how you responded. Did you shut down and withdraw into yourself, or numb your pain with drugs or alcohol? Or, just maybe, rather than shutting down, you opened to the pain that inevitably accompanies life's breakdowns; and in so doing, your breakdown became a catalyst for awakening?

Breakdowns aren't limited to personal upheavals; they can also occur at a global scale. For more than half a century, scientists worldwide have been monitoring Earth's declining health, calling attention to breakdowns in Earth's atmosphere, oceans, forests, soils and more. The evidence is now unequivocal and mounting: We are debilitating Earth, making her sicker and sicker; and though we desperately need Earth for our survival, Earth really does not need us.

People from all walks of life are now openly acknowledging that our civilization may not survive the ecological crisis that now envelops us. In other words, life as we have come to understand and experience it may be ending. This is not alarmism so much as a candid assessment of where things stand. As lawyer and environmental advocate Gus Speth reminds us: "The only thing we have to do to be sure we will leave a ruined world for our children and our grandchildren is to do exactly what we are doing now."[2]

These sorts of frightening assessments could lead us to shut down and look away; but just as with personal breakdowns, we can choose to face the pain, using it as a catalyst for our own awakening.

Permission to Feel: It is by fearlessly giving ourselves permission to feel the heartbreak of these times that we awaken. Activist, author and ecopsychologist Joanna Macy expresses it this way:

> If we felt the pain of loss each time an ecosystem was destroyed, a species wiped out, or a child killed by war or starvation, we wouldn't be able to continue living the way we do. It would tear us apart inside. The losses continue because they are not registered, they aren't marked, they aren't seen as important. By choosing to honor the pain of loss rather than discounting it, we might begin to break the spell that numbs us to the dismantling of our world.[3]

Macy has spent many decades creating safe spaces—think of them as truth-telling circles—where people gather to give voice to their pain for the world.[4]

Imagine yourself in one of these circles now. You have joined with a dozen other people to give voice to the grief you feel for the broken state of the world using a time-tested model for authentic communication known as "Council." Your host welcomes you and introduces you to the Four Agreements of Council:

- Truthspeaking: Speak your truth from your heart—i.e., from your personal experience.
- Brevity: Say it once and be done—i.e., hearts speak few words.
- Spontaneity: Speak what arises as your truth in the moment— i.e., don't plan what to say.
- Deep Listening: Listen with an open, empathic heart, absent judgment.

After nodding your consent to these guidelines, you sit together in silence, gazing into the center of the circle, where you see an unlit candle that is surrounded by four objects: a large porcelain bowl, a thick stick, a cluster of dry leaves and a large stone. Each object has been chosen to evoke a distinct emotion: the dry leaves for feelings of sadness, the stout stick for the expression of anger, the cold stone for fear, and the empty bowl for acknowledging feelings of emptiness.

An elder moves to the center, lights the candle, and says, "This truth-telling circle is dedicated to the healing of the world." In the long silence that follows, you open to the emotions that arise as your gaze falls, in turn, on the hard stone, the empty bowl, the stout stick and the dry leaves.

Eventually, a young man moves to the middle of the circle and, cradling the bowl, speaks of the emptiness and hopelessness he feels: "I want to do something to stop the mess that we are in, but nothing I can do will make a difference; it's already too late." Then, abruptly, he grabs the thick stick and, shaking it fiercely, shouts: "We're fucked! WE'RE FUCKED…." When his anger subsides, the others respond with, "We hear you."

A bit later, a mother, holding her newborn daughter, moves to the center and picks up the cold stone. Then, holding her child so that all can see, says: "Look at this child. What will become of her? See her innocence, her goodness? This is the truth of each of us. This is the truth of Earth, our Mother." Then, she lays down the stone and clutching her child confides: "I am so afraid for my baby; she didn't ask for this broken world. Oh, God, why have we done this to her? Why are we doing this to each other? Why are we doing this to our precious Earth?"

Speaking in this bold way, we break free of the social conditioning that has taught us that emotions like sadness, anger, fear and emptiness should be avoided at all costs. The deeper truth, though, is that these hard emotions connect us to ourselves and to the preciousness of life. After all, our capacity to speak of the sadness we feel for Earth's wounds is rooted in our own embodied connection to Earth. It is the same with the anger we feel for the ongoing abuse of Earth. This anger signals our capacity to express and act passionately on behalf of Life. Similarly, the temerity to voice our fears reveals our capacity to trust in the power of truthspeaking as a means of tapping into our shared humanity. Even the emptiness symbolized by the bowl can be seen as an affirmation that something new and life-giving will emerge as we give ourselves permission to voice our pain.[5]

Making it Personal: You, yourself, can begin to engage in this process of putting words to your feelings about the state of the world. Here are four prompts that might help:

i. How would you voice your <u>sadness</u> for the deteriorating state of Earth if you were holding those dry, shriveled leaves in your hands?
ii. What words would you put to your <u>anger</u> for our human abuse of Earth if you were firmly grasping that thick stick?
iii. How would you speak of your <u>fear</u> for those alive today and for future generations, if you were holding that cold stone against your heart?
iv. What words would you conjure to express your <u>emptiness</u> and sense of helplessness if you were cradling that empty bowl in your lap?

Of course, it would be easy to pass over these prompts, but refusing to face the reality and heartbreak of these times, won't make either go away! Instead it will generate more numbness within us. But we don't need to go dead! It's not yet too late for us to heal ourselves and the world! This healing will begin as we summon the courage to feel and express our pain, standing to declare:

No! No more! Not on my watch!
I refuse to censor my heart's deep knowing because of fear!
I refuse to mask my pain for the world through mindless consumption!
I refuse to leave a broken world to future generations!
I refuse to remain silent!

You could begin to "come out" to yourself right now by fetching a stone, a stick, a bowl and dry leaves; and, then, as you cradle each, in turn, sit with the four questions (above), softening and opening to whatever arises. For example, if you are moved to weep or scream or moan or curse or rant or pound, trust that this is your body's deep knowing—deep intelligence—expressing itself. Trust, too, that by daring to behave in this radically human way, you will be creating the conditions to hasten your own awakening, while contributing to our collective liberation.

The Great Turning: That we are beginning to acknowledge and give voice to our collective pain for the world is a good sign, because it is our pain and heartbreak that will stir us to action and make us whole. Indeed, once we have a clear idea of the problems we are facing, we can begin to imagine and give form to the world for which our hearts are longing.[6]

And, so—given that you have now taken the time to sit with and examine your pain for the world—I ask you: How might you transform this pain into a New Story of what it means to be fully human in these heartbreaking times? Use the following open sentences as gateways into this question:

- In the New Story, humans everywhere will see and treat Earth with

  _____.

- In the New Story, humans will see and treat each other with _____

  _____.

- The principal purpose of humans in the New Story is to _____

  _____.

- The New Story is calling me to _____

  _____.

- One thing I can do today to hasten the emergence of the New Story is _____.

Your willingness to engage with these open sentences is indicative of your readiness to stand up and act in defense of life. If you stand, you won't be alone. There are now millions of people throughout the world who are finding their voices, as they stand and turn toward one another. Joanna Macy refers to this phenomenon as *The Great Turning*; and here is how Universalist Unitarian Minister Christine Fry describes it:

> You've asked me to tell you of The Great Turning, of how
> we saved the world from disaster. The answer is both
> simple and complex:
> We turned.
> For hundreds of years we had turned
> away as life on earth grew more precarious.
> We turned away from the homeless men on the streets,
> the stench from the river, the children orphaned in Iraq,
> the mothers dying of AIDS in Africa.
> We turned away because that is what we had been taught.
> To turn away, from the pain, from the hurt in another's eyes,
> from the drunken father or the friend betrayed.

Always we were told, in actions louder than words, to turn away, turn
     away.
And so we became a lonely people caught up in a world moving too
     quickly,
too mindlessly toward its own demise.
Until it seemed as if there was no safe place to turn.
No place, inside or out, that did not remind us of fear or terror,
despair and loss, anger and grief.
Yet one of those days someone did turn.
Turned to face the pain.
Turned to face the stranger.
Turned to look at the smoldering world
and hatred seething in too many eyes.
Turned to face himself, herself.
And then another turned.
And another. And another.
And as they wept, they took
each other's hands.
Until whole groups of people were turning.
Young and old, gay and straight. People
of all colors, all nations, all religions.
Turning not only to the pain and hurt
but to the beauty, gratitude and love.
Turning to one another with
forgiveness and a longing
for peace in their hearts.
At first the turning made people dizzy, even silly.
There were people standing to the side gawking, criticizing,
trying to knock the turners down.
But the people kept getting up, kept helping one
another to their feet. Their laughter and kindness brought others
into the turning circle until even the naysayers began to smile and sway.
As the people turned, they began to spin, reweaving the
web of life, mending the shocking tears, knitting it back
together with the colors of the earth, sewing on tiny
mirrors so the beauty of each person, each creature, each
plant, each life form might be seen and respected.
And as the people turned, as they spun
like the earth through the universe, the web wrapped
around them like a soft baby blanket, making it clear all
were loved, nothing separate.
And as this love reached into every crack and crevice, the
people began to wake and wonder, to breathe and give

thanks, to work and celebrate together.
And so the world was saved, but only as long as you, too,
sweet one, remember to turn.
        —Christine Fry[7]

This story of *The Great Turning* is already announcing that it's time to risk being open and vulnerable, time to stand together to acknowledge that our current pursuit of constant growth, never-ending consumption and ever-widening inequality is life-denying and heartbreakingly immoral.

Wrap-Up

The conditions in which we find ourselves are the conditions through which we must find our true selves and our genuine way of being in this world.... In the end, what we fear will not go away for it indicates what we must go through in order to awaken, become more genuine, and live more fully.
        —Michael Meade[8]

There is no doubt that, given enough time, Planet Earth will eventually recover from today's human-induced abuses; but the long-term prospects for our species are less certain. Like so many of Earth's other life forms, we too may soon become an "endangered species."

Still, we beseech you, Dear Reader: Never underestimate the power of standing up to declare your allegiance to LIFE. For it is through the courageous act of standing that we might heal both ourselves and the world.

If you have ever been at the curtain call of a theatrical performance, you've probably witnessed how the act of standing up can be electrifyingly transformative. Take a moment to imagine yourself there now: It's a packed house. The show has concluded, and the cast is being greeted with cheers. You too are clapping enthusiastically, ready to join in a standing ovation but, alas, no one is standing.

Though you want to stand, you are afraid of being judged by others, so you remain seated. Then, unexpectedly, your feelings of appreciation supersede your fear of standing out; and the next thing you know you are standing and turning to those around you, with unfiltered exuberance.

It feels so right, so honest, to be expressing yourself in this way. Then, to your surprise, you watch as several other people, close by, join you in standing. Then, simultaneously, virtually everyone in the theater is on their feet, roaring their appreciation.

Amazed, you ask yourself, "How did this happen? Did I cause it?" The answer is "yes!" All those who finally stood surely appreciated the performance, as you did, but they needed a nudge to stand. That's what you gave them. And this was possible because you allowed yourself to be moved by your feelings of gratitude.

May it be that we each summon the courage to stand and to join our heads, our hands, and our hearts in the creation of a world overflowing with gratitude not greed, humility not hubris and love not loathing.

It All Comes Down to Choice

I (co-author, Melissa) was conditioned to believe that my destiny in life would be the result of making good decisions. I was wrong. Here's my story.

"Do you want to try something?" Will asked. Then, he added, "Before you answer, I just want to warn you that this exercise could change everything. It did for me."

What do you say to something like that? Was I ready to have everything change? And what would that even mean? How could everything change just by trying some exercise with this person who was, essentially, a stranger?

"Yeah, let's do it," I heard myself answering.

Hearing my "Yeah," Will looked me in the eye and said, "Choose: chocolate or vanilla?"

Huh? What was he talking about?

Seeing that I was perplexed, Will simply nodded reassuringly and repeated, "Choose: chocolate or vanilla?"

His question made me think of ice cream so I answered, "Vanilla."

"Why did you choose vanilla?" he asked, a hint of a smile turning up the corners of his mouth.

"Because I like vanilla ice cream better than chocolate."

"Ok, so it was taste that was the deciding factor for you."

I answered back that I supposed that was true. He asked again, "Choose: chocolate or vanilla?" Chocolate was my answer this time, because it came first in the question.

"So, placement in the sentence was the deciding factor?"

Again, I confirmed this. My brain was working overtime, trying to come up with the point of this game, earnest in my desire to solve the puzzle. Deciphering the "deciding factor" seemed to be the key. But I couldn't see any holes, any ways that one answer was better than another. Randomly, I picked chocolate again, feeling rising exasperation. I justified my answer with the explanation that chocolate was a more interesting color than the white of vanilla. Will told me that "aesthetics" was my deciding factor. My confirmation allowed him to ask again:

"Choose: chocolate or vanilla?"

"Chocolate."

"Why?" he asked.

My exasperation turned into mild frustration, and, truthfully, I was at a loss for a good explanation, so I blurted out, "Because I have to pick one, it seems."

"Ah," he said. "Take that a little further."

"Chocolate, because…" I trailed off, still not really sure where I was going with this. Taking a deep breath, I sat for a moment, and in the stillness something just clicked. "Because I <u>choose</u> chocolate."

"Yes," he confirmed, "It is the fact that you <u>CHOOSE</u> it that is important, not what you chose or why you picked it."

Something in my expression must have told him that I hadn't fully grasped the point of this exercise, so Will asked, "Do you know the difference between 'choosing' something and 'deciding' on something?"

I admitted that I didn't.

"Well, 'decide' comes from Latin, meaning 'to cut off or to kill' like the 'cide' in 'pesticide' or 'homicide'; something is eliminated. Better yet, think of it this way…." Will reached out, arranging three coffee mugs into a line on the table.

"Now, suppose I were to ask you to take one of these three mugs. In a decision, you have three options. You eliminate one," He moved one cup away. "Then another," He removed a second cup, "and you are left with your decision. In this example, you are left to make the most of the one cup that remains."

"So, really, how is that any different than choosing?" I asked.

"Because in choosing," Will placed the three cups back in a line on the table before me, "you deliberate, consider your options, then simply pick the one you want with all your being, without eliminating the others. You take it, not because it's left over, but because you WANT it. You see, in our lives, it's all about the way in which we show up."

That was it. I got it, really got it. I had been offered a job recently and had taken it. I had other options, and after weighing the pros and cons of each, I made my decision. In other words, I didn't CHOOSE to take this job. Instead, I eliminated the various alternatives, one by one, and decided to take what was left.

When I told people about my new job, I received impressed nods. They said that my job seemed amazing and important. How wonderful for me. How I must love the flexibility, the freedom. How young I was to have such a job. Yet, I didn't feel important, empowered, or even particularly happy. If the work was so important, why did I feel rather empty about it and disconnected from the whole thing? Because I hadn't chosen it! It wasn't my passion or my vision; I was working to bring someone else's dream to fruition.

This prompted me to review my life, noticing how I felt at times when I had chosen things, compared to when I had decided upon things. Doing so, it was apparent that the difference was, to use Will's words, in how I showed up. When I chose something, I "showed up" filled with commitment, excitement, and energy. Even things that would ordinarily sound boring, hard or painful, became compelling, even fun; those were rich, full experiences for me. And the reverse was true for the things I had done based on decisions; I often experienced those things as pretty much lifeless and underwhelming.

Yet still, I had, for the most part, continued to live my life deciding and then making the best of what I had. The gift that Will gave me in this exercise was a very simple—though by no means easy—realization: If I really wanted to live my life, I must choose something, and it didn't matter at all what! The important thing was to choose, and then commit.

Describing his personal "a-ha" moment around the power of choice, Will shared the following story with me:

> My wife, Heather, chose our daughter, Fern. You see, Fern is one of our three children, and she has Down Syndrome. Heather has done an exceptional job as Fern's parent, but I have struggled. In fact, it was only when I did this "Chocolate-Vanilla" exercise at a Landmark Forum Workshop that I realized that while Heather had truly chosen Fern, I had not! When I shared this realization with Heather, she held me in her arms, and I cried and cried. Heather already knew that I had not chosen to be a father to Fern. And yet I could not hear her. I mean, I was trying so damn hard to be Fern's father, giving it all I had. Or so I thought. But I had not chosen Fern; rather I had decided to be a good father, to accept her, to do all the right things like get down on my knees and give her a hug when I came home from work. But, oh my, now

I know what a difference <u>choice</u> makes, how it eradicates blame and victimhood, making room for unconditional love.[1]

Like Will, I too realized that I had not chosen that new job I mentioned earlier, but instead, had made a decision to simply accept it. Choice finally entered in when I *chose* to quit that job because I knew, in my gut, that it wasn't right for me. With this "no," I was choosing to say "yes" to myself, "yes" to trusting my intuition, and "yes" to embracing the unknown. As for Will, he chose to say "yes" to Fern—to commit to Fern, his own flesh and blood, from the core of his being. In both cases, our choices were profoundly liberating.

Choosing to Awaken: Awakening is not a decision based on pros and cons; it's a choice that arises from the core of our being. When we forthrightly choose a life path, we do so cognizant of the challenges and hardships and sacrifices that this will bring. We manifest our choice as we choose to show up, committed, with a full-throated YES to life. In this way, we are available to be cracked open, expanded, changed, transformed.

And, as Will's story with his daughter, Fern, exemplifies, even if you are attempting to make the most of something, or working with the dregs of a decision, it's never too late to own your decision, by reframing it as something that you actively choose. Then, everything that follows—your demeanor, your actions, your sorrows and joys, and, especially, your ability to be transformed—will emerge from that choice.

However, as I have found, it can be just as important to choose to say "no" to a decision and chart a new path. Now, two years after my own choice to quit that job I can say that it was right because it flowed from my heart and rose from my core. And it wasn't easy! It meant giving up daily routines, proximity to loved ones, and financial security. It also required vulnerability, because I had to accept possible failure and the criticism of others. Frankly, it felt, and still sometimes feels, like cracking open my ribs to reveal my heart; it would be safer to keep my heart hidden, because then it could never be shattered. But I am done with that. It is time for me to remove the shackles, time to surrender to the pull of destiny.

Remove the Shackles[2]

It is time to remove
the shackles.

The angel at your left ear finally reports:

"The bindings have reached their expiration date."

Free your Self

You are not the property of others,
of culture,
of dogma,
of your limiting beliefs and fears.

Stop volunteering
to wilt in the dungeon.

Let the gallows be nothing
more than a guano-encrusted pigeon perch.

Give the heavy, cold chains
that have weighed you down
back to the wounded-child-Master
link by link,
like prayer beads
intended for a long meditation
on compassion.

Refrain from thrashing
yourself
with shame
for where you have been.

Instead,
release yourself to live,
from this moment forward,
in communion with
empathy and joy.

Turn towards the
tens of millions still bodily
enslaved
and so many more
indentured in soul.

Become an abolitionist
of what no longer serves.

I know,

You now know
how to set Humanity free.

                    —Jamie Reaser

Wrap-Up

Destiny is not a matter of chance; it is a matter of choice. It
is not a thing to be waited for.
—William Jennings Bryan[3]

Recall the statement, "What we believe, we become," that was introduced in Part I of this book. Now, consider that this statement describes
the operating system of our lives. Yes, it is our beliefs, more than anything else, that determine our lives, our destinies. And for those seeking
to awaken, there is an important corollary, namely: We have the freedom,
if we take it, to CHOOSE our beliefs! And by choosing our beliefs, we
choose the values, ideals and principles for which we stand and live by.
Ultimately, it is through our choices that we gain the power to show up
in the world as our unique, one-of-a-kind, precious selves—and this is all
the world asks...

Coda
Personal and Cultural Transformation

Recall, now, the story from the Introduction to Part V, about a powerful Wizard who, because he had been wronged in the past, poisoned the Kingdom's well with a secret potion that drove everyone mad. The only people who were spared from insanity were the King and Queen because they happened to have a private well from which they drank.

As the story goes, when the King discovered that his people had all gone crazy, he began to issue edicts to keep them safe; but because his subjects were truly insane, they concluded that it was the King who was crazy and marched on his castle, demanding that he step down.

Watching as the commoners approached the castle, the Queen convinced the King that to stay in power, their only option was to drink from the poisoned well and, in so doing, prove that they were just like everyone else and, therefore, fit to rule.

This is precisely what they did, and upon drinking the poisoned water, they, too, became mad. As such, they were able to communicate in ways that made sense to their subjects. Then, believing that the King and Queen had finally come to their senses, the people allowed them to remain on the throne. But things got worse rather than better. Mired in insanity, the Kingdom became more and more plagued by anger, hatred, chaos, hunger and disease until it finally imploded on itself.

This could be what lies in store for us, too. But another outcome is possible! In this spirit, Melissa has transformed the ending of the Poison Well story. In the new version, rather than enjoining the King to join their subjects in insanity by drinking from the poison well, the Queen caught the King's arm and suggested, "Let us step down as the people want. This way we can travel throughout the kingdom and figure out what's causing the madness and how we might bring our people back to sanity."

The King agreed and, under the cover of night, dressed as commoners, the royal couple left the castle in a horse-drawn wagon filled with water from their private well. Together, they wandered for many months hoping to find at least one person who wasn't crazy. Finally, in a remote corner of the Kingdom, they came to a house made of stone that had its own well. It turned out to be the home of the Wizard!

When they knocked on his door, he was furious to discover that his potion had not affected them, and he ordered them to go away and leave him alone. But the couple refused to leave because it was clear that this man had not lost his senses and, therefore, might offer them a clue as to what was behind all the madness.

The royal couple stayed close to the Wizard over the course of many long months, assisting him in his garden, sharing meals with him, and, in general, helping him appreciate how good it feels to live in community with people who take care of each other. They hoped that through their deepening connection, the Wizard might share what, if anything, he knew about the Kingdom's madness.

And their plan worked! Eventually, a day came when the Wizard, deeply moved by the compassion of the King and Queen, confessed that he was the one who poisoned the Kingdom's well, causing the epidemic of insanity. The royal couple, listening with open hearts, was touched by the Wizard's confession. At the end, in a moment of profound vulnerability, the Wizard went on to confide that his reason for inflicting insanity on others was because he had been miserable, having lost his sense of meaning and purpose in life.

Seeking redemption, the Wizard resolved to create a new potion with the power to reverse the insanity. True to his word, he put this elixir in the Kingdom's well and soon, everyone's sanity was restored. Once they were in their right minds again, the people welcomed the King and Queen back to the castle, where they governed in peace until the end of their days.

What's different in Melissa's revised version of the story is the choices made by the King and Queen. Rather than conforming by joining their subjects in insanity, as occurred in the original story, they chose to say "no" to the status quo—i.e., "no" to becoming insane like everyone else in the Kingdom. Then, they surrendered their royal trappings and wandered in search of a cure for the insanity epidemic. And when they finally located the broken-down Wizard, they chose to treat him, not as a villain, but instead as an embodiment of the disconnection and pain that, in some measure, lies within each of us. As such, they realized that the cure for the wizard's suffering wasn't condemnation, but compassion. Ultimately, it was their capacity for unconditional love that brought redemption to the Wizard and transformation to the entire Kingdom.

There is an obvious parallel between this fable about a kingdom made insane by a poison potion and the strife and alienation that now plague humankind, the world over. Indeed, we have now reached a point where our population has become so large, our military weaponry so lethal, our environmental insults so devastating and our greed, arrogance and ignorance so rampant that our long-term survival as a species is now in the balance. It is our life-denying beliefs/stories grounded in separation, entitlement and fear that are poisoning our minds and hearts, while also poisoning our Mother, Earth.

Is redemption and transformation still possible? Will we come back to our right minds? Do we care enough? Do we have enough courage, enough love?

Epilogue

The deepest human resources tend to awaken amidst the greatest human disasters.

—Michael Meade[1]

"Mohini" was the name given to a regal white tiger who once lived at the National Zoo in Washington, D.C. For much of her life, Mohini was locked away in a standard 12 × 12-foot cage, where she paced back and forth, relentlessly. But, then, one day the zoo staff decided they wanted something better for Mohini and set about creating an outdoor park for her, complete with hills and trees and a pond. However, when Mohini was released into this new setting, she retreated to a secluded corner of the compound, where she spent the rest of her life pacing back and forth until she had worn an area, 12 × 12 feet, bare of grass.

Just like Mohini, we have been born into a story that cages us in, telling us what to believe and how to act. Tara Brach, who tells Mohini's story, laments "Perhaps the biggest tragedy in our lives is that freedom is possible, yet we can pass our years trapped in the same old patterns; and then, like Mohini, we grow incapable of accessing the freedom and peace that are our birthright."[2]

As a college teacher, I note that my students are aware of the wounds and pain of our times; and when I ask them to tell me about the world they long for, they often speak forthrightly saying things like:

- I want a world where there are no weapons, no wars, no hatred.
- I want a world where children are cherished and nurtured and where elders are respected.
- I want a world where everyone is "family," and where people share rather than hoard.
- I want a world free of rushing, where we take time for play and art and friendship.

What's heartbreaking, however, is how students respond to the follow-up question—"Do you believe that your vision for this more beautiful world

237

is achievable?" Here, most admit to despair having, in some measure, lost their faith in humankind and in the future.

When I hear their lament that "there is nothing one person can do" I sometimes ask, "How does this belief serve you?" This provocation usually makes it clear that saying "there is nothing I can do" gets us off the hook, freeing us from any responsibility to act.

Should this "learned helplessness" continue to spread, it may well spell our death warrant as a species, because we have now come to a point where we must act responsibly or perish—must evolve or die!

Indeed, we have entered what scientists call the Anthropocene, a new era in Earth's history where our species, *Homo sapiens*, has grown so mighty that we dominate Earth's biology and geological cycles, holding in our hands the power to upend the biosphere.

This is a bottleneck moment. We can take the known path, continuing to be passive spectators caught in the soulless, life-denying stories of Economism and Separation or we can choose to turn toward each other and toward Earth, summoning the audacity to co-create a new story in the service of life, wholeness and healing.

I place my faith in humankind, choosing to believe that all the pain and suffering that separates us from each other and from life, itself, is the precise catalyst that we now need to grow beyond our adolescence as a species and to rise up and make manifest the goodness that lies at the heart of the human spirit. In her poem, "The Rising Times,"[3] Jamie Reaser provides these words of encouragement:

> These are the rising times, the rising
>   of the sweet potency within your Soul.
> The rising of humanity
> to meet its greatest potential.
>
> You know it.
> You feel it.
> Deep within your root,
> there is a quivering.
> It's true.
>
> It's that uncertainty.
> It's that chaos.
> It's that which you fear
> will shake you to your core.
>
> Bless you,

I hope it will.

These are the rising times.
Let your authentic power rise.
Let your voice fly on
impassioned thermals,
high,
like a hawk kettling amidst the gods.

These are the rising times.
Stand up for what you believe in.
Stand up for those who have
been beaten down,
whatever their creed or form.

Stand up because humans are
not designed to crawl indefinitely,

And now is the time.

These are the rising times.

These are the rising times.
Raise your arms high above your head.
Look up.
You're a vast being in a vast universe.
How lucky you are to be here now.
Be here now.

These are the rising times.

Glory to the phoenix for
teaching us that ashes are not
an end point,
but a bed for consummating that
which is destined to be reborn.
Believe in the heat and glow.

These are the rising times—
and I'll stand beside you
as we see these times through.
Standing together—
that's all She has ever wanted for us.

Stand up and stand together.
It's really that simple for us
to become fully human.
The Sun has been showing us how

every morning,
and the Moon, every night—
Rising…

Did you realize?

These are the rising times.
                              —Jamie Reaser

In this final poem, Reaser is offering each of us a new way of imagining our future. On the one hand, we could stay put—stuck in the stagnant and limiting mindsets of *economism*, *separation* and *not-enoughness*. On the other hand, we could choose to turn toward each other, with the shared mission of co-creating a world of peace and love and harmony that is humanity's birthright and highest calling.

Which will it be for you? You could close this book and return to your previous life, untouched. But, instead, what if you were to stand up and embrace your one-and-only life with passion and purpose? We hope that you chose the latter so that you can continue to walk with us and many others along the ever-unfolding path of awakening.

Acknowledgments

We begin by offering our gratitude to a group of contemporary writers who have served as our teachers insofar as their insights have affected the content, as well as the ethos, of this book. So it is, that we bow deeply to: Joanna Macy, Phillip Shepherd, Byron Katie, Bill Plotkin, Eckhart Tolle, Joseph Campbell, Wendell Berry, Michael Meade, and Parker Palmer.

The initial impetus for writing this book grew from my [Uhl] work with students at Penn State over the past three decades. So, to the thousands of young people that I have had the joy of teaching and working with, I say "Thank you"; your impact is scribed into each page of this book.

Together, we offer a special *shoutout* to the following students who generously took time to comment on early drafts of this book's thirty-one stepping stones: Chloe DeOnna, Erin Fackenthal, Samantha Kaup, Katie Thomas, Sarah Hammaker, Kirsten O'Hanlon, Brandon Valentin, Courtney Zacherl, Alexa Frumer, Morgan Leap, Alex Liney, Nina Fischetti, and Gaby Bedeian.

We also wish to offer a special acknowledgment to Tressa J. Gibbard, for offering a thorough, no-holds barred critique of the book's first draft. Similarly, our appreciation goes to Johanna Jackson, who took the time to both engage with and critique many of the book's practices and exercises; and to Greg Lankenau, Matt McNees, Steven Lachman, Tim Dougherty, Peter Yu, Bill Zimmerman, Helen Mogford, and Webb Cam, we thank you for your enormously helpful reviews of the book's first draft.

We are also indebted to Rachel Thor for the acuity with which she rounded and smoothed out the book's rough edges, patiently calling attention to text passages that required rewriting, while also contributing material containing her own hard-earned insights.

Others who have contributed personal stories to this book's contents include Curran Hunter, Jamie Quail, Christy Carfagno, Annamarie DiRaddo, Haley Hoch, Antonia Bartolomeo, Kaitlyn Spangler, Johanna Jackson, Christine Fry, and Joyce Keller. Thank you one and all.

We also wish to extend a robust bow of gratitude to Jamie Reaser, who generously gave us permission to weave six of her extraordinary poems into the larger story that is this book.

Beyond this, we acknowledge Molly Haight and Curran Hunter for their skillful editing assistance.

Finally, there are those dear to our hearts who have played unique roles in each of our individual journeys of awakening. So it is that I (Christopher) wish to offer a belated bow of gratitude to my deceased parents (Vince and Fran) who planted and nurtured the seeds of awakening in me, starting in my teen years and extending through my thirties. Indeed, it was their unwavering trust in me that provided me with the assurance that I belonged and that I was enough and that my life mattered.

In a related vein, Melissa is eternally grateful to her parents, Lynda and Stephen, for their support, in all its shapes and forms, throughout the process of writing this book. Beyond the hundreds of times she made them read through chapters, listen to prose, or talk ideas through with her, their steady support of her life choices, and their overall emotional and financial support, were essential to her part in this endeavor.

Lastly, we offer thanks to: Anne Depue, our agent, for her skillful coaching and to Natalie Foreman and Lisa Camp at McFarland for believing in this project and guiding us through the publication process.

Chapter Notes

Prologue

1. Pema Chödrön, *Start Where You are: A Guide to Compassionate Living* (Boston: Shambhala Publications, 2004) 1.

Asleep or Awake?

1. Stephen Gillian and Robert Dilts, *The Hero's Journey: A Voyage to Self-Discovery* (Bethel, CT: Crown Publishing Company, 2009) 1.
2. Inspired by Natalie Goldberg, *Writing Down the Bones* (Boston: Shambhala Publications, 1986).
3. https://en.wikiquote.org/wiki/Martha_Graham
4. https://slate.com/culture/2011/06/-part-4-walking-to-walden-isn-t-enough.html

What We Believe We Become

1. Text in brackets has been paraphrased.
2. Jean Liedloff, *The Continuum Concept: In Search of Happiness Lost* (New York: Addison-Wesley Publishing Company, 1977) 10.
3. Bruce H. Lipton, *The Biology of Belief* (Carlsbad, CA: Hay House Inc., 2005) 133–134.
4. C.J. Bruce Moseley, M.D., Kimberly O'Malley, Ph.D., Nancy J. Petersen, Ph.D., Terri J. Menke, Ph.D., Baruch A. Brody, Ph.D., David H. Kuykendall, Ph.D., John C. Hollingsworth, Dr. P. H., Carol M. Ashton, M.D., M.P.H., and Nelda P. Wray, M.D., M.P.H., "A Controlled Trial of Arthroscopic Surgery for Osteoarthritis of the Knee," *The New England Journal of Medicine*, July 11, 2002, Volume 347, no. 2: 81–88.
5. This exploration of limiting beliefs is inspired by Byron Katie's book, *Loving What Is: Four Questions that Can Change Your Life* (New York: Three Rivers Press, 2002).
6. https://www.goodreads.com/author/quotes/2782.Viktor_E_Frankl

Questions Rather Than Answers

1. https://en.wikipedia.org/wiki/The_unexamined_life_is_not_worth_living
2. Tobin Hart, *From Information to Transformation: Education for the Evolution of Consciousness* (New York: Peter Lang, 2007) 131.
3. R.M. Rilke, *Letters to a Young Poet*, translated by M.D Herter (New York: Norton, 1993).
4. http://www.weegeesachtjen.com/2014/01/a-100-questions-an-exercise-in-self-reflection/
5. One of my students, in reflecting on his experience with this exercise, wrote: "That whole writing 100-questions thing… I complained about that to my friends, but when I sat down and actually did it, I was shocked at how much came out."
6. Amanda Lang, *The Power of Why* (New York: Harper Collins, 2010).
7. *Ibid.*, Lang, 36.
8. Derrick Jensen, *Walking on Water: Reading, Writing and Revolution* (Vermont: White River Junction, 2004).
9. Neil Postman and Charles Weingartner, *Teaching as a Subversive Activity* (New York: Delta Publishing, 1969) 23.

Education for What?

1. David McCullough, Jr., *You are Not so Special and Other Encouragements* (New York:HarperCollins, 2014).
2. https://www.youtube.com/watch?v=9M4tdMsg3ts

3. Donald Finkel, *Teaching with Your Mouth Shut* (Portsmouth, NH: Boynton/Cook Publishers, 2000) 7.

4. Matt Hern, *Field Day: Getting Society Out of School* (Vancouver, BC: New Star Books, 2003) 65.

5. Portions of the Sudbury School story appear in: Christopher Uhl with Dana L. Stuchul, *Teaching as if Life Matters: The Promise of a New Education Culture* (Baltimore: Johns Hopkins Press, 2011) 11.

6. Daniel Greenberg, *Free at Last: The Sudbury Valley School* (Framingham, MA: Sudbury Valley School Press, 1987) 15.

7. *Ibid.*,16–17.

8. For an excellent overview of the research on Sudbury School see: Peter Gray, *Free to Learn* (New York: Basic Books, 2013).

9. https://www.goodreads.com/quotes/-671411-whatever-an-education-is-it-should-make-you-a-unique

Truthspeaking as a Catalyst for Awakening

1. https://www.brainyquote.com/quotes/james_e_faust_621206

2. Tamarack Song, *Sacred Speech: The Way of Truthspeaking* (Three Lakes, WI: Teaching Drum Outdoor School, 2004).

3. This manner of speaking has been dubbed "non-violent communication" and has been used successfully in conflict situations, including war, to help move through hostility to understanding. For a full explanation of this practice see: Marshall Rosenberg, *Nonviolent Communication: A Language of Compassion* (Encintas, CA, PuddleDancer Press, 1999).

4. https://www.azquotes.com/author/-15512-Cornel_West

The Story that Lives Us

1. The ideas in this stepping stone are also explored in my book *Developing Ecological Consciousness: Becoming Fully Human* (Lanham, MD: Rowman and Littlefield, 2020).

2. Quoted in Sabrina Hassumani, S. Rushdie: *A Postmodern Reading of his Major Works* (Cranbury, NJ: Associated University Presses, 2002) 104.

3. Robin Wall Kimmerer, *Braiding Sweetgrass: Indigenous Wisdom, Scientific Knowledge, and the Teachings of Plants* (Minneapolis, MN: Milkweed Editions, 2013) 17.

4. Daniel Quinn, *Ishmael* (New York: Bantam, Turner, 1992) 35–36.

5. A similar version of this thought experiment is recounted in my book *Developing Ecological Consciousness: The End of Separation* (New York: Rowman and Littlefield, 2013) 182–187.

6. Economism is a term that is sometimes used in critiques of capitalist economics to point to the social and psychic damage that occurs when all of life's richness, wonder and complexity is reduced to economic dimensions. See: https://en.wikipedia.org/wiki/Economism

7. https://www. america.org/explore/-research-publications/an-economy-for-the-1/

8. https://www.thoughtco.com/is-burning-money-illegal-3367953

9. https://www.theatlantic.com/education/archive/2015/06/in-defense-of-a-try-hard-generation/394535/

10. Herman Daily, *From Uneconomic Growth to a Steady-State Economy* (Northampton, MA: Edward Elgar Publishing, 2014); also see: https://steadystate.org/wp-content/uploads/CASSE_Brief_SSE.pdf

11. Thomas Berry, *The Dream of the Earth* (San Francisco: Sierra Club Books, 1988) 123–124.

Coda: Waking Up

1. https://www.goodreads.com/quotes/-7625719-no-one-can-build-you-the-bridge-on-which-you

Breakdown as a Catalyst for Self-Discovery

1. http://boardofwisdom.com/togo/Quotes/ShowQuote?msgid=599045#.-WVFjPD-XK0c

2. If you find that you have answered "no" to most of these questions, you might see this as an opportunity to be fully hon-

est with yourself (See Truthspeaking, Part I) by pausing to ask yourself questions like: What growth opportunity am I avoiding in my life? What am I afraid of? What's a door that I am reluctant to open? When my friend and colleague, Rachel Thor, asks these kinds of questions of herself, she notes: "I find that the answer is usually the very first thought or image that comes to my mind! So, the challenge for me is to stay with what first arises."

3. Bill Plotkin, *Soulcraft: Crossing into the Mysteries of Nature and Psyche* (Novato, CA: New World Library, 2003) 62.

4. *Ibid.*, 62–63.

5. *Ibid.*, 63.

6. Jamie Reaser, *Note to Self: Poems for Changing the World from the Inside Out* (Danvers, MA: Hireath Press, 2011) 4–6.

7. Martha Beck, *Finding Your Own North Star: Claiming the Life You Were Meant to Live* (New York: Three Rivers Press, 2001).

8. Michael Meade, *Fate and Destiny: The Two Agreements of the Soul* (Seattle: GreenFire Press, 2010) 155.

Rites of Passage as Catalysts for Awakening

1. Dan Millman, https://www.optimize.me/quotes/dan-millman/18631-every-positive-change-every-jump-to-a-h/

2. Michael Meade, *Why the World Doesn't End: Tales of Renewal in Times of Loss* (Seattle, WA: GreenFire Press, 2012).

3. This event was part of a three-day rite of passage called "The Crossings: Marking the Move to Manhood" organized by the Men's Covenant Group of the State College Presbyterian Church and inspired, in part, by the work of Richard Rohr (https://www.illuman.org/mens-rites-of-passage/).

4. Inspired in part by Bill Plotkin, *Soulcraft: Crossing into the Mysteries of Nature and Psyche* (Novato, CA: New World Library, 2003).

5. Paulo Coelho, "Closing Cycles" http://paulocoelhoblog.com/2016/12/27/-closing-cycles/

Success from the Inside Out

1. https://en.wikiquote.org/wiki/Howard_Thurman

2. Naomi Remen, "The Recovery of the Sacred," *In Context*, no. 39, 1994) 29.

3. https://www.ramdass.org/zumbach-the-tailor/

4. http://www.wordtrade.com/religion/worldreligion/amiramdassR.htm

5. For a fuller elaboration, see: Christopher Uhl and Dana L. Stuchul, *Teaching as if Life Matters* (Baltimore, MD: Johns Hopkins Press, 2011).

6. David Orr, *Earth in Mind* (Washington D.C.: Island Press, 1994) 12.

The Seed in Each of Us

1. Michael Meade, *Fate and Destiny: The Two Agreements of the Soul* (Seattle: Mosaic Multicultural Foundation, 2010) 106.

2. Sobonfu Some, *The Spirit of Intimacy: Ancient African Teachings in the Ways of Relationships* (New York: Harper, 1997) 56.

3. See Part I, steppingstone, "Education for What?"

4. https://www.britannica.com/topic/tabula-rasa

5. David McCullough, Jr., *You Are Not So Special and Other Encouragements* (New York: Harper Collins, 2014) 5.

6. *Ibid.*, 5

7. Bo Lozoff, *It's a Meaningful Life: It Just Takes Practice* (New York: Penguin Putnam Inc., 2000) 144–5.

8. *Ibid.*, 145.

9. David Whyte, *Crossing the Unknown Sea: Work as a Pilgrimage of Identity* (New York: Riverhead Books, 2001) 70–71.

10. Jake's website: http://www.corvuesignbuild.com/.

11. Puanani Burgess, "Blessings Revealed," *YES! A Journal of Positive Futures*, Winter 2009.

12. James Hillman, *The Soul's Code: In Search of Character and Calling* (New York: Random House, 1996).

13. Satish Kumar, *You Are Therefore I Am* (Foxhole, Dartington: Green Books Ltd, 2002).

14. Marc Gafni, *Soul Prints: Your Path to Fulfillment* (New York: Pocket Books, 2001) xiv and 30.

15. https://www.goodreads.com/work/quotes/50823097-the-genius-myth. Michael Meade, *The Genius Myth* (Seattle: Greenfire Press, 2016).

16. Bill Plotkin, *Soulcraft: Crossing into the Mysteries of Nature and Psyche* (Novato, CA: New World Library, 2003) 13.

Hearing the Call

1. https://www.brainyquote.com/quotes/quotes/j/josephcamp378372.html

2. Gregg Levoy, *Callings: Finding and Following an Authentic Life* (New York: Three Rivers Press, 1997) 206.

3. *Ibid.*

4. Marc Gafni, *Soul Prints: Your Path to Fulfillment* (New York: Pocket Books, 2001) xxix–xxx.

5. We will return to the topic of slowing down/hushing in the stepping stone, "Living Life Now" in Part III.

6. http://www.calledthejourney.com/blog/2014/12/17/frederick-buechner-on-calling

7. Levoy, p. 123.

8. Inspired by Bill Plotkin, *Soulcraft: Crossing into the Mysteries of Nature and Psyche* (Novato, CA: New World Library, 2003) 192.

9. *Ibid.*,15.

10. John Davis, "The medicine walk: An exploration of ecopsychology and rites of passage" (unpublished manuscript), n.d. (Naropa University, Boulder, CO) 1.

11. Steven Foster and Meredith Little, *The Roaring of The Sacred River: The Wilderness Quest for Vision and Self-Healing* (New York: Prentice Hall Press, 1989).

12. *Ibid.*

13. This description is inspired by Plotkin, p. 243.

14. Davis, p. 2.

From Breakdown to Breakthrough

1. https://www.goodreads.com/quotes/1825889-we-must-be-willing-to-get-rid-of-the-life

2. All Polk quotes from: https://www.nytimes.com/2014/01/19/opinion/sunday/-for-the-love-of-money.html

3. *Ibid.*

4. *Ibid.*

5. *Ibid.*

6. *Ibid.*

7. *Ibid.*

8. *Ibid.*

9. http://www.outsidelands.org/1971_oil_spill.php; https://en.wikipedia.org/wiki/1971_San_Francisco_Bay_oil_spill

10. http://www.grist.org/news/maindish/2005/05/10/hertsgaard-francis/

11. John Francis tells his story in *Planetwalker: How to Change Your World One Step at a Time* (Point Reyes Station, CA: Elephant Mountain Press, 2005).

12. *Ibid.* 44.

13. http://www.grist.org/news/maindish/2005/05/10/hertsgaard-francis/

14. https://www.theguardian.com/lifeandstyle/2016/nov/25/i-didnt-speak-for-17-years-experience-planetwalker#img-1

15. Contributed by Christy Carfagno; paraphrased in places.

16. Michael Meade, *Why the World Doesn't End: Tales of Renewal in Times of Loss* (Seattle: GreenFire Press, 2012) 45.

Coda: Breakdown

1. Jamie Reaser, *Note to Self: Poems for Changing the World from the Inside Out* (Danvers, MA: Hireath Press, 2011) 123–124.

Introduction

1. Compiled from direct translations at: http://www.sacred-texts.com/ane/ishtar.htm; and from this retelling: Bierlein, J.F. *Parallel Myths* (New York: Random House Publishing Group, 1994).

Transcending Dualism

1. Byron Katie, *A Mind at Home with Itself* (New York: Harper-Collins, 2017) 196.

2. Martha Beck, *Finding Your Own North Star: Claiming the Life You Were Meant to Live* (New York: Three Rivers Press, 2001) 78–79.

3. Jeanne Segal, *Raising Your Emo-*

tional Intelligence (New York: Henry Holt, 1997).

4. http://www.ashidakim.com/zen koans/zenindex.html

5. http://www.azquotes.com/quotes/topics/dualism.html

6. In Part III we are offering our own interpretation of the Ishtar myth, distinct from other renderings.

Recovering Imagination and Play

1. Lewis Carroll, *Alice's Adventures in Wonderland and Through the Looking Glass* (New York: Bantan Classic Edition, 1981); http://www.goodreads.com/quotes/-9467-alice-laughed-there-s-no-use-trying-she-said-one-can-t

2. Contributed by Hayly Hoch and inspired by Brene Brown, *Daring Greatly: How the Courage to Be Vulnerable Transforms the Way We Live, Love, Parent, and Lead* (New York: Penguin, 2012).

3. See: https://www.helpguide.org/articles/emotional-health/laughter-is-the-best-medicine.htm; and https://www.ccpa-accp.ca/the-benefits-of-laughter/

4. https://move-with-me.com/play/play-quotes/

Reclaiming Wildness

1. J. Lee, "Honoring the World: An Interview with Author Scott Russell Sanders" in *Stonecrop* (Denver: River Lee Book Company, 1997) 29.

2. This elaboration is thanks to my colleague Rachel Thor.

3. Bill Plotkin, *Wild Mind: A Field Guide to the Human Psyche* (Novato, CA: New World Library, 2013) 57.

4. Tobin Hart, *The Secret Spiritual World of Children* (Novato, CA: New World Library, 2003) 47.

5. Some trees, like willows, rely on wind for pollination.

6. Inspired by an experience I had in a workshop led by Philip Shepherd.

7. Henry David Thoreau, "Walking." In *Civil Disobedience and Other Essays* (New York: Dover Thrift Editions, 1993

Discovering Full-Body Intelligence

1. http://www.azquotes.com/quote/681420

2. For information on the heart brain see: http://www.mindfulmuscle.com/heart-has-consciousness-knows-before-brain/ For information on the gut/enteric brain see: https://www.scientificamerican.com/article/gut-feelings-the-second-brain-in-our-gastrointestinal-systems-excerpt/

3. Philip Shepherd, *New Self New World: Recovering Our Senses in the Twenty-First Century* (Berkeley, CA: North Atlantic Books, 2010).

4. *Ibid.*

5. *Ibid.*

6. *Ibid.*, p. 220.

7. *Ibid.*

8. https://simplelifestrategies.com/the-most-important-question-to-ever-ask-according-to-albert-einstein/

9. Christopher Uhl, "The Root Cause of Climate Change, " *Minding Nature*, 9.1, 2016, 21–26.

10. http://www.huffingtonpost.com/richard-m-cohen/living-in-our-heads_b_5459708.html

Opening to Love

1. https://www.brainyquote.com/quotes/quotes/w/williambut383082.html

2. Karen Armstrong, *Twelve Steps to a Compassionate Life* (New York: Random House, 2010).

3. https://www.garrisoninstitute.org/blog/insight-of-interbeing/

4. *Ibid.*

5. David Deida, *Blue Truth: A Spiritual Guide to Life & Death and Love & Sex* (Boulder, CO: Sounds True, 2005) 21.

6. https://richardchadek.com/blog/

7. Gerald May, *The Awakened Heart: Opening Yourself to the Love You Need* (New York: HarperCollins, 1991) 2.

Living Life Now

1. Annie Dillard, *The Writing Life* (New York: HarperCollins, 1989).

2. Gene Weingarten, "Pearls Before Breakfast," *The Washington Post*, April 8, 2007).

3. *Ibid.*

4. Eckhart Tolle, *The Power of Now* (Novato, CA, New World Library, 1999) 27.

5. Stephan Rechtschaffen, *Time-shifting* (New York, Doubleday, 1996) 5.

6. http://www.4hourworkday.org/workhoursontherise.html

7. https://www.amazon.com/5-Minute-Snuggle-Stories/dp/1423167651

8. Thich Nhat Hanh, *Peace Is Every Step: The Path of Mindfulness in Everyday Life* (New York: Bantan Book, 1991) 26–27.

9. As described in the Part III stepping stone, "Discovering Full-Bodied Intelligence."

10. Michael Lerner, *Spirit Matters* (Charlottesville, VA: Hampton Roads, 2000) 299.

11. *Ibid.*, 300–301.

12. Goodhew, L., & Loy, D. "Momo, Dogen, and the Commodification of Time," *KronoScope,* Volume 2/1, 2002 p 106); and http://www.jonathantan.org/handouts/buddhism/Loy-Momo.pdf

13. Philip Shepherd, *New Self New World* (Berkley, CA:North Atlantic Books, 2010) 27.

Befriending Our Shadow

1. Kopp, S. B. "Tale of a descent into hell" In: C. Zweig and J. Abrams (Eds.), *Meeting the Shadow: The Hidden Power of the Dark Side of Human Nature* (New York, NY: G.P. Putnam's Sons, 1991) 243–48.

2. Toub, G. "The usefulness of the useless" In: C. Zweig and J. Abrams (Eds.), *Meeting the Shadow: The Hidden Power of the Dark Side of Human Nature* (New York, NY: G.P. Putnam's Sons, 1991) 250–56.

3. Robert Bly, *A Little Book on the Human Shadow* (New York: Harper & Row, 1998).

4. John Wellwood, *Love and Awakening: Discovering the Sacred Path of Intimate Relationship* (New York: Harper Collins, 1996); and Debbie Ford, *The Dark Side of the Light Chasers* (New York: Riverhead, 1998).

5. As my colleague Rachel Thor pointed out to me: "This locking also includes rooms that would have caused us pain. For example, some people lock the room of their open-hearted love after experiencing heartbreak; others lock away their shinning beauty after experiencing rape. In other words, we may even lock away culturally desirable traits, under certain circumstances.

6. Ford, *The Dark Side of the Light Chasers.*

7. Anodea Judith, *Eastern Body Western Mind: Psychology and the Chakra System as a Path to the Self* (Berkeley, CA: Celestial Arts, 2004) 118.

8. Ford, *The Dark Side of the Light Chasers.*

9. *Ibid.*

10. Edited slightly with permission.

11. http://worldmythology.wikifoundry.com/page/Ishtar+In+The+Underworld

Coda: A Curriculum for Waking Up

1. http://www.quotehd.com/quotes/herman-hesse-quote-some-of-us-think-holding-on-makes-us-strong-but-sometimes-it

Introduction

1. Jamie Reaser, *Note to Self: Poems for Changing the World from the Inside Out* (Danvers, MA: Hiraeth Press, 2011).

Each Day as a Call to Presence

1. Joseph Campbell with Bill Moyer, *The Power of Myth* (New York: Random House, 1991) 3.

2. Thanks to Rachel Thor for suggesting this incremental approach toward body acceptance with its emphasis on conjuring gratitude for function rather than appearance.

3. James Farrell, *Nature of College: How a New Understanding of Campus Life Can Change the World* (Minneapolis: Milkweed Editions, 2010).

4. For a list of cosmetic chemical additives that can jeopardize health and well-being go to: http://www.davidsuzuki.org/issues/health/science/toxics/dirty-dozen-cosmetic-chemicals/. Also see: http://www.breastcancer.org/risk/factors/cosmetics

5. None of this is to say that wearing makeup is bad or wrong. Even Kaitlyn, when I ran into her on the eve of her graduation, acknowledged that she sometimes puts on makeup for special occasions because it's fun and it feels good.

6. https://www.goodreads.com/quotes/341620-the-little-things-the-little-moments-they-aren-t-little

Stuff

1. https://quotefancy.com/quote/761164/Alan-Cohen-Abundance-is-not-a-number-or-acquisition-It-is-the-simple-recognition-of

2. See: Marie Kondo, *The Life-Changing Magic of Tidying Up* (Berkeley, CA: Ten Speed Press, 2016).

3. https://www.google.com/search?client=firefox-b-1-d&q=price+of+new+house+in+U.S.%3F

4. However, this does not include annual tax and insurance payments; nor does it consider the need to rent space for the placement of one's Tiny House.

5. http://finance.yahoo.com/news/this-couple-built-their-own-tiny-home-for-less-than--10-000-162920658.html

6. http://www.blessthistinyhouse.com/

7. For more info and/or photos of lavvus see http://lavvu.com/

8. For more info and/or photos of clocháns visit http://www.learn.columbia.edu/ma/htm/sr/ma_sr_discuss_ia_sysconst.htm

9. http://www.dancingrabbit.org/about-dancing-rabbit-ecovillage/eco-living/building/natural-building/gobcobatron/

10. http://www.goodreads.com/quotes/-134739-the-things-you-own-end-up-owning-you-it-s-on

11. Joshua F. Millburn and Ryan Nicodemus, *Minimalism: Live a Meaningful Life* (Missoula: Asymmetrical Press, 2016).

Food

1. Derrick Jensen, *The Myth of Human Supremacy* (New York: Seven Stories Press, 2016).

2. Michael Pollan, *In Defense of Food* (New York: Penquin Books, 2008).

3. Wendell Berry, *Sex, Economy, Freedom & Community* (New York: Pantheon Books, 1993) xvii.

4. See: http://lubbockonline.com/local-news/2014-08-09/drying-times-could-rapidly-depleting-ogallala-aquifer-run-dry; www.nrcs.usda.gov; and Joel Cohen, *How Many People Can the Earth Support?* (New York: W.W. Norton, 1995).

5. This sentence is worth reading a second time, so here goes: "The cumulative amount of energy (mostly in the form of fossil fuels) used to grow, process, package, and transport the food that we consume in the U.S. is ten times greater than the nutritional energy actually contained in the food itself." In other words, the industrial food system requires ten times more energy to operate than it actually produces in the form of food.

6. Brian Halweil, *Eat Here: Reclaiming Homegrown Pleasures in a Global Supermarket* (Washington, D.C.: Worldwatch Institute, 2004).

7. To locate CSAs and farmer's markets in your area go to: www.localharvest.org

8. For a video of our expanding garden go to: https://www.youtube.com/watch?feature=player_embedded&v=0DqbN4GKhBQ#

9. http://twenty-somethingtravel.com/2010/07/wwoof/

10. For more information on WWOOFing go to: https://www.wwoof.it/en?gclid=Cj0KEQjwv_fKBRCG8a3ao-OQuZ8BEiQAvpHp6FBmQJZfEIfokBWOzNUY0LXqIyL5D8TqKYbjz6T6CxoaAnJZ8P8HAQ

11. Joan Halifax, *Being with Dying: Cultivating Compassion and Fearlessness in the Presence of Death* (Boston: Shambhala Publications, 2008).

12. Anna Thomas, *Love Soup* (New York: W.W. Norton & Company, 2009).

Transportation

1. Edward Abbey, *Desert Solitaire* (New York: Touchstone, 1968).

2. https://www.google.com/search?q=st atistics+harmful+effects+of+car+use&ie=-utf-8&oe=utf-8#q=average+carbon+dioxid e+emissions+from+cars+in+u.s.+

3. Katie Avord, *Divorce Your Car: Ending the Love Affair with the Automobile* (Gabriola Island, British Columbia: New Society Publishers, 2000).

4. https://www.google.com/search?q= people+dying+in+car+related+accident s+in+U.S.&ie=utf-8&oe=utf-8' also see: https://www.cdc.gov/motorvehiclesafety/ pedestrian_safety/index.html

5. This discussion was inspired by Ivan Illich, *Energy and Equity* (New York: Harper Collins, 1974). Note: If your annual income is six figures or higher, your mph speed will be somewhat higher than 15 mph.

6. http://www.zipcar.com/meetthe fleetboston

7. http://www.zipcar.com/is-it&gclid=-CO7doe-lxMYCFYGRHwodXx8Oqg http://org.elon.edu/sustainability/ documents/zipcar%20faqs.pdf

8. http://www.thestreet.com/story/ 11278169/1/zipcar-faces-increased-compet ition.html

9. Train/bus mile/gallon estimates based on operation at full capacity. http://truecostblog.com/2010/05/27/fuel-efficiency-modes-of-transportation-ranked-by-mpg/

10. Avord, *Divorce Your Car.*

11. *Ibid.*

12. http://www.theguardian.com/ environment/2013/oct/04/swapping-car-bike-stories-blog

13. *Ibid.*

14. https://www.google.com/search?q=p eople+dying+in+car+related+accidents+in +U.S.&ie=utf-8&oe=utf-8

15. James McGurn, *On Your Bicycle* (London: John Murray Publishers Ltd., 1987).

Community

1. Sobonfu Some, *The Spirit of Intimacy: Ancient African Teachings in the Ways of Relationships* (New York: Harper, 1997) 22.

2. https://www.psychologytoday.com/ us/blog/envy/201902/loneliness-new-epidemic-in-the-usa; also see: Robert Putman, *Bowling Alone: The Collapse and Revival of American Community* (New York: Simon & Schuster, 2000).

3. Turner, Toko-pa, *Belonging: Remembering Ourselves Home* (Salt Spring Island, BC: Her Own Room Press, 2017) 14.

4. I do not wish to suggest that the only way to create "community" is within place-based neighborhoods. I know people who are spread about but who are still connected by virtue of a shared vision and values. They connect regularly using internet resources and they also gather once or twice a year in retreat-like settings to support each other, celebrate life and co-create new possibilities.

5. Botsman and Rogers, *What's Mine Is Yours: The Rise of Collaborative Consumption* (New York: HarperCollins, 2010).

6. http://transitionus.org/transition-101

7. John McKnight and Peter Block, "What Happy Families Know: The Good Life? It's Close to Home," *Yes! Magazine* Winter, 2011, pp 48–50.

8. Wendell Berry, *Conversations with Wendell Berry*, ed. Morris Allen Grubbs (Jackson: University Press of Mississippi, 2007).

Happiness from the Inside Out

1. https://www.facebook.com/Dale CarnegieTraining/posts/10152721453110148

2. Contrast the descriptor "material goods" with the descriptor "stuff." The first wording implies that possessions are "good"; the second creates space to distinguish between "good" stuff and "bad" stuff.

3. Adapted from "I Am" documentary, directed by Tom Shadyak.

4. National Opinion Research Council.

5. Although there are several versions of this story, the original version is attributed to German storyteller Heinrich Boll (author) and Leila Vennewitz (translator), *The Collected Stories of Heinrich*

Boll (Brooklyn, NY: MelvilleHouse, 2011) 794–794.

6. http://www.ted.com/talks/david_steindl_rast_want_to_be_happy_be_grateful?language=en

7. http://www.versiondaily.com/-gratitude-and-happiness-the-link-based-on-neuroscience/

8. http://www.raimon-panikkar.org/english/XL-el-espiritu

9. http://izquotes.com/quote/30467

Coda: Awakening in Action

1. Jamie Reaser, *Note to Self: Poems for Changing the World from the Inside Out* (Danvers, MA: Hiraeth Press, 2011).

Introduction

1. From Paulo Coelho, *Veronika Decides to Die* (New York, NY: Harper-Collins, 1998).

A New Story of Self

1. Sydney Harris, American journalist and author as cited in: http://www.motivation-for-dreamers.com/the-real-you.html

2. Eckhart Tolle, *A New Earth* (New York: Penguin Group, 2005) p. 43.

3. Michael Singer, *The Untethered Soul: The Journey Beyond Yourself* (Oakland, CA: New Harbinger Publications, 2007) 9.

4. Tolle, *A New Earth.*

5. Inspired by Arjuna Ardagh, *The Translucent Revolution* (Novato, CA: New World Library, 2005).

6. Tolle , *A New Earth,*108–09.

7. In this spirit, consider the words of Teilhard de Chardin: "I took the lamp and, leaving the zone of everyday occupations and relationships where everything seems clear, I went down into my inmost self, to the deep abyss whence I feel dimly that my power of action emanates. But as I moved further and further away from the conventional certainties by which social life is superficially illuminated, I became aware that I was losing contact with myself. At each step of the descent a new person was disclosed within me of whose name I was no longer sure, and who no longer obeyed me. And when I had to stop my exploration because the path faded from beneath my steps, I found a bottomless abyss at my feet, and out of it came—arising I know not from where—the current which I dare to call my life." http://www.headless.org/-english-new/Reflections/saturn373.htm

8. Derrick Jensen, *A Language Older Than Words* (New York, NY: In Context Books, 2000) 126–127.

A New Story of the Human Other

1. https://www.google.com/search?client=firefox/

2. Satish Kumar, *You Are Therefore I Am: A Declaration of Dependence* (Foxhole, Dartington, Devon: Green Books Ltd., 2004) 110.

3. Daniel Goldman, *Social Intelligence: The New Science of Human Relationships* (New York: Bantam Dell, 2006) 43.

4. Wade Davis, *Light at the Edge of the World* (Vancouver: Douglas & McIntyre, 2007) 138.

5. Robert Holden, *Success Intelligence* (New York: Hay House, 2006).

6. https://www.azquotes.com/quotes/topics/interbeing.html

A New Story of Earth

1. Toko-pa Turner, *Belonging: Remembering Ourselves Home* (Salt Spring Island, British Columbia: Her Own Room Press, 2017) 232.

2. http://thegreatstory.org/Earthname.html (slightly modified)

3. Some plants and animals are hermaphroditic, meaning that they possess both male and female reproductive organs.

4. Robin Wall Kimmerer, *Braiding Sweetgrass: Indigenous Wisdom, Scientific Knowledge, and the Teachings of Plants* (Canada: Milkweed Editions, 2013) 57.

5. *Ibid.*, 55.

6. http://earthheart.org/url/berry.htm

7. Kimmerer, *Braiding Sweetgrass.*

8. This story is paraphrased from

Susan Strauss, *The Passionate Fact* (Golden, CO: North American Press, 1996) 9.

9. Inspired by David Abram, *Becoming Animal: An Earthly Cosmology* (New York: Pantheon Books, 2010).

10. *Ibid.*

11. Paraphrased from Christopher Uhl, *Developing Ecological Consciousness: The End of Separation* (Lanham, MD: Rowman & Littlefield, 2013) 30–31.

12. From Ms. Curran Hunter.

13. Adapted from a story related by Chellis Glendinning, *My Name Is Chellis & I'm in Recovery from Western Civilization* (Boston: Shambhala Publications, 1994).

14. Richard Nelson, *The Island Within* (New York: Vintage, 1991) 249.

A New Story of the Universe

1. Brian Thomas Swimme, and Mary Evelyn Tucker, *Journey of the Universe* (New Haven, CT: Yale University Press, 2011) 2.

2. Hydrogen, the most abundant atom in the universe, was formed within minutes of the Big Bang. https://www.google.com/search?client=firefox-b-1-d&q=what+percent+of+the+universe+is+hydrogen

3. https://www.space.com/16943-supernova-explosion-solar-system-formation.html

4. Genesis 1:3; ttps://biblehub.com/genesis/1-3.htm

5. Michael Dowd, *Thank God for Evolution* (Tulsa, Okla: Council Oak Books, LLC, 2007) p. 79; also see: http://www.thegreatstory.org/morequotes.html

6. For a refresher on dualism, see "Transcending Dualism" in Part III.

7. http://www.fbchsv2.org/blindfaith/2010/10/20/mysterium-tremendum-et-fascinans/

8. The following thought experiment is drawn in part from my book, *Developing Ecological Consciousness: The End of Separation* (Lanham, MD: Rowman and Littlefield, 2013).

9. https://www.azquotes.com/author/-21199-Thomas_Berry

10. Thomas Berry, *The Great Work* (New York: Bell Tower, 1999).

Healing

1. https://www.azquotes.com/quote/575369

2. https://www.scribd.com/document/162632542/If-Your-House-is-on-Fire

3. Joanna Macy and Chris Johnstone, *Active Hope: How to Face the Mess We Are in Without Going Crazy* (Novato, CA: New World Library, 2012) 79.

4. Details for this Truthspeaking ceremony are laid out in: J. Macy and M. Brown, *Coming Back to Life: Practices to Reconnect, Our Lives, Our World* (Gabriola Island, BC, Canada: New Society Publishers, 2014) 119–122.

5. Macy and Johnstone, *Active Hope*, p. 79.

6. *Ibid.*, p. 3.

7. Christine Fry (October 19, 2004) http://thewaybackhome.ca/the-great-turning/?shared=email&msg=fail

8. Michael Meade, *Why the World Doesn't End, Tales of Renewal in Times of Loss* (Seattle: Mosaic Multicultural Foundation, GreenFire Press, 2012).

It All Comes Down to Choice

1. Will shares this addendum to Heather's story: "Before we had kids, Heather knew that she was at increased odds for having a kid with Down Syndrome. When she asked a friend, who had a Down Syndrome child, what it was like, the woman said "It is like being invited to a club that I never knew existed and it has been the best thing ever." Heather's response at the time was: "I never want to belong to that club." But lo and behold, today, Heather has become the vice president of the local chapter of the Down Syndrome Society; she has raised money by organizing "Buddy Walks" for this organization; and she has written a memoir entitled, *This Is What Perfect Looks Like*, about her experience as Fern's mother. Clearly, Heather has CHOSEN Fern.

2. Jamie Reaser, *Note to Self: Poems for Changing the World from the Inside Out* (Danvers, MA: Hireath Press, 2011) 21.

3. https://en.wikiquote.org/wiki/William_Jennings_Bryan

Epilogue

1. Michael Meade, *Genius Transforms the World* (Seattle, WA: GreenFire Press, Mosaic Cultural Foundation, 2016) Chapter 1.

2. Tara Brach, *Radical Acceptance: Embracing Your Life with the Heart of the Buddha* (New York: Bantam Books, 2003) 26.

3. Jamie Reaser, *Note to Self: Poems for Changing the World from the Inside Out* (Danvers, MA: Hiraeth Press, 2011).

Bibliography

Abbey, Edward. *Desert Solitaire*. New York: Touchstone, 1968.

Abram, David. *Becoming Animal: An Earthly Cosmology*. New York: Pantheon Books, 2010.

Ardagh, Arjuna. *The Translucent Revolution*. Novato: New World Library, 2005.

Armstrong, Karen. *Twelve Steps to a Compassionate Life*. New York: Random House, 2010.

Avord, Katie. *Divorce Your Car: Ending the Love Affair with the Automobile*. Gabriola Island: New Society Publishers, 2000.

Beck, Martha. *Finding Your Own North Star: Claiming the Life You Were Meant to Live*. New York: Three Rivers Press, 2001.

Berry, Thomas. *The Dream of the Earth*. San Francisco: Sierra Club Books, 1988.

Berry, Thomas. *The Great Work*. New York: Bell Tower, 1999.

Berry, Wendell. *Conversations with Wendell Berry*. Jackson: Jackson University Press of Mississippi, 2007.

Berry, Wendell. *Sex, Economy, Freedom & Community*. New York: Pantheon Books, 1993.

Bly, Robert. *A Little Book on the Human Shadow*. New York: Harper & Row, 1998.

Botsman, Rachel, and Roo Rogers. *What's Mine is Yours: The Rise of Collaborative Consumption*. New York: HarperCollins Publishers, 2010.

Brach, Tara. *Radical Acceptance: Embracing Your Life with the Heart of the Buddha*. New York: Bantam Books, 2003.

Brown, Brene. *Daring Greatly: How the Courage to Be Vulnerable Transforms the Way We Live, Love, Parent, and Lead*. New York: Penguin Publishing Group, 2012.

Campbell, Joseph, with Bill Moyer. *The Power of Myth*. New York: Random House, 1991.

Chödrön, Pema. *Start Where You Are: A Guide to Compassionate Living*. Boston: Shambhala Publications, 2004.

Daily, Herman. *From Uneconomic Growth to a Steady-State Economy*. Northhampton: Edward Elgar Publishing, 2014.

Deida, David. *Blue Truth: A Spiritual Guide to Life & Death and Love & Sex*. Boulder: Sounds True, 2005.

Dillard, Annie. *The Writing Life*. New York: HarperCollins Publishers, 1989.

Dowd, Michael. *Thank God for Evolution*. San Francisco: Council Oak Books, 2007.

Farrell, James. *Nature of College: How a New Understanding of Campus Life Can Change the World*. Minneapolis: Milkweed Editions, 2010.

Finkel, Donald. *Teaching with Your Mouth Shut*. Portsmouth: Boynton/Cook Publishers, 2000.

Ford, Debbie. *The Dark Side of the Light Chasers*. New York: Riverhead, 1998.

Foster, Steven, and Meredith Little. *The Roaring of The Sacred River: The Wilderness Quest for Vision And Self-Healing*. New York: Prentice Hall Press, 1989.

Francis, John. *Planetwalker: How to Change Your World One Step at a Time*. Point Reyes Station: Elephant Mountain Press, 2005.

Gafni, Marc. *Soul Prints: Your Path to Fulfillment*. New York: Pocket Books, 2001.

Gillian, Stephen, and Robert Dilts. *The Hero's Journey: A Voyage to Self-Discovery*. Bethel: Crown Publishing Company LLC, 2009.

Glendinning, Chellis. *My Name Is Chellis & I'm in Recovery from Western Civilization*. Boston: Shambhala Publications, 1994.

Goldberg, Natalie. *Writing Down the Bones*. Boston: Shambhala Publications, 1986.

Gray, Peter. *Free to Learn*. New York: Basic Books, 2013.

Greenberg, Daniel. *Free at Last: The Sudbury Valley School*. Framingham: Sudbury Valley School Press, 1987.

Halifax, Joan. *Being with Dying: Cultivating*

Compassion and Fearlessness in the Presence of Death. Boston: Shambhala Publications, 2008.

Hanh, Thich Nhat. *Peace Is Every Step: The Path of Mindfulness in Everyday Life.* New York: Bantan Book, 1991.

Hart, Tobin. *From Information to Transformation: Education for the Evolution of Consciousness.* New York: Peter Lang, 2007.

Hart, Tobin. *The Secret Spiritual World of Children.* Novato: New World Library, 2003.

Hern, Matt. *Field Day: Getting Society Out of School.* Vancouver: New Star Books, 2003.

Hillman, James. *The Soul's Code: In Search of Character and Calling.* New York: Random House, 1996.

Holden, Robert. *Success Intelligence.* New York: Hay House, 2006.

Illich, Ivan. *Energy and Equity.* New York: Harper Collins, 1974.

Jensen, Derrick. *A Language Older Than Words.* New York: In Context Books, 2000.

Jensen, Derrick. *The Myth of Human Supremacy.* New York: Seven Stories Press, 2016.

Jensen, Derrick. *Walking on Water: Reading, Writing and Revolution.* White River Junction: Chelsea Green, 2004.

Judith, Anodea. *Eastern Body Western Mind: Psychology and the Chakra System as a Path to the Self.* Berkeley: Celestial Arts, 2004.

Katie, Byron. *Loving What Is: Four Questions That Can Change Your Life.* New York: Three Rivers Press, 2002.

Katie, Byron. *A Mind at Home with Itself.* New York: Harper-Collins, 2017.

Kimmerer, Robin Wall. *Braiding Sweetgrass: Indigenous Wisdom, Scientific Knowledge, and the Teachings of Plants.* Minneapolis: Milkweed Editions, 2013.

Kondo, Marie. *The Life-Changing Magic of Tidying Up.* Berkeley: Ten Speed Press, 2016.

Kumar, Satish. *You Are Therefore I Am.* Foxhole: Green Books Ltd, 2002.

Lang, Amanda. *The Power of Why.* New York: Harper Collins, 2010.

Lerner, Michael. *Spirit Matters.* Charlottesville, VA: Hampton Roads, 2000.

Levoy, Gregg. *Callings: Finding and Following an Authentic Life.* New York: Three Rivers Press, 1997.

Liedloff, Jean. *The Continuum Concept: In Search of Happiness Lost.* New York: Addison-Wesley Publishing Company, 1977.

Lipton, Bruce. *The Biology of Belief.* Carlsbad: Hay House Inc., 2005.

Lozoff, Bo. *It's a Meaningful Life: It Just Takes Practice.* New York: Penguin Putnam, 2000.

Macy, Joanna, and Chris Johnstone. *Active Hope: How to Face the Mess We're in Without Going Crazy.* Novato: New World Library, 2012.

Macy, Joanna, and Molly Brown. *Coming Back to Life: Practices to Reconnect, Our Lives, Our World.* Gabriola Island: New Society Publishers, 2014.

May, Gerald. *The Awakened Heart: Opening Yourself to the Love You Need.* New York: HarperCollins, 1991.

McCullough Jr., David. *You Are Not So Special and Other Encouragements.* New York: HarperCollins, 2014.

McGurn, James. *On Your Bicycle.* London: John Murray Publishers Ltd., 1987.

Meade, Michael. *Fate and Destiny: The Two Agreements of the Soul.* Seattle: GreenFire Press, 2010.

Meade, Michael. *The Genius Myth.* Seattle: Greenfire Press, 2016.

Meade, Michael. *Why the World Doesn't End: Tales of Renewal in Times of Loss.* Seattle: GreenFire Press, 2012.

Millburn, Joshua F., and Ryan Nicodemus. *Minimalism: Live a Meaningful Life.* Missoula: Asymmetrical Press, 2016.

Nelson, Richard. *The Island Within.* New York: Vintage, 1991.

Orr, David. *Earth in Mind.* Washington D.C.: Island Press, 1994.

Plotkin, Bill. *Soulcraft: Crossing into the Mysteries of Nature and Psyche.* Novato: New World Library, 2003.

Plotkin, Bill. *Wild Mind: A Field Guide to the Human Psyche.* Novato: New World Library, 2013.

Pollan, Michael. *In Defense of Food.* New York: Penguin Books, 2008.

Postman, Neil, and Charles Weingartner. *Teaching as a Subversive Activity.* New York: Delta Publishing, 1969.

Quinn, Daniel. *Ishmael.* New York: Bantam, Turner, 1992.

Reaser, Jamie. *Note to Self: Poems for Changing the World from the Inside Out.* Danvers: Hireath Press, 2011.

Rechtschaffen, Stephan. *Timeshifting.* New York: Doubleday, 1996.

Rilke, R.M. *Letters to a Young Poet.* New York: Norton, 1993.

Rosenberg, Marshall. *Nonviolent Communication: A Language of Compassion.* Encintas: PuddleDancer Press, 1999.

Segal, Jeanne. *Raising Your Emotional Intelligence.* New York: Henry Holt, 1997.

Shepherd, Philip. *New Self New World: Recovering Our Senses in the Twenty-First Century.* Berkeley: North Atlantic Books, 2010.

Singer, Michael. *The Untethered Soul: The Journey Beyond Yourself.* Oakland: New Harbinger Publications, Inc., 2007.

Some, Sobonfu. *The Spirit of Intimacy: Ancient African Teachings in the Ways of Relationships.* New York: Harper, 1997.

Song, Tamarack. *Sacred Speech: The Way of Truthspeaking.* Three Lakes: Teaching Drum Outdoor School, 2004.

Swimme, Brian Thomas, and Mary Evelyn Tucker. *Journey of the Universe.* New Haven: Yale University Press, 2011.

Thomas, Anna. *Love Soup.* New York: W.W. Norton & Company, 2009.

Tolle, Eckhart. *A New Earth.* New York: Penguin Group, 2005.

Tolle, Eckhart. *The Power of Now.* Novato: New World Library, 1999.

Turner, Toko-pa. *Belonging: Remembering Ourselves Home.* Salt Spring Island: Her Own Room Press, 2017.

Wellwood, John. *Love and Awakening: Discovering the Sacred Path of Intimate Relationship.* New York: HarperCollins, 1996.

Whyte, David. *Crossing the Unknown Sea: Work as a Pilgrimage of Identity.* New York: Riverhead Books, 2001.

About the Authors

Christopher Uhl: In my twenties and thirties I studied ecology and aided in conservation efforts in the rain forests of Brazil. In my forties, as a professor of biology at Penn State University, I spearheaded a movement to "green" the university by researching and championing sustainability practices. As a teacher at Penn State, over the past three decades, I have emphasized questions rather than answers and risk-taking rather than conformity.

My passion for teaching motivated me to write *Teaching as If Life Matters: The Promise of a New Education Culture* (with Dana L. Stuchul) and *Developing Ecological Consciousness: Becoming Fully Human* (with Jennifer Anderson).

Melissa DiJulio: I am an ecopsychologist, storyteller, and writer, trying to live my way into the answers to questions like, "How can humans fit, harmoniously, into the larger tapestry of the biosphere?" and "What is the role of stories in navigating these uncertain times?"

To further explore AWAKENING practices and possibilities, visit https://www.awaken101.us/